T0210879

Lecture Notes in Computer Science 10110

Commenced Publication in 1973
Founding and Former Series Editors:
Gerhard Goos, Juris Hartmanis, and Jan van Leeuwen

FoLLI Publications on Logic, Language and Information

Subline of Lectures Notes in Computer Science

More information about this series at http://www.springer.com/series/7407

Thomas Zeume

Small Dynamic Complexity Classes

An Investigation into Dynamic
Descriptive Complexity

 Springer

Author

Thomas Zeume
Fakultät für Informatik
TU Dortmund
Dortmund, Nordrhein-Westfalen
Germany

This work was carried out at:
Department of Computer Science,
TU Dortmund University in Dortmund, Germany
and accepted there as a PhD thesis.

ISSN 0302-9743   ISSN 1611-3349   (electronic)
Lecture Notes in Computer Science
ISBN 978-3-662-54313-9   ISBN 978-3-662-54314-6   (eBook)
DOI 10.1007/978-3-662-54314-6

Library of Congress Control Number: 2017930617

LNCS Sublibrary: SL1 – Theoretical Computer Science and General Issues

Printed on acid-free paper

This Springer imprint is published by Springer Nature
The registered company is Springer-Verlag GmbH Germany
The registered company address is: Heidelberger Platz 3, 14197 Berlin, Germany

Preface

On the first few days of my PhD studies in the summer of 2009, my adviser Thomas Schwentick introduced me to dynamic complexity. Very recently Wouter Gelade, Marcel Marquardt, and Thomas had obtained a very nice characterization of regular languages in terms of dynamic complexity, and also a lower bound for the dynamic complexity of the alternating reachability problem. Many interesting problems in this area seemed to be awaiting a solution; and so I attempted to prove a lower bound for reachability. I was not successful. After two (at the end frustrating) months, I abandoned this project.

In the following two-and-a-half years I almost forgot about dynamic complexity. Decidability issues for the two-variable fragment of first-order logic turned out to be a much more accessible and fruitful field. Thomas and I obtained promising results, and a PhD in this field did not seem to be too far away. This was the moment when Thomas asked whether I would be interested in applying for funds from the DFG. If successful, such funding could relieve me from my teaching obligations.

We decided to have a second, deeper look into dynamic complexity, and to apply for funds for an extensive study of the power of logics in dynamic settings. At that time, the decision to spend more time on dynamic complexity was not easy for me. I was in the third year of my PhD and already had results and further ideas for two-variable logics; and it was not clear whether an application for funding would be successful. On the other hand, I now had more experience, which might be helpful for attacking the very same problems that I had tried to solve at the beginning of my PhD. I do not regret the decision.

With the thesis at hand I want to document the progress in dynamic complexity that we have made in the last two-and-a-half years. The focus of this thesis is on small dynamic descriptive complexity classes, in particular on lower bound methods for them. A short summary of results on decidability issues for two-variable logic is presented at the end of the thesis.

I am very grateful to Thomas Schwentick for all his support throughout the years of my PhD studies, and for being a great example of how to be a researcher and teacher. I thank the referees Erich Grädel and Thomas Schwentick as well as Cornelia Tadros and Jens Teubner for their work in my defense committee. Further, I thank Samir Datta, Sebastian Siebertz, and Nils Vortmeier for many fruitful discussions about dynamic complexity. I also thank the numerous colleagues at Dortmund and in the logic and database community for making the last years a great time. Moreover, I thank Katja Losemann and Nils Vortmeier for proofreading parts of this work. I acknowledge the financial support by the German DFG under grant SCHW 678/6-1.

My warmest thanks goes to my family, to Katja, and to all my friends who supported me during the past couple of years.

January 2015   Thomas Zeume

Contents

1 Introduction 1
  1.1 Introduction 1

2 Dynamic Complexity: Definitions and Examples 11
  2.1 Preliminaries 11
  2.2 The Dynamic Complexity Framework 13
  2.3 Three Basic Dynamic Complexity Classes 15
    2.3.1 The Class DYNFO 15
    2.3.2 The Class DYNPROP 17
    2.3.3 The Class DynQF 18
  2.4 Variants of the Dynamic Complexity Framework 21
  2.5 A Case Study: Graph Queries. 24
    2.5.1 Regular Path Queries. 25
    2.5.2 Beyond Regular Path Queries 27
  2.6 Outlook and Bibliographic Remarks 34

3 Relating Small Dynamic Complexity Classes 35
  3.1 A Hierarchy of Dynamic Classes 40
    3.1.1 Tools for Collapsing Dynamic Classes. 42
    3.1.2 Eliminating Negations and Inverting Quantifiers 45
    3.1.3 Eliminating Disjunctions 47
    3.1.4 Simulating Functions by Conjunctive Queries. 57
  3.2 Short Interlude: Δ-Semantics 60
  3.3 Relating Dynamic Classes and Static Classes 67
    3.3.1 A Dynamic Characterization of First-Order Logic 69
    3.3.2 DYNPROP Captures Semi-positive $\exists^*$FO Under Insertions 73
  3.4 Eliminating Built-In Arithmetic. 76
  3.5 Outlook and Bibliographic Remarks 80

4 Lower Bounds for Dynamic Complexity Classes 83
  4.1 Quantifier-Free Update Programs 86
    4.1.1 The Substructure Lemma. 89
    4.1.2 Applications of the Substructure Lemma 91
    4.1.3 An Arity Hierarchy for Quantifier-Free Programs 106
    4.1.4 Fragments of Quantifier-Free Programs 108

4.2 Quantifier-Free Update Programs with Functions   112

    4.2.1 A Generalization of the Substructure Lemma   114

    4.2.2 Applying the Generalized Substructure Lemma.   116

    4.2.3 Why Lower Bounds for Binary Functions
             Are Hard to Prove   122

4.3 First-Order Update Programs   124

    4.3.1 Applying Static Lower Bound Methods   125

    4.3.2 Two Approaches for Restricted Initializations   131

4.4 Outlook and Bibliographic Remarks   136

5 Conclusion   139

References   143

Subject Index   147

Chapter 1
Introduction

1.1 Introduction

In many of today's data management scenarios the data is subject to frequent modifications, and it is often essential to react to those changes quickly. When a train is canceled on short notice, travelers need to find alternative connections as fast as possible. When a web server is temporarily not available, data packages have to be rerouted immediately. Also data in social networks is subject to frequent changes: modifications of the relationships of users lead to numerous consequences including the necessity of updating the visibility of sensitive data.

Recomputation of a query result from scratch after each small change of the data is often not possible in such scenarios due to the large amount of data at hand and efficiency considerations. Very often it is also not necessary: the breakdown of a single train does affect only a very small fraction of the whole train network. Thus it is reasonable to try to dynamically update essential information in an incremental fashion by reusing information that has been computed already before. Ideally such a dynamic update should use less resources than recomputation from scratch.

Approaches for such dynamic updates often store, besides the relevant data, additional information in order to facilitate the update process. This information is called *auxiliary data*. When updating the result of a query after a modification of the data occurred, an update process has access to both the modification and the stored auxiliary data. The auxiliary data, however, has to be updated as well. In Fig. 1.1 the dynamic point of view is juxtaposed to the classical static point of view.

Two fundamentally different approaches for dynamically updating the result of a query have been studied, an *algorithmic approach* and a *declarative approach*.

The algorithmic approach is not subject of this work. In this approach the goal is to develop algorithms that need less resources for recomputing query results after modifications than a naïve algorithm that recomputes results from scratch. A good starting point for readers interested in upper bounds for dynamic algorithms is [RZ08, DI08]; a good starting point for lower bound techniques is the survey by Miltersen on cell probe complexity [Mil99].

© Springer-Verlag GmbH Germany 2017
T. Zeume, *Small Dynamic Complexity Classes*, LNCS 10110
DOI: 10.1007/978-3-662-54314-6_1

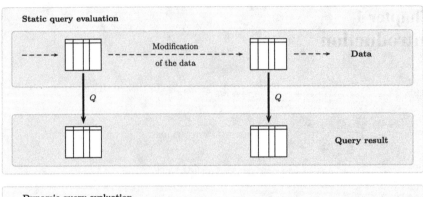

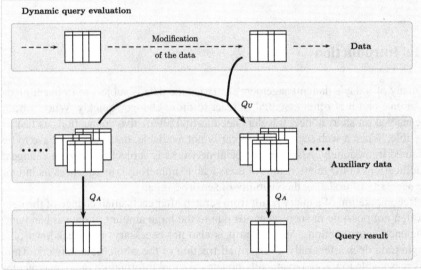

Fig. 1.1 Updating the result of a query $\mathcal{Q}$ in the static and dynamic setting after modifying the data. In the static setting the query is re-evaluated from scratch after each modification; in the dynamic setting some auxiliary data is updated by a query $\mathcal{Q}_U$, and the result of $\mathcal{Q}$ is obtained by evaluating another query $\mathcal{Q}_A$ on the auxiliary data. In our framework the result of $\mathcal{Q}$ will be part of the auxiliary data.

The objective of this work is to advance the understanding of the declarative approach. Here, declarative means that updates of the auxiliary information are specified by some logical formalism. In this approach the input data and the auxiliary data is stored in (logical) structures. When the underlying input structure is modified, i.e. a tuple is inserted into or deleted from some input relation, then every auxiliary relation is updated through a logical query that can refer to the modification, the previous content of the input relations and the previous content of the auxiliary relations. The aim is to be able to extract the updated query result from one of the auxiliary relations at each moment.

The focus of this work is on first-order definable update queries. This setting was independently formalized by Dong, Su and Topor [DT92, DS93] and Patnaik and Immerman [PI94]. Both formalizations are very similar. We use the formalization by Patnaik and Immerman throughout this work, henceforth called the *dynamic (descriptive) complexity framework*. In this framework first-order formulas are the basic update mechanism. We call a set of first-order formulas for updating the auxiliary relations *dynamic first-order program* and the class of queries maintainable by such dynamic programs is called DYNFO. For a discussion of the differences of the two formalizations we refer to the later discussion in Sect. 2.4.

Different aspects of dynamic descriptive complexity have been studied over the last twenty years. The main focus of research has been to see how strong this formalism is, and how it relates to the power of static logical formalisms. Our main objective is to advance those two lines of research.

Before discussing the aspirations and contributions of this work in detail, it is instructive to see this approach at work, to see some merits of the dynamic descriptive complexity approach, and to have a short look at previous and related work. We start with an illustrative example.

Example 1.1. Consider a graph G into which edges are inserted dynamically. For the moment we disallow deletions of edges. In the following, our goal is to maintain the transitive closure of G using a dynamic program with first-order update formulas. The transitive closure is maintained by such a dynamic program, if one of its auxiliary relations always (that is, after every possible insertion sequence) stores the transitive closure of G.

It turns out that if edges may only be inserted (and not deleted), then it is sufficient to store the current transitive closure relation in an auxiliary relation T. In other words, T shall contain all pairs (a, b) of nodes that are connected by a path in the current graph G. Now, when an edge (c, d) is inserted into G, the relation T has to be updated. The following very simple rule updates T: there is a path from a to b after inserting (c, d) if (1) there has been a path from a to b before the insertion, or (2) there has been a path from a to c and a path from d to b before the insertion. See Fig. 1.2 for an example of an edge insertion and the corresponding update of T.

This rule can be easily specified by a first-order update formula:

$$\phi^T_{\text{INS}_E}(u, v; x, y) \stackrel{\text{def}}{=} T(x, y) \vee \big(T(x, u) \wedge T(v, y)\big)$$

The interpretation of the update formula $\phi^T_{\text{INS}_E}(u, v; x, y)$ is as follows: when inserting an edge (u, v) into E, then the tuple (x, y) will be present in the updated relation T if $\phi^T_{\text{INS}_E}(u, v; x, y)$ holds. Thus, after the insertion of (u, v), the relation T is replaced by the relation defined by $\phi^T_{\text{INS}_E}(u, v; x, y)$.   □

Using first-order formulas as an update mechanism must appear as a weird choice to readers not too familiar with logic. Yet, there are some strong arguments for choosing first-order logic as the basic update language for the dynamic descriptive complexity framework.

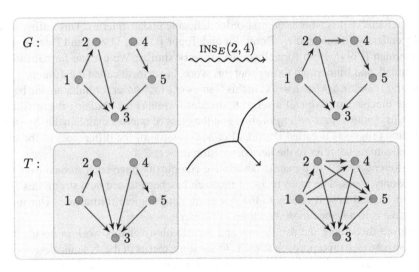

Fig. 1.2 Update of the transitive closure T of a graph G after inserting the edge $(2, 4)$.

Why Dynamic Descriptive Complexity Matters

We present two perspectives on first-order logic that indicate that it is indeed a good choice.

The relational database model due to Codd [Cod70] has, since its introduction in the 1970's, revolutionized the field of database systems. One of the most influential query languages for relational databases in use today, SQL, has a strong connection to first-order logic. The core of SQL, the relational algebra, has many characterizations (see, e.g., [AHV95]); one of them being first-order logic. In other words, a query can be stated in core-SQL if and only if it is expressible in first-order logic[1]. Even more, some very popular syntactic fragments of core-SQL, such as conjunctive queries and unions of conjunctive queries, directly correspond to well-defined fragments of first-order logic. As it is well known that certain queries such as the transitive closure query cannot be expressed in first-order logic, they can also not be stated in the core of SQL.

Thus studying which queries can be maintained by first-order update formulas in the dynamic complexity framework has an immediate impact on the power of core-SQL in a dynamic setting: if a query can be maintained via first-order update formulas, then it can also be maintained using core-SQL queries. In Example 1.1 we have already seen that the transitive closure query, while not expressible in first-order logic, can be easily expressed in the dynamic complexity framework under insertions. The update formula updating the transitive closure after an edge insertion can be easily translated into an SQL query, see Fig. 1.3. In fact, very recently it

---

[1] More precisely, core-SQL is equivalent to domain-independent first-order logic. For simplicity we ignore this technical issue here.

```
SELECT *
  FROM (
        SELECT *
        FROM   T
     UNION
        SELECT T1.x, T2.y
        FROM   T as T1, T as T2
        WHERE  T1.y = u AND T2.x = v
       )
```

Fig. 1.3 An SQL query for selecting tuples in the transitive closure of a graph after inserting the edge (u, v). This query corresponds to the first-order update formula $\phi^T_{\text{INS}_E}(u, v; x, y) \stackrel{\text{def}}{=} T(x, y) \vee \left(T(x, u) \wedge T(v, y)\right)$.

has been shown that this query can even be maintained by first-order updates under both insertions and deletions [DKM+15] (a rough proof sketch for this result is presented in Sect. 2.6). More connections between dynamic descriptive complexity and relational databases will be discussed below in the paragraph on related work.

Another motivation for studying first-order logic as an update mechanism is its close connection to parallel computation models. Circuits have been studied as a model for parallelism for several decades (see, e.g., [Vol99]). The uniform variant of the circuit complexity class AC^0 corresponds to first-order logic complemented by basic arithmetic, that is, built-in addition and multiplication relations [BIS90]. Circuits in AC^0 are of constant depth and may have polynomially many $\wedge$-, $\vee$- and $\neg$-gates; the $\wedge$- and $\vee$-gates may have unbounded fan-in. Such circuits can be simulated by parallel random access machines (short: PRAMs) with polynomially many processors in constant time (see, e.g., [Vol99]). In particular first-order logic can be evaluated by such random access machines in constant time.

Thus if a query can be maintained via first-order update formulas, it can be dynamically recomputed by a highly parallel program in constant time as well. Although it is not immediately clear how to implement first-order update programs in real systems, results from dynamic descriptive complexity offer a foundation for future work towards fast, parallel dynamic programs for important queries. The construction of such programs is highly relevant in todays huge, distributed databases.

Those two motivations offer a strong incentive to study dynamic descriptive complexity with first-order update formulas in detail. We will now discuss prior and related work.

Short History of Dynamic Complexity Theory

Several aspects of dynamic complexity have been studied over the last two decades. The major directions are depicted in Fig. 1.4. We discuss those directions now.

Maintainability of Basic Queries. Most of the attention devoted to dynamic complexity has been on investigating which queries can be maintained by first-order updates

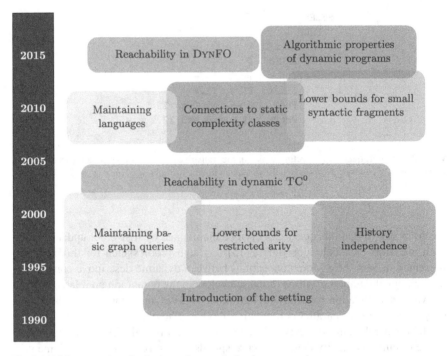

Fig. 1.4 Main research topics in dynamic complexity theory over time.

or even weaker update languages. Typical graph queries as well as formal languages have been studied.

Among graph queries, the reachability query is the best studied query. Already with the introduction of the dynamic complexity framework, dynamic first-order programs for maintaining the reachability query for acyclic and undirected graphs have been known [DS95, PI97]. Later Hesse showed that reachability (on arbitrary graphs) can be maintained using TC^0-circuits as update mechanism [Hes03a], where TC^0-circuits are defined like AC^0-circuits except that they can also use majority gates. Very recently reachability was shown to be maintainable in a non-uniform variant of DYNFO extended by a parity quantifier [DHK14]. Finally, in so far unpublished work, reachability was shown to be in DYNFO [DKM+15]. Reachability has been studied also for restricted update formalisms. Hesse showed that reachability on deterministic graphs can be maintained by quantifier-free update formulas (the corresponding dynamic complexity class is called DYNPROP), and on undirected graphs with quantifier-free update formulas that can also use auxiliary functions (the corresponding dynamic complexity class is called DYNQF) [Hes03b]. Moreover other graph queries such as 2-colorability and the tree-isomorphism query have been studied, and shown to be contained in DYNFO [DS98, Ete98].

The maintainability of formal languages has been studied as well. Already Patnaik and Immerman observed that regular languages can be maintained in DYNFO [PI97]. A more extensive study of languages conducted by Gelade, Marquardt and Schwentick revealed that regular languages are exactly the languages that can be maintained in DYNPROP [GMS12]. They also showed that all context-free languages can be maintained in DYNFO; and that certain context-free languages can be maintained in DYNQF.

Other maintainability results for dynamic descriptive complexity have been obtained in, e.g., [KW03, WS07, GS12].

Lower Bounds. Lower bounds have been studied as well, though proving lower bounds for DYNFO turned out to be very hard. Therefore several restrictions of DYNFO have been studied, among them the restriction of the arity of auxiliary relations [DS98, DLW03] and syntactic restrictions of first-order update formulas [GMS12]. For a more detailed overview over previous work on lower bounds we refer to Chap. 4, which is devoted to lower bounds and methods for proving them.

Other Aspects. A lot of other aspects have been studied as well. Among them notions of reducibility and complete problems for dynamic complexity classes [PI97, HI02, WS07], the (in)dependence of the auxiliary relations from the actual input relations [DS97, DS98, GS12], and the relation of dynamic and static complexity classes [PI94, Ete98, WS07, GMS12]. For a detailed overview over the latter aspect we refer to Chap. 3.

Related Work

The development of the dynamic complexity framework has been influenced by several very similar settings from database theory and computational complexity theory. In the following we present some of them and highlight their relation to the dynamic complexity framework. We remark that the following classification is quite artificial as it is neither clear how to draw a strict line between dynamic descriptive complexity and those related areas nor is it desirable to do so.

Incremental View Maintenance. Dynamic complexity is closely related to the incremental maintenance of views. The goal in incremental view maintenance is to keep a materialized view, defined by some fixed query, updated after the database has been modified (see, e.g., [GMS93, SI84]). Most of the work in incremental view maintenance has been done from an algorithmic perspective. Usually only the database and the current view are used for updating views in this setting, but sometimes also auxiliary data may be used.

An algebraic perspective of incremental view maintenance under Δ-semantics has been studied in [Koc10]. Parts of the latter work have also been implemented, leading to significant performance gains for query evaluation compared to static query evaluation, see e.g. [KAK+14].

Updating with SQL-like Languages. In the dynamic complexity framework updates are specified by first-order logic. However, many features of SQL such as the GROUPBY and HAVING clauses as well as aggregate functions such as TOTAL and COUNT are not captured by first-order logic. In [LW97b], Libkin and Wong have shown that those constructs can be modeled by equipping the relational calculus with bag semantics and aggregate functions. The resulting query language, $\mathcal{NRC}$, and its restriction to flat relations, $\mathcal{SQL}$, have been studied as update mechanism as well. For example, it has been shown that $\mathcal{NRC}$ and $\mathcal{SQL}$ are equally expressive in the dynamic context [LW97a], and that $\mathcal{SQL}$-updates capture the polynomial time hierarchy [LW99]. The latter implies that reachability can be maintained using SQL as update language [DLSW99].

This setting differs from the dynamic complexity framework in two aspects: it uses a stronger update mechanism and it assumes that the domain has an infinite supply of fresh domain elements (which can be used in auxiliary relations even though they are not used in the actual database).

Theory of Incremental Computation. The dynamic descriptive complexity class DYNFO is equivalent to a dynamic version of the circuit class AC^0 for a large class of queries (see Sect. 3.4 for details). In [MSVT94], Miltersen et al. proposed a framework for studying dynamic complexity classes based on larger static complexity classes, that is, classes beyond AC^0. It is easy to see that PTIME coincides with the class of queries maintainable with polynomial time updates. Therefore classes with logarithmic space and time updates (on random access machines) have been studied in [MSVT94]. Some of the constructions and reduction concepts from [MSVT94] have been reused by Patnaik and Immerman in [PI97].

This concludes the related work. We now state the goals of this work.

Purpose and Outline of this Work

As stated above our main objective is to advance the understanding of the power of the dynamic descriptive complexity framework. Our focus is on proving lower bounds. To this end also a good knowledge about small descriptive complexity classes is essential.

Our first central goal arises from the fact that very few lower bound methods for dynamic complexity are known, and that applying the available methods to a given query is usually not easy. The goal is easy to state.

Goal 1. *Provide new lower bound methods and new lower bounds for dynamic complexity.*

Above we have seen that dynamic programs with first-order update formulas are very powerful. They can maintain recursive queries such as reachability, and they can maintain all AC^0-properties. No meaningful lower bounds for full DYNFO are known so far. This indicates that lower bounds for first-order updates are not easy to achieve, and that a more concerted approach is necessary. Our approach towards new lower bound methods is to study small syntactic fragments of DYNFO first. The hope is that lower bound methods for small fragments will serve as a solid foundation for proving lower bounds for larger fragments. As starting point we choose the quantifier-free fragment of DYNFO, since some lower bounds for this fragment have been already achieved [GMS12].

When trying to generalize lower bound methods to larger fragments it is essential to choose a suitable next candidate fragment. This is the motivation for our second central goal, namely to gain a clear understanding of small dynamic complexity classes.

Goal 2. *Understand how small dynamic complexity classes relate with respect to each other, and how they relate with respect to static complexity classes.*

One chapter is devoted to each of the two goals. Our contributions are presented in an informal way at the beginning of each of those chapters. In addition to the contributions for those two goals, we present a case study that examines how queries on graph databases can be maintained in the dynamic complexity framework.

The structure of the rest of this work is as follows.

In Chap. 2, "Dynamic Complexity: Definitions and Examples", a formal introduction into the dynamic complexity framework will be given. The basic dynamic complexity classes used in this work are defined and many examples given. The chapter is concluded by a longer example section that explores which queries on graph databases can be maintained by dynamic programs. In this section we also present an overview of the proof that the reachability query can be maintained by first-order update formulas.

In Chap. 3, "Relating Small Dynamic Complexity Classes", the relationship between various small dynamic complexity classes are explored. Most of them are motivated from database theory. Also the expressive power of traditional static descriptive complexity classes is compared to the power of those dynamic classes. As an interlude, the relationship of absolute and Δ-semantics is studied. Further we take a quick glance at the relationship between restricted initialization mappings. Our main result presented here is one of the three steps for maintaining Reachability with first-order update formulas.

Chapter 4, "Lower Bounds for Dynamic Complexity Classes", is devoted to the development of new techniques for proving lower bounds for quantifier-free update programs, quantifier-free update programs with auxiliary functions and first-order update programs. Furthermore most prior techniques for proving lower bounds are presented.

Both Chaps. 3 and 4 start with an informal introduction aimed at an occasional reader. The informal introduction clearly states the goals that shall be achieved in this chapter, and it states our contributions in an informal fashion. Precise results are given in subsequent sections. Each such section contains precise theorem statements close to its beginning. If proofs of those theorems are more involved, then they are sometimes distributed into subsections[2]. Chapters end with a conclusion section that

---

[2]If the statement of a theorem is repeated, it is marked by (R).

discusses possible future work and open questions. It also contains bibliographical remarks.

In order to not distort the flow of reading too much, references within the text are usually only given to work in which the author was not involved. In the bibliographical remarks in the conclusion of each chapter there will be a detailed exposition of who contributed to which result and where results have been published before.

Bibliographic Remarks

Parts of the beginning of this introduction as well as Fig. 1.1 have been used in a project proposal to the German Research Foundation (DFG) prepared by Thomas Schwentick and the author.

Chapter 2
Dynamic Complexity: Definitions and Examples

In this chapter the dynamic complexity framework is defined formally; and many examples for its expressive power are presented. As the dynamic complexity framework is based on notions from database theory and finite model theory, we will shortly review necessary foundations from those two areas first. Afterwards we will introduce the formal dynamic complexity framework, define three basic dynamic complexity classes and present simple examples for each of them. The formal framework has several aspects that can be varied; those will be discussed subsequently.

In order to get some familiarity with the setting, this chapter will be concluded by an extensive case study on path queries for graph databases. Recently query languages for graph databases have drawn considerable attention from the database theory community (see e.g. [MW95, AV99, ACP12, LM13, Woo12, Bae13] for surveys). Graph databases can contain huge amounts of data and therefore evaluating queries in parallel and, if possible, dynamically is highly desired. This motivates to study graph query languages from the dynamic complexity perspective. We will see how to maintain regular path queries as well as certain non-regular path queries using dynamic programs. The maintenance of regular path queries relies on the recent result that reachability can be maintained in by first-order update formulas. An overview for the proof of this result is presented. Rather than giving a complete picture for graph queries, we aim at developing some intuition of the capabilities of dynamic programs. This intuition will be of help in Chaps. 3 and 4.

Parts of this chapter originated in joint work with Samir Datta, Raghav Kulkarni, Anish Mukherjee and Thomas Schwentick; and discussions with Katja Losemann. For detailed bibliographic remarks we refer to the end of this chapter.

2.1 Preliminaries

In this section we review basic definitions in order to fix notations. We list definitions that are used throughout the whole work; specific notations are introduced in later chapters.

© Springer-Verlag GmbH Germany 2017
T. Zeume, *Small Dynamic Complexity Classes*, LNCS 10110
DOI: 10.1007/978-3-662-54314-6_2

Basic Notations

Let A be a finite set. We denote by A^k the set of all k-tuples over A and by $[A]^k$ the set of all k-element subsets of A. For two tuples $\bar{a} = (a_1, \ldots, a_k)$ and $\bar{b} = (b_1, \ldots, b_\ell)$ over A, the $(k + \ell)$-tuple obtained by concatenating $\bar{a}$ and $\bar{b}$ is denoted by $(\bar{a}, \bar{b})$. We slightly abuse set theoretic notations and write $c \in \bar{a}$ if $c = a_i$ for some i, and $\bar{a} \cup \bar{b}$ for the set $\{a_1, \ldots, a_k, b_1 \ldots, b_\ell\}$. The tuple $\bar{a}$ is $\prec$-ordered with respect to a linear order $\prec$ of A, if $a_1 \prec \ldots \prec a_k$. If π is a function on A, we denote $(\pi(a_1), \ldots, \pi(a_k))$ by $\pi(\bar{a})$.

Structures and First-order Logic

We shortly review basic notions from finite model theory. We emphasize that in this work we are solely interested in finite structures. For a detailed introduction to the field we refer the reader to [EF05, Lib04].

A *(relational) schema* τ consists of a set τ_{rel} of relation symbols and a set τ_{const} of constant symbols together with an arity function $\text{Ar} : \tau_{\text{rel}} \to \mathbb{N}$. A *domain D* is a finite set. A *database* $\mathcal{D}$ over schema τ with domain D is a mapping that assigns to every relation symbol $R \in \tau_{\text{rel}}$ a relation of arity $\text{Ar}(R)$ over D and to every constant symbol $c \in \tau_{\text{const}}$ an element (called *constant*) from D.

A τ-*structure* $\mathcal{S}$ is a pair $(D, \mathcal{D})$ where $\mathcal{D}$ is a database over schema τ and D is a domain. For a relation symbol $R \in \tau$ and a constant symbol $c \in \tau$ we denote by $R^{\mathcal{S}}$ and $c^{\mathcal{S}}$ the relation and constant, respectively, that are assigned to those symbols in $\mathcal{S}$. The substructure $\mathcal{S}'$ of $\mathcal{S}$ induced by some $D' \subseteq D$ is denoted by $\mathcal{S} \upharpoonright D'$. In this work we always assume that the domain of a substructure contains all constants from the structure itself.

Let $\mathcal{S}$ and $\mathcal{T}$ be two structures over schema τ with domains S and T, respectively. A mapping $\pi : S \to T$ *preserves* a relation symbol $R \in \tau$ of arity m, when $\bar{a} \in R^{\mathcal{S}}$ if and only if $\pi(\bar{a}) \in R^{\mathcal{T}}$ for all m-tuples $\bar{a}$. It preserves a constant symbol c if and only if $\pi(c^{\mathcal{S}}) = c^{\mathcal{T}}$. The structures $\mathcal{S}$ and $\mathcal{T}$ are *isomorphic via* π, denoted by $\mathcal{S} \simeq_\pi \mathcal{T}$, if π is a bijection from S to T that preserves all relation and constant symbols in τ. The bijection $id[\bar{a}, \bar{b}]$ from S to S with $\bar{a} = (a_1, \ldots, a_k)$ (where all a_i are pairwise distinct) and $\bar{b} = (b_1, \ldots, b_k)$ (where all b_i are pairwise distinct) will be used a couple of times; it maps a_i to b_i, b_i to a_i and every other element of S to itself.

The set of *first-order formulas* over schema τ is defined inductively as follows:

- Every *atomic formula* of the form $R(t_1, \ldots, t_k)$ or $t_1 = t_2$, where all t_i are either constant symbols or variables, is a first-order formula.
- Every *composed formula* of the form $\neg\varphi$, $\varphi \wedge \psi$, or $\exists x\varphi$ is a first-order formula.

The abbreviations $\vee$, $\to$, $\leftrightarrow$ and $\forall x$ are defined as usual.

Let $\mathcal{S} \stackrel{\text{def}}{=} (D, \mathcal{D})$ be a τ-structure, φ a first-order formula over τ with free variables $x_1, \ldots, x_k$, and α an assignment that maps every x_i to an element from D. By $(\mathcal{S}, \alpha) \models \varphi$ we indicate that $(\mathcal{S}, \alpha)$ is a model of φ. Often we write also

$(\mathcal{S}, \bar{a}) \models \varphi$ or $\mathcal{S} \models \varphi(\bar{a})$ where $\bar{a} \overset{\text{def}}{=} (\alpha(x_1), \ldots, \alpha(x_k))$. The model relation $\models$ is defined as usual.

An *m-ary query* $\mathcal{Q}$ on τ-structures is a mapping that is closed under isomorphisms and assigns a subset of D^m to every τ-structure over domain D. *Closure under isomorphisms* means that $\pi(\mathcal{Q}(\mathcal{S})) = \mathcal{Q}(\pi(\mathcal{S}))$ for all isomorphisms π. Often we will denote $\mathcal{Q}(\mathcal{S})$ by $\text{ANS}(\mathcal{Q}, \mathcal{S})$. A query $\mathcal{Q}$ is *definable* (alternatively: *expressible*) in first-order logic if there is a first-order formula $\varphi(\bar{x})$ such that $\text{ANS}(\mathcal{Q}, \mathcal{S}) = \{\bar{a} \mid (\mathcal{S}, \bar{a}) \models \varphi(\bar{x})\}$ for all structures $\mathcal{S}$.

The *k-ary atomic type* $\langle \mathcal{S}, \bar{a} \rangle$ of $\bar{a} \in D^k$ with respect to a structure $\mathcal{S}$ over τ is the conjunction of all atomic formulas $\varphi(\bar{x})$ over τ for which $\mathcal{S} \models \varphi(\bar{a})$.

Standard Structures and Queries

The following structures and queries will be used throughout this work. A (directed) *graph* G is a pair (V, E) where V is a finite set and E is a subset of V^2. Graphs can be encoded as structures over schema $\{E\}$ where E is a binary relation symbol (to be interpreted by the set of edges). Usually we identify graphs and their corresponding structures.

An *s-t-graph* is a graph with two distinguished nodes s and t. Such graphs can be encoded by structures over schema $\{E, s, t\}$ where E is as before and s and t are two constant symbols (to be interpreted by two distinguished nodes). A *k-layered s-t-graph* G is an *s-t*-graph in which $V - \{s, t\}$ is partitioned into k layers $A_1, \ldots, A_k$ such that every edge is from s to A_1, from A_k to t or from A_i to A_{i+1} for some $i \in \{1, \ldots, k-1\}$.

The *reachability query* REACH, the *k-clique query* k- CLIQUE and the *k-colorability query* k-COL are defined as usual. A tuple (a, b) is in REACH(G) if b can be reached from a in G. The *s-t-reachability query* s-t-REACH is a Boolean query which is true for an *s-t*-graph G, if and only if $(s, t) \in \text{REACH}(G)$. A graph $G = (V, E)$ is in k- CLIQUE if V contains k nodes $v_1, \ldots, v_k$ such that $(v_i, v_j) \in E$ or $(v_j, v_i) \in E$ for all $1 \le i < j \le k$.

A *k-node-coloring col* of G is a mapping that assigns to every node of V a color from $\{1, \ldots, k\}$. Such a coloring is admissible, if all nodes a and b with $(a, b) \in E$ are colored by different colors. A graph is *k-node-colorable*, if it admits a *k*-node-coloring. The graph $G = (V, E)$ is in k-COL if it is *k*-node-colorable.

2.2 The Dynamic Complexity Framework

After the informal discussion of the dynamic complexity framework in the introduction chapter, we present the basic formal framework now. In Example 1.1, the structure subjected to modifications was a graph and modifications were restricted to be insertions. In the general dynamic complexity framework, arbitrary structures

are subject to both tuple insertions and tuple deletions. We present a variant of the
framework introduced by Patnaik and Immerman [PI94].

A *dynamic instance* of a query $\mathcal{Q}$ is a pair $(\mathcal{D}, \alpha)$, where $\mathcal{D}$ is a database over some
finite domain D and α is a sequence of modifications to $\mathcal{D}$. Here, a *modification* is
either an insertion of a tuple over D into a relation of $\mathcal{D}$ or a deletion of a tuple from a
relation of $\mathcal{D}$. The result of $\mathcal{Q}$ for $(\mathcal{D}, \alpha)$ is the relation that is obtained by first applying
the modifications from α to $\mathcal{D}$ and then evaluating $\mathcal{Q}$ on the resulting database. We use
the Greek letters α and β to denote modifications as well as modification sequences.
The database resulting from applying a modification α to a database $\mathcal{D}$ is denoted
by $\alpha(\mathcal{D})$. The result $\alpha(\mathcal{D})$ of applying a sequence of modifications $\alpha \stackrel{\text{def}}{=} \alpha_1 \ldots \alpha_m$
to a database $\mathcal{D}$ is defined by $\alpha(\mathcal{D}) \stackrel{\text{def}}{=} \alpha_m(\ldots(\alpha_1(\mathcal{D}))\ldots)$.

Dynamic programs, to be defined next, consist of an initialization mechanism
and an update program. The former yields, for every (input) database $\mathcal{D}$, an initial
state with initial auxiliary data. The latter defines how the new state of the dynamic
program is obtained from the current state when applying a modification.

A *dynamic schema* is a tuple $(\tau_{\text{inp}}, \tau_{\text{aux}})$ where τ_{inp} and τ_{aux} are the schemas of
the input database and the auxiliary database, respectively. While τ_{inp} may contain
constants, we do not allow constants in τ_{aux} in the basic setting. We always let
$\tau \stackrel{\text{def}}{=} \tau_{\text{inp}} \cup \tau_{\text{aux}}$.

Definition 2.2.1 (Update program). *An* update program P *over a dynamic schema*
(τ_{inp}, τ_{aux}) *is a set of first-order formulas (called* update formulas *in the following)*
that contains, for every relation symbol R in τ_{aux} and every $\delta \in \{\text{INS}_S, \text{DEL}_S\}$ with
$S \in \tau_{inp}$, an update formula $\phi_\delta^R(\bar{x}; \bar{y})$ over the schema τ where $\bar{u}$ and $\bar{x}$ have the
same arity as S and R, respectively.

A *program state* $\mathcal{S}$ over dynamic schema $(\tau_{\text{inp}}, \tau_{\text{aux}})$ is a structure $(D, \mathcal{I}, \mathcal{A})$ where
D is a finite domain, $\mathcal{I}$ is a database over the input schema (the *current database*)
and $\mathcal{A}$ is a database over the auxiliary schema (the *auxiliary database*).

The semantics of update programs is as follows. Let P be an update program,
$\mathcal{S} = (D, \mathcal{I}, \mathcal{A})$ be a program state and $\alpha = \delta(\bar{a})$ a modification where $\bar{a}$ is a tuple
over D and $\delta \in \{\text{INS}_S, \text{DEL}_S\}$ for some $S \in \tau_{\text{inp}}$. If P is in state $\mathcal{S}$ then the application
of α yields the new state $\mathcal{P}_\alpha(\mathcal{S}) \stackrel{\text{def}}{=} (D, \alpha(\mathcal{I}), \mathcal{A}')$ where, in $\mathcal{A}'$, a relation symbol
$R \in \tau_{\text{aux}}$ is interpreted by $\{\bar{b} \mid \mathcal{S} \models \phi_\delta^R(\bar{a}; \bar{b})\}$. The effect $P_\alpha(\mathcal{S})$ of applying a
modification sequence $\alpha \stackrel{\text{def}}{=} \alpha_1 \ldots \alpha_m$ to a state $\mathcal{S}$ is the state $P_{\alpha_m}(\ldots(P_{\alpha_1}(\mathcal{S}))\ldots)$.

Definition 2.2.2 (Dynamic program). *A* dynamic program *is a triple* (P, INIT, Q),
where

- *P is an update program over some dynamic schema (τ_{inp}, τ_{aux}),*
- *INIT is a mapping that maps τ_{inp}-databases to τ_{aux}-databases, and*
- *$Q \in \tau_{aux}$ is a designated query symbol.*

A dynamic program $\mathcal{P} = (P, \text{INIT}, Q)$ *maintains* a query $\mathcal{Q}$ if, for every dynamic
instance $(\mathcal{D}, \alpha)$, the relation $\text{ANS}(\mathcal{Q}, \alpha(\mathcal{D}))$ coincides with the query relation $Q^\mathcal{S}$
in the state $\mathcal{S} = P_\alpha(\mathcal{S}_{\text{INIT}}(\mathcal{D}))$ where $\mathcal{S}_{\text{INIT}}(\mathcal{D})$ is the initial state for $\mathcal{D}$, that is,
$\mathcal{S}_{\text{INIT}}(\mathcal{D}) \stackrel{\text{def}}{=} (D, \mathcal{D}, \text{INIT}(\mathcal{D}))$.

In Example 1.1 we have already seen how to maintain reachability in graphs under insertions. Now we present a simple dynamic program for maintaining the parity of a unary relation as another example. This already gives a glimpse of the power of dynamic programs with first-order update formulas, as parity and reachability are not expressible in first-order logic (even with arbitrary built-in predicates) [Ajt83, FSS84].

Example 2.2.3. The parity query asks whether the number of elements in a unary relation U is divisible by two. A dynamic program can maintain the parity of U using a single 0-ary auxiliary relation Q as follows:

$$\phi^Q_{\mathrm{INS}_U}(u; x, y) \stackrel{\mathrm{def}}{=} (\neg U(u) \wedge \neg Q) \vee (U(u) \wedge Q)$$

$$\phi^Q_{\mathrm{DEL}_U}(u; x, y) \stackrel{\mathrm{def}}{=} (U(u) \wedge \neg Q) \vee (\neg U(u) \wedge Q) \qquad\qquad \square$$

The following notions will be useful at several places. Two programs $\mathcal{P}$ and $\mathcal{P}'$ with the same input schema and with designated query symbols Q and Q' of the same arity are *equivalent* if Q and Q' store the same relation after the application of every modification sequence.

The *dependency graph* of a dynamic program $\mathcal{P}$ with auxiliary schema τ has the vertex set $V = \tau$ and an edge (R, R') if the relation symbol R' occurs in one of the update formulas for R. The *deletion dependency graph* is defined as the dependency graph except that only update formulas for delete operations are taken into account.

2.3 Three Basic Dynamic Complexity Classes

It is natural to look at the classes of queries that can be maintained by dynamic programs. In the following we introduce the dynamic complexity classes DYNFO, DYNPROP and DYNQF. These are the basic complexity classes studied in this work. They been introduced in [PI94, Hes03b].

2.3.1 The Class DYNFO

We start with the class of queries maintainable by dynamic programs with first-order updates.

Definition 2.3.1 (DynFO). DYNFO *is the class of all dynamic queries that can be maintained by dynamic programs with first-order update formulas and arbitrary initialization mappings.*

The role of the initialization mapping will be discussed later in this section. We remark that the class DYNFO is the prototype of dynamic complexity classes defined by referring to a static class C; in this case FO. More generally, in the dynamic class DYNC updates from class C are allowed. In Chap. 3 we will encounter several other classes of the form DYNC where C is a fragment of FO.

The dynamic complexity class DYNFO and all other classes presented in the following also come in a variant where the arity of the auxiliary relations is restricted. A dynamic program is k-*ary* if the arity of its auxiliary relation symbols is at most k. By k-ary DYNFO we refer to dynamic queries that can be maintained with k-ary DYNFO-programs.

As we already have seen above, the parity query is in DYNFO; even in 0-ary DYNFO. Many other queries have been shown to be in DYNFO as well, e.g. two-colorability of graphs [DS98] and all context-free languages are in DYNFO [GMS12]. Very recently reachability for arbitrary (directed) graphs has been shown to be maintainable in DYNFO [DKM+15].

As an example we show how reachability on acyclic graphs can be maintained in DYNFO. The technique used in this example will be the foundation for some results for maintaining graph queries on acyclic graphs in Sect. 2.6.

Example 2.3.2. We follow the argument from [PI97] and construct a dynamic DYNFO-program with one binary auxiliary relation T which is intended to store the transitive closure of an acyclic graph.

Insertions can be handled straightforwardly as in the introductory example at the beginning of this section: after inserting an edge (u, v) there is a path from x to y if, before the insertion, there has been a path from x to y or there have been paths from x to u and from v to y. There is a path p from x to y after deleting an edge (u, v) if there was a path from x to y before the deletion and (1) there was no such path via (u, v), or (2) there is an edge (z, z') on p such that u can be reached from z but not from z'. If there is still a path p from x to y, such an edge (z, z') must exist on p, as otherwise u would be reachable from y contradicting acyclicity. All conditions can be checked using the transitive closure of the graph before the deletion of (u, v). The update formulas for T are as follows:

$$\phi^T_{\mathrm{INS}_E}(u, v; x, y) \stackrel{\mathrm{def}}{=} T(x, y) \vee \big(T(x, u) \wedge T(v, y)\big)$$

$$\phi^T_{\mathrm{DEL}_E}(u, v; x, y) \stackrel{\mathrm{def}}{=} T(x, y) \wedge \Big(\big(\neg T(x, u) \vee \neg T(v, y)\big)$$
$$\vee \exists z \exists z' \big(T(x, z) \wedge E(z, z') \wedge (z \neq u \vee z' \neq v)$$
$$\wedge T(z', y) \wedge T(z, u) \wedge \neg T(z', u)\big)\Big) \qquad \square$$

Those examples already show that DYNFO is very powerful. This is the reason why several restrictions of DYNFO have been studied.

2.3.2 The Class DYNPROP

Disallowing quantifiers in update formulas yields the class DYNPROP. Thus, in DYNPROP, update formulas can only access the inserted or deleted tuple $\bar{a}$ and the currently updated tuple $\bar{b}$ of an auxiliary relation.

Definition 2.3.3 (DynProp). DYNPROP *is the class of all dynamic queries that can be maintained by dynamic programs with quantifier-free first-order update formulas and arbitrary initialization mappings.*

By k-ary DYNPROP we refer to dynamic queries that can be maintained with k-ary quantifier-free dynamic programs.

At first glance the restriction to quantifier-free programs appears severe. However, Example 2.2.3 shows that the parity query is also in DYNPROP, and Example 1.1 shows that reachability can be maintained in DYNPROP under insertions. Using a slightly more involved construction, Hesse proved that reachability on deterministic graphs can be maintained in DYNPROP [Hes03b]. Gelade et al. showed that on strings, all regular languages can be maintained in DYNPROP [GMS12]. Thus quantifier-free programs are already quite expressive; and, as we will see later, proving lower bounds for quantifier-free programs is non-trivial.

The following example illustrates a technique to maintain lists with quantifier-free dynamic programs which is used in some of our upper bound results. This technique was introduced in [GMS12, Proposition 4.5].

Example 2.3.4. We provide a DYNPROP-program $\mathcal{P}$ for the dynamic variant of the Boolean query NONEMPTYSET. This query asks, for a unary relation U subject to insertions and deletions of elements, whether U is empty. Of course, this query is trivially expressible in first-order logic, but not without quantifiers.

The program $\mathcal{P}$ uses the auxiliary schema $\tau_{\text{aux}} = \{Q, \text{FIRST}, \text{LAST}, \text{LIST}\}$, where Q is the query bit (i.e. a 0-ary relation symbol), FIRST and LAST are unary relation symbols, and LIST is a binary relation symbol. The idea is to store in a program state S a list of all elements currently in U. The list structure is stored in the binary relation LIST^S such that a tuple (a, b) is in LIST^S if a and b that are adjacent in the list. The first and last element of the list are stored in FIRST^S and LAST^S, respectively. We note that the order in which the elements of U are stored in the list depends on the order in which they are inserted into the set.

For a given instance of NONEMPTYSET the initialization mapping initializes the auxiliary relations accordingly.

In the following we assume for simplicity that only elements that are not already in U are inserted. The given formulas can be extended easily to the general case. A similar assumption is made for deletions.

Insertion of a into U. A newly inserted element is attached to the end of the list. Therefore the FIRST-relation does not change except when the first element is inserted into an empty set U. Furthermore, the inserted element is the new last element of the list and has a connection to the former last element. Finally, after inserting an element into U, the query result is 'true':

$$\phi_{\mathrm{INS}_U}^{\mathrm{FIRST}}(a; x) \overset{\text{def}}{=} (\neg Q \wedge a = x) \vee (Q \wedge \mathrm{FIRST}(x))$$

$$\phi_{\mathrm{INS}_U}^{\mathrm{LAST}}(a; x) \overset{\text{def}}{=} a = x$$

$$\phi_{\mathrm{INS}_U}^{\mathrm{LIST}}(a; x, y) \overset{\text{def}}{=} \mathrm{LIST}(x, y) \vee (\mathrm{LAST}(x) \wedge a = y)$$

$$\phi_{\mathrm{INS}_U}^{Q}(a) \overset{\text{def}}{=} \top.$$

Deletion of a from U. How a deleted element a is removed from the list, depends on whether a is the first element of the list, the last element of the list or some other element of the list. The query bit remains 'true', if a was not the first *and* last element of the list.

$$\phi_{\mathrm{DEL}_U}^{\mathrm{FIRST}}(a; x) \overset{\text{def}}{=} (\mathrm{FIRST}(x) \wedge a \neq x) \vee (\mathrm{FIRST}(a) \wedge \mathrm{LIST}(a, x))$$

$$\phi_{\mathrm{DEL}_U}^{\mathrm{LAST}}(a; x) \overset{\text{def}}{=} (\mathrm{LAST}(x) \wedge a \neq x) \vee (\mathrm{LAST}(a) \wedge \mathrm{LIST}(x, a))$$

$$\phi_{\mathrm{DEL}_U}^{\mathrm{LIST}}(a; x, y) \overset{\text{def}}{=} x \neq a \wedge y \neq a \wedge \big(\mathrm{LIST}(x, y) \vee (\mathrm{LIST}(x, a) \wedge \mathrm{LIST}(a, y))\big)$$

$$\phi_{\mathrm{DEL}_U}^{Q}(a) \overset{\text{def}}{=} \neg(\mathrm{FIRST}(a) \wedge \mathrm{LAST}(a)) \qquad\qquad \square$$

2.3.3   The Class DynQF

Quantifier-free programs, as the one above, can only access the inserted or deleted tuple and the currently updated tuple of an auxiliary relation. Dynamic programs with first-order update formulas, on the other hand, have great freedom in choosing tuples to access. In the following we consider a class of queries maintainable by programs that lay in between those two extremes.

To define this class of dynamic programs, we extend the class of programs with quantifier-free update formulas as follows. In addition to auxiliary relations, we allow auxiliary functions to be stored as auxiliary data. With auxiliary functions further elements might be accessed via function terms over the modified tuple and the currently updated tuple. Thus, in a sense, auxiliary functions can be seen as adding weak quantification to quantifier-free formulas. When full first-order updates are available, auxiliary functions can be simulated in a straightforward way by auxiliary relations. However, without quantifiers this is not possible.

The class of queries maintainable by quantifier-free programs extended by auxiliary functions is called DYNQF. Before giving the formal definition of DYNQF, we formalize the extension of the basic dynamic complexity framework by functions. We follow the approach from [GMS12].

When talking about DYNQF, the auxiliary schema τ_{aux} is the union of a relational schema τ_{rel} and a *functional schema* τ_{fun}. It has an associated arity function Ar :

$\tau_{\text{rel}} \cup \tau_{\text{fun}} \mapsto \mathbb{N}$. A database $\mathcal{D}$ over such a schema with domain D is a mapping that assigns to every relation symbol $R \in \tau_{\text{rel}}$ a relation of arity $\text{Ar}(R)$ over D and to every k-ary function symbol $f \in \tau_{\text{fun}}$ a k-ary function from D^k to D. We observe that constants can be modeled by 0-ary functions.

In the following, we extend our definition of update programs with relational auxiliary schemas to programs with auxiliary schemas with function symbols. It is straightforward to extend the definition of update formulas for auxiliary relations: they simply can make use of function terms. However, following the spirit of DYNPROP, a more powerful update mechanism for auxiliary functions is used which allows case distinctions in addition to composition of function terms.

Definition 2.3.5 (Update term). *Update terms are inductively defined as follows:*

(1) Every variable and every constant is an update term.
(2) If f is a k-ary function symbol and $t_1, \ldots, t_k$ are update terms, then $f(t_1, \ldots, t_k)$ is an update term.
(3) If ϕ is a quantifier-free update formula (possibly using update terms) and t_1 and t_2 are update terms, then $\text{ITE}(\phi, t_1, t_2)$ is an update term.

The semantics of update terms associates with every update term t and interpretation $I = (\mathcal{S}, \beta)$, where $\mathcal{S}$ is a state and β a variable assignment, a value $[\![t]\!]_I$ from $\mathcal{S}$. The semantics of (1) and (2) is straightforward. If $I \models \phi$ holds, then $[\![\text{ITE}(\phi, t_1, t_2)]\!]_I$ is $[\![t_1]\!]_I$, otherwise $[\![t_2]\!]_I$.

The extension of the notion of update programs for auxiliary schemas with function symbols is now straightforward. An update program still has an update formula ϕ_δ^R (possibly using update terms instead of only variables and constants) for every relation symbol $R \in \tau_{\text{aux}}$ and every $\delta \in \{\text{INS}_S, \text{DEL}_S\}$ with $S \in \tau_{\text{inp}}$. Furthermore, it has, for every such δ and every function symbol $f \in \tau_{\text{aux}}$, an update term $t_\delta^f(\bar{x}; \bar{y})$. For a modification $\delta(\bar{a})$ it redefines f for each tuple $\bar{b}$ by evaluating $t_\delta^f(\bar{a}; \bar{b})$ in the current state.

Definition 2.3.6 (DynQF). DYNQF *is the class of queries maintainable by quantifier-free update programs with (possibly) auxiliary functions and arbitrary initialization mappings.*

The class k-ary DYNQF is defined via update programs that use auxiliary functions and relations of arity at most k.

We remark that our definition of DYNQF is slightly stronger than the usual definition. Here we allow for using update terms in update formulas for relations whereas in [GMS12] only terms are allowed. This strengthens several of our later results.

Auxiliary functions are quite powerful. While only regular languages can be maintained in DYNPROP, all Dyck languages, among other non-regular languages, can be maintained in DYNQF [GMS12]. Furthermore, undirected reachability can be maintained in DYNQF with built-in arithmetic [Hes03b, Corollary 4.9].

The following example provides an impression of the expressive power of DYNQF.

Example 2.3.7. Consider the unary graph query $\mathcal{Q}$ that returns all nodes a of a given graph G with maximal outdegree.

We construct a unary DYNQF-program $\mathcal{P}$ that maintains $\mathcal{Q}$ in a unary relation denoted by the designated query symbol Q. The program uses two unary functions SUCC and PRED that shall encode a successor and its corresponding predecessor relation on the domain. For simplicity, but without loss of generality, we therefore assume that the domain is of the form $D = \{0, \ldots, n-1\}$. For every state $\mathcal{S}$, the function $\text{SUCC}^{\mathcal{S}}$ is then the standard successor function on D (with $\text{SUCC}^{\mathcal{S}}(n-1) = n-1$), and $\text{PRED}^{\mathcal{S}}$ is the standard predecessor function (with $\text{PRED}^{\mathcal{S}}(0) = 0$). Both functions are initialized accordingly. In the following we refer to *numbers* and mean the position of elements in SUCC. The program uses constants for representing the numbers 0 and 1.

The program $\mathcal{P}$ maintains two unary functions #EDGES and #NODES. The function #EDGES counts, for every node a, the number of outgoing edges of a; more precisely #EDGES$(a) = b$ if and only if b is the number of outgoing edges of a. The function #NODES counts, for every number a, the number of nodes with a outgoing edges; more precisely #NODES$(a) = b$ if and only if b is the number of nodes with a outgoing edges. A constant MAX shall always point to the number i such that i is the maximal number of outgoing edges from some node in the current graph.

When inserting an outgoing edge (u, v) for a node u that already has a outgoing edges, the counter #EDGES of u is incremented from a to $a+1$ and all other edge-counters remain unchanged. The counter #NODES of a is decremented, the counter of $a+1$ is incremented, and all other node-counters remain unchanged. The number MAX increases if, before the insertion, u was a node with maximal number of outgoing edges. This yields the following update terms:

$$t_{\text{INS}_E}^{\text{#EDGES}}(u, v; x) \stackrel{\text{def}}{=} \text{ITE}\Big(\neg E(u, v) \wedge x = u, \text{SUCC}(\text{#EDGES}(x)), \text{#EDGES}(x)\Big)$$

$$t_{\text{INS}_E}^{\text{#NODES}}(u, v; x) \stackrel{\text{def}}{=} \text{ITE}\Big(\neg E(u, v) \wedge x = \text{#EDGES}(u), \text{PRED}(\text{#NODES}(x)),$$

$$\text{ITE}\big(\neg E(u, v) \wedge x = \text{SUCC}(\text{#EDGES}(u)),$$

$$\text{SUCC}(\text{#NODES}(x)), \text{#NODES}(x)\big)\Big)$$

$$t_{\text{INS}_E}^{\text{MAX}}(u, v) \stackrel{\text{def}}{=} \text{ITE}\Big(\text{MAX} = \text{#EDGES}(u) \wedge \neg E(u, v), \text{SUCC}(u), \text{MAX}\Big)$$

The update formula for the designated query symbol Q is as follows:

$$\phi_{\text{INS}_E}^{Q}(u, v; x) \stackrel{\text{def}}{=} t_{\text{INS}_E}^{\text{#EDGES}}(u, v; x) = t_{\text{INS}_E}^{\text{MAX}}(u, v)$$

The update terms for deletions are very similar:

$$t_{\text{DEL}_E}^{\#\text{EDGES}}(u, v; x) \overset{\text{def}}{=} \text{ITE}\Big(E(u, v) \wedge x = u, \text{PRED}(\#\text{EDGES}(x)), \#\text{EDGES}(x)\Big)$$

$$t_{\text{DEL}_E}^{\#\text{NODES}}(u, v; x) \overset{\text{def}}{=} \text{ITE}\Big(E(u, v) \wedge x = \#\text{EDGES}(u), \text{PRED}(\#\text{NODES}(x)),$$

$$\text{ITE}\big(E(u, v) \wedge x = \text{PRED}(\#\text{EDGES}(u)),$$

$$\text{SUCC}(\#\text{NODES}(x)), \#\text{NODES}(x)\big)\Big)$$

$$t_{\text{DEL}_E}^{\text{MAX}}(u, v) \overset{\text{def}}{=} \text{ITE}\Big(\text{MAX} = \#\text{EDGES}(u) \wedge E(u, v) \wedge \#\text{NODES}(\text{MAX}) = 1,$$

$$\text{PRED}(\text{MAX}), \text{MAX}\Big)$$

The update formula for the designated query symbol Q under deletion is as follows:

$$\phi_{\text{DEL}_E}^{Q}(u, v; x) \overset{\text{def}}{=} t_{\text{DEL}_E}^{\#\text{EDGES}}(u, v; x) = t_{\text{DEL}_E}^{\text{MAX}}(u, v) \qquad \qquad \square$$

2.4 Variants of the Dynamic Complexity Framework

Many variations of the basic dynamic complexity framework presented above have been studied. In the following we discuss three aspects of the basic framework that can be varied: the type of the domain; the initial state of a dynamic program and the power of the initialization mapping; and, closely related, whether built-in relations are available. For each of the aspects we also say which variants we consider in this work and explain why we chose those variants.

Choosing a Domain

While in the framework of Patnaik and Immerman as well as in our framework fixed and finite domains are used, the first-order incremental evaluation system framework (short: FOIES) introduced by Dong, Su and Topor [DT92, DS93] uses active domains, where the domain accessible by the update formulas contains only elements currently used in input relations. The choice of domains is the main diference between our basic framework and the FOIES framework. We discuss both choices in the following.

In this work, we will almost exclusively use finite and fixed domains and thus follow the approach taken by Patnaik and Immerman [PI94]. Here, fixed means that domains do not change while modifications are applied. Yet a dynamic program has to work uniformly for all domain sizes in order to maintain a query. Choosing fixed domains for a dynamic setting might appear counterintuitive at first sight.

After all, dynamic complexity is about dynamically changing structures, in particular structures might grow without any a priori bound on the size of the domain when tuples are inserted. However, it turns out that fixed and finite domains are sufficient to study the underlying dynamic mechanisms of dynamic programs. They also offer a strong connection to logics and circuit complexity, which will be used a couple of times in this work. Very often upper and lower bounds obtained for fixed, finite domains can be easily transferred to settings where the domain can depend on the input database, and vice versa.

When using active domains, only elements used in the input database are contained in the domain. When a tuple containing a so far unused element a is inserted into the input database, then a is also inserted into the domain accessible to the update formulas. This setting is a little closer to real database systems but most results in dynamic complexity hold equally for both fixed, finite domains and active domains.

Initializations

How the initial state of a dynamic program looks like depends on two choices: the set of permissible input databases and the power of the initialization mapping. We first highlight some possible options for those two choices, how those options have been combined in previous work and how they relate to each other; then we discuss which initialization settings we use in this work and why.

In our basic framework the initial input database can be arbitrary. Always starting from scratch, that is from an initially empty input database, is another option.

The initialization mapping in our basic dynamic complexity classes may assign arbitrary complex auxiliary relations. Other options are to restrict the mapping to be computable in some static complexity class, to be permutation-invariant (short: invariant initialization), or to always assign empty initial auxiliary relations. Intuitively a permutation-invariant initialization mapping maps isomorphic databases to isomorphic auxiliary databases. A particular case of permutation-invariant initialization mappings, studied in [GS12], is when the initialization is specified by some logical formalism.

Several combinations of those options have been used in the literature. We state some examples only. In [PI97], DYN- FO is defined as the class of (Boolean) queries that can be maintained for empty initial input databases with first-order update formulas and a first-order definable initialization mapping. Furthermore, a larger class DYN- FO$^+$ that extends DYN- FO by polynomial-time computable initialization mapping has been studied by Patnaik and Immerman. Also [Ete98] considers empty initial databases. In [WS07], general instances (with non-empty initial databases) are allowed, and auxiliary data is initialized by a mapping computable in some given complexity class. In [GS12], also general instances are allowed, but the initialization mapping has to be defined by logical formulas and is thus always permutation-invariant.

Some of the initialization settings are the same. First we note that for arbitrary initialization mappings, the same queries can be maintained regardless of whether one starts from an empty or from a non-empty initial database. This is because the initialization for a non-empty database can be obtained as the auxiliary relations obtained after inserting all tuples of the database into the empty one. Furthermore, it is easy to see that applying an invariant initialization mapping to an empty database is pretty much useless, as, all tuples with the same constants at the same positions are treated in the same way. Therefore, queries maintainable in DYNFO with empty initial database and invariant initialization can also be maintained from initially empty input and auxiliary database. We do not formally prove this here.

We shortly discuss which settings are used in this work. For upper bounds, we try to make the initialization as weak as possible. Yet, the weakest setting we use is the original setting of Patnaik and Immerman, that is, the setting with initially empty input database and first-order definable initialization mapping [PI97]. If a query can be maintained, for example, in this setting with first-order update formulas, we say that it can be maintained *in* DYNFO *from scratch*.

When proving lower bounds, we try to make the initialization as strong as possible. This is motivated by the fact that lower bounds in settings with restricted initialization might depend on the restriction. Thus our goal is to use the setting with arbitrary initial input databases and arbitrary initialization mappings for lower bounds whenever possible. An inexpressibility result in this setting shows that a query cannot be maintained dynamically at all.

In this work the basic dynamic complexity classes use the setting with arbitrary initial input databases and arbitrary initialization mapping as default. We explicitly state when a result does not adhere to this setting.

Built-In Relations

When studying fragments of DYNFO with restricted arity, it is sometimes useful to allow for special built-in relations of larger arity. For example, a lower bound proof for unary DYNPROP could look like it depends on the fact that no linear order was present on the domain (as binary relations are not allowed in unary DYNPROP). Then proving a lower bound for unary DYNPROP with a built-in linear order can refute this.

For the study of dynamic complexity classes with built-in relations we extend dynamic schemas to triples $(\tau_{\text{inp}}, \tau_{\text{aux}}, \tau_{\text{bi}})$ where τ_{bi} is the schema for the built-in database. The built-in relations are initialized by an initialization mapping that only depends on the domain (and not on the input database). In contrast to the auxiliary database, the built-in database never changes throughout a "computation", that is, update formulas for built-in relations R are of the form $\phi_\delta^R(\bar{u}; \bar{x}) = R(\bar{x})$ for all modifications δ.

In this work, the main dynamic classes do not allow built-in relations. At times we also consider dynamic programs with non-empty built-in schemas. We denote the extension of a dynamic complexity class that allows programs with non-empty built-in schemas by a superscript *, as in DYNPROP*. For classes with restricted arity of the auxiliary schema, the restriction does not apply to the built-in schema. For example, dynamic programs for queries in binary DYNPROP* can only use binary auxiliary relations, but built-in relations of arbitrary arity.

We use built-in databases only to strengthen some results in one of two possible ways, (1) by showing upper bounds in which (some) auxiliary relations or functions need not to be updated or (2) by showing inexpressibility results that hold for auxiliary schemas of bounded arity but with built-in relations of unbounded arity. In general, built-in data can be "simulated" by auxiliary data. However, this needs not to hold, e.g., if the auxiliary schema is more restricted than the built-in schema.

2.5 A Case Study: Graph Queries

The goal of this section is to develop a better intuition for the capabilities of dynamic programs. To this end we will study graph query languages from the perspective of dynamic complexity. We refer to the introduction of this chapter for a motivation for studying graph query languages in this context.

Formally, a *graph database* is a labeled graph $G = (V, E)$ where V is the set of nodes and E is a set of labeled edges $(x, \sigma, y) \subseteq V \times \Sigma \times V$ for some alphabet Σ. Here σ is called the *label* of edge (x, σ, y). The graph underlying a labeled graph is obtained by removing all labels from the database. A labeled graph is acyclic if its underlying graph is acyclic; it is undirected if, for each $\sigma \in \Sigma$, the projection of G to edges labeled by σ is undirected.

A path p in G is labeled with a word $w = \sigma_1 \dots \sigma_\ell$ if the edges $e_1, \dots, e_\ell$ along p are labeled with $\sigma_1, \dots, \sigma_\ell$. We also say that p is a *w-path*. A path is an *L-path*, for a formal language L, if it is a w-path for some $w \in L$.

Here we focus on path-based graph query languages. Every formal language L can be seen as a path query that selects a pair (x, y) of nodes from a given labeled graph if there is an L-path from x to y. Usually we identify a path query with its defining formal language. A path query is called *regular path query* if L is regular, similarly for context-free path queries and other classes of formal languages. A conjunctive regular path query is a query of the form $\mathcal{Q}(\bar{\S}) \overset{\text{def}}{=} \exists \bar{\ddagger} \bigwedge_{\rangle} \dagger_\rangle \mathcal{L}_\rangle \dagger'_\rangle$ where each L_i is a regular language, and each y_i, y'_i is either contained in $\bar{x}$ or in $\bar{z}$. Informally, a tuple $\bar{x}$ is selected by the query if there is a tuple $\bar{z}$ such that for each i there is an L_i-path from y_i to y'_i. For a more thorough introduction to graph queries we refer to [Bae13].

In dynamic complexity, even maintaining path queries as simple as $L(a^*)$ was, until recently, not possible using first-order update formulas because this requires to maintain reachability. Very likely this is the reason why graph queries have (almost) not been studied at all in dynamic complexity.

Some related work has been done before. Already Patnaik and Immerman pointed out that regular languages can be maintained in DYNFO [PI97]. Later Gelade et al. systematically studied formal languages in the dynamic complexity framework [GMS12]. They showed, among other results, that regular languages coincide with DYNPROP, and that all context-free languages can be maintained in DYNFO. A result for path queries has been obtained by Weber and Schwentick in [WS07]: the Dyck language D_2 can be maintained in DYNFO on acyclic graphs.

Here we present some further results for maintaining graph queries. As our main goal is to develop some intuition, those results are not meant to be exhaustive.

It turns out that regular path queries can be evaluated dynamically in a highly parallel fashion.

Theorem 2.5.1. *(a) When only insertions are allowed then every regular path query can be maintained from scratch in* DYNPROP.
(b) Every conjunctive regular path query can be maintained from scratch in DYNFO.

The proof of the second part relies on the very recent result that reachability can be maintained from scratch in DYNFO [DKM+15]. This result will not be proved in detail here.

Theorem 2.5.2. *Reachability can be maintained in* DYNFO *from scratch.*

Proof overview. The proof has three main steps.

Step 1. Show that reachability can be maintained in DYNFO if the rank of a matrix subject to modifications can be maintained in DYNFO.
Step 2. Construct a DYNFO-program with built-in arithmetic that maintains the rank of a matrix.
Step 3. Show that if a domain independent query is in DYNFO with built-in arithmetic then it can be maintained in DYNFO from scratch (and, in particular, without built-in arithemtic).

The statement of the theorem follows from Steps (1)–(3) since the reachability query is domain independent. In Section 3.4 we present Step 3 in detail.   □

Capturing non-regular path queries by one of our basic dynamic complexity classes seems to be significantly harder. We provide only some preliminary results for restricted classes of graphs and modifications.

Theorem 2.5.3. *(a) Context-free path queries can be maintained from scratch in* DYNFO *on acyclic graphs.*
(b) There is a non-context-free path query that can be maintained from scratch in DYNFO *on acyclic graphs.*
(c) There is a non-context-free path query that can be maintained from scratch in DYNFO *when only insertions are allowed.*

Part (a) of the theorem generalizes results and techniques from [GMS12, WS07].

2.5.1   Regular Path Queries

In this subsection we prove Theorem 2.5.1. For proving the first part of the theorem, the following notion will be useful. Let $\mathcal{A}$ be a deterministic finite state automaton (short: DFA) and let G be a labeled graph. Then a path p in G can be *read by* $\mathcal{A}$ *starting in a state* q *and ending in a state* r if $\mathcal{A}$ can reach state r from state q by reading the label sequence of p.

Proposition 2.5.4. *When only insertions are allowed then every regular path query can be maintained in* DYNPROP *from scratch.*

Proof. Let L be a regular path query and let $\mathcal{A} = (Q, \Sigma, \delta, s, F)$ be a DFA with $L = L(\mathcal{A})$. We construct a DYNPROP-program $\mathcal{P}$ that maintains L.

The program $\mathcal{P}$ has input schema $\{E_\sigma \mid \sigma \in \Sigma\}$ and an auxiliary schema that contains a binary relation symbol $R_{q,r}$ for every tuple $(q, r) \in Q^2$, as well as a binary designated query symbol R. The simple idea is that in a state S with underlying labeled graph G, the relation $R_{q,r}^{\mathcal{S}}$ contains all tuples $(a, b) \in V^2$ such that $\mathcal{A}$, for some labeled path p from a to b, can read p by starting in state q and ending in state r.

The update formulas for the relations $R_{q,r}$ are slightly more involved than the formulas for maintaining reachability under insertions (see Example 1.1). This is because $\mathcal{A}$ might reach a state r from a state q only by reading a labeled path from a to b that contains one or more loops. The crucial observation is, however, that for deciding whether (a, b) is in $R_{q,r}$ it suffices to consider paths that contain the node a at most $|Q|$ times (as paths that contain a more than $|Q|$ times can be shortened). This suffices to maintain the relations $R_{q,r}$ dynamically.

The update formulas for $R_{q,r}$ and R are as follows:

$$\phi_{\mathrm{INS}_{E_\sigma}}^{R_{q,r}} (u, v; x, y) \stackrel{\mathrm{def}}{=} R_{q,r}(u, v) \vee \bigvee_{q',r'} \left(R_{q,q'}(x, u) \wedge \varphi_{q',r'}^{|Q|}(u, v) \wedge R_{r',r}(v, y) \right)$$

$$\phi_{\mathrm{INS}_{E_\sigma}}^{R} (u, v; x, y) \stackrel{\mathrm{def}}{=} \bigvee_{f \in F} \phi_{\mathrm{INS}_{E_\sigma}}^{R_{s,f}} (u, v; x, y)$$

Here the formula $\varphi_{q',r'}^{|Q|}(u, v)$ shall only be satisfied by tuples (a, b) for which there exists a path p from a to b such that $\mathcal{A}$ can read p by starting in q' and ending in r'. It shall be satisfied by all such tuples with a witness path p that contains node a at most $|Q|$ times.

We inductively define, for every $1 \leq i \leq |Q|$ and all $q, r \in Q$, the slightly more general formulas $\varphi_{q,r}^i(u, v)$ as follows:

$$\varphi_{q,r}^1(u, v) \stackrel{\mathrm{def}}{=} [(q, \sigma, r) \in \delta] \vee R_{q,r}(u, v)$$

$$\varphi_{q,r}^i(u, v) \stackrel{\mathrm{def}}{=} \varphi_{q,r}^{i-1}(u, v) \vee \bigvee_{q',r'} \left(\varphi_{q,q'}^1(u, v) \wedge R_{q',r'}(v, u) \wedge \varphi_{r',r}^{i-1}(u, v) \right) \qquad \square$$

We conjecture that DYNPROP cannot maintain regular path queries for both insertions and deletions. This would imply that reachability can be maintained in DYNPROP which is very unlikely. A first step towards verifying this conjecture is done in Sect. 4.1.2 where we show that reachability cannot be maintained in binary DYNPROP.

However, regular path queries with insertions and deletions can be maintained in
DYNFO. The main ingredient for the proof is that reachability can be maintained in
DYNFO.

Proposition 2.5.5. *Every conjunctive regular path query can be maintained from
scratch in* DYNFO.

Proof sketch. Since DYNFO is closed under conjunctions and existential quantification, it suffices to show that regular path queries can be maintained in DYNFO.
We reduce the maintenance of regular path queries to reachability. The approach is
very similar to the approach taken in [KW03] for showing that dynamic LTL model
checking can be maintained by a TC^0-update mechanism.

The product graph $G \times \mathcal{A}$ of a labeled graph $G = (V, E)$ and an DFA $\mathcal{A} =
(Q, \Sigma, \delta, s, F)$ has nodes $V \times Q$, and the edge set contains a tuple $((u, q), (v, r))$ if
and only if there is a $\sigma \in \Sigma$ such that both $(u, \sigma, v) \in E$ and $(q, \sigma, r) \in \delta$. It can be
easily verified that there is a path from node a to node b in G labeled by $w \in L(\mathcal{A})$
if and only if there is a path from (a, s) to (b, f) in $G \times \mathcal{A}$ for some accepting state
$f \in F$ of $\mathcal{A}$.

Now, let L be a regular path query and let $\mathcal{A} = (Q, \Sigma, \delta, s, F)$ be an DFA with
$L = L(\mathcal{A})$. We construct a DYNFO-program $\mathcal{P}$ that maintains L. The program $\mathcal{P}$ has
input schema $\{E_\sigma \mid \sigma \in \Sigma\}$, yet it also stores an encoding of $G \times \mathcal{A}$ in its state. This
can be easily achieved, for example, by using a 4-ary auxiliary relation $R_{G \times \mathcal{A}}$ that
contains the tuples of $G \times \mathcal{A}$. For this it has to be assumed, without loss of generality,
that G contains at least $|Q|$ nodes and that each $q \in Q$ is identified with a unique
node. The result of a fixed regular path query for labeled graphs G with less than $|Q|$
nodes can be easily encoded by a first-order formula.

The crucial observation is that the modification of a single labeled edge in G leads
to at most $|Q|$ modifications in $G \times \mathcal{A}$. Thus, due to REACH $\in$ DYNFO [DKM+15] and
the closure of DYNFO under bounded expansion first-order reductions (see [PI97]),
the transitive closure of $G \times \mathcal{A}$ can be maintained in a relation T.

Now, this relation can be used to maintain the regular path query via

$$\phi_\delta^Q(u, v; x, y) = \bigvee_{f \in F} T'((x, s), (y, f))$$

where updating T with modification δ yields T'.   □

2.5.2   Beyond Regular Path Queries

The maintenance of non-regular path queries is more difficult. Here we prove the
results stated in Theorem 2.5.3. All of them are either for restricted graph classes or
for restricted modification sequences. We start with proving part (a).

Proposition 2.5.6. *Context-free path queries can be maintained from scratch in* DYNFO *on acyclic graphs.*

It is known that context-free languages are in DYNFO [GMS12] and that the Dyck language with two types of parentheses can be maintained on acyclic graphs [WS07]. We combine the techniques used in those two proofs in order to prove Proposition 2.5.6.

In the following we fix a context-free language L and a grammar $\mathcal{G} = (V, \Sigma, S, P)$ for L. We assume, without loss of generality, that $\mathcal{G}$ is in Chomsky normal form, that is, it has only rules of the form $X \to YZ$ and $X \to \sigma$. Further if $\epsilon \in L$ then $S \to \epsilon$ and no right-hand side of a rule contains S. We write $V \Rightarrow^* w$ if $w \in (\Sigma \cup V)^*$ can be derived from $Z \in V$ using rules of $\mathcal{G}$.

The dynamic program maintaining L on acyclic graphs will use 4-ary auxiliary relation symbols $R_{Z \to Z'}$ for all $Z, Z' \in V$. The intention is that in every state $\mathcal{S}$ with input database G, the relation $R_{Z \to Z'}^{\mathcal{S}}$ contains a tuple (x_1, y_1, x_2, y_2) if and only if there are strings $s_1, s_2 \in \Sigma^*$ such that $Z \Rightarrow^* s_1 Z' s_2$ and there is an s_i-path p_i from x_i to y_i for $i \in \{1, 2\}$. The paths p_1 and p_2 are called *witnesses* for $(x_1, y_1, x_2, y_2) \in R_{Z \to Z'}^{\mathcal{S}}$. Later we will see that whether two nodes are connected by an L-path after an update can be easily verified using those relations.

It turns out that for updating the relations $R_{Z \to Z'}^{\mathcal{S}}$ it is necessary to have access to $(2k + 2)$-ary relations $R_{X \to Y_1, \ldots, Y_k}^{\mathcal{S}}$, for $k \in \{1, 2, 3\}$, which contain a tuple $(x_1, y_1, \ldots, x_{k+1}, y_{k+1})$ if and only if there are strings $s_1, \ldots, s_{k+1} \in \Sigma^*$ such that $X \Rightarrow^* s_1 Y_1 s_2 \ldots s_k Y_k s_{k+1}$ and there is an s_i-path p_i from x_i to y_i in the input database underlying $\mathcal{S}$.

Next, in Lemma 2.5.7, we prove that every relation $R_{X \to Y_1, \ldots, Y_k}^{\mathcal{S}}$ is first-order definable from the relations $R_{Z \to Z'}^{\mathcal{S}}$ (and thus only relations $R_{Z \to Z'}^{\mathcal{S}}$ have to be stored as auxiliary data). This lemma is inspired by Lemma 7.3 from [WS07], and its proof is a generalization of the technique used in the proof of Theorem 4.1 in [GMS12]. Afterwards we prove Proposition 2.5.6 by showing how to use the relations $R_{Z \to Z'}^{\mathcal{S}}$ to maintain L and how to update the relations $R_{Z \to Z'}^{\mathcal{S}}$ using the formulas that define relations of the form $R_{X \to Y_1, Y_2}^{\mathcal{S}}$ and $R_{X \to Y_1, Y_2, Y_3}^{\mathcal{S}}$.

Lemma 2.5.7. *For a grammar $\mathcal{G}$ in Chomsky normal form, $k \geq 2$ and variables $X, Y_1, \ldots, Y_k$ there is a first-order formula $\varphi_{X \to Y_1, \ldots, Y_k}$ over schema $\tau = \{R_{Z \to Z'} \mid Z, Z' \in V\}$ that defines $R_{X \to Y_1, \ldots, Y_k}$ in states $\mathcal{S}$ where the relations $R_{Z \to Z'}^{\mathcal{S}}$ are as described above.*

Proof sketch. We explain how $\varphi_{X \to Y_1, Y_2, Y_3}$ tests whether a tuple is contained in $R_{X \to Y_1, Y_2, Y_3}^{\mathcal{S}}$. The construction for general k is analogous.

If a tuple $(x_1, y_1, x_2, y_2, x_3, y_3, x_4, y_4)$ is contained in $R_{X \to Y_1, Y_2, Y_3}^{\mathcal{S}}$ witnessed by s_i-paths p_i from x_i to y_i such that $X \Rightarrow^* s_1 Y_1 s_2 Y_2 s_3 Y_3 s_4$, then in the derivation tree of $s_1 Y_1 s_2 Y_2 s_3 Y_3 s_4$ from X there is a variable U such that $U \to U_1 U_2$ and either (1) Y_1 and Y_2 are derived from U_1, and Y_3 is derived from U_2; or (2) Y_1 is derived from U_1, and Y_2 and Y_3 are derived from U_2. In case (1), the derivation subtree starting from U_1 contains a variable W such that $W \to W_1 W_2$ and Y_1 is derived from W_1 and

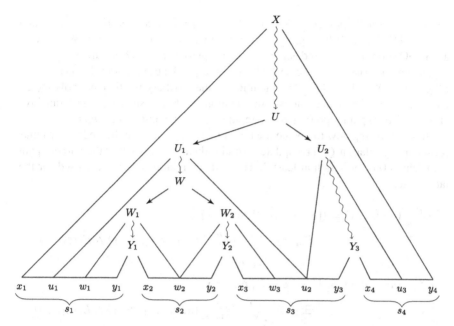

Fig. 2.1 Illustration of when a tuple $(x_1, y_1, x_2, y_2, x_3, y_3, x_4, y_4)$ is contained in $R_{X \to Y_1, Y_2, Y_3}$ in Lemma 2.5.7.

Y_2 is derived from W_2. Analogously for case (2). The derivation tree of X for case (1) is illustrated in Fig. 2.1.

The formula $\varphi_{X \to Y_1, Y_2, Y_3}$ is the disjunction of formulas ψ_1 and ψ_2, responsible for dealing with the cases (1) and (2) respectively. We only exhibit ψ_1, the formula ψ_2 can be constructed analogously. The formula ψ_1 guesses the variables U, U_1, U_2, W, W_1 and W_2, and the start and end positions of strings derived from those variables. Whether $(x_1, y_1, x_2, y_2, x_3, y_3, x_4, y_4)$ is contained in $R^{\mathcal{S}}_{X \to Y_1, Y_2, Y_3}$ can then be tested using the relations $R_{Z \to Z'}$. For simplicity the formula ψ_1 reuses the element names x_i and y_i as variable names and is defined as follows:

$$\psi(x_1, y_1, \ldots, x_4, y_4) = \exists u_1 \exists u_2 \exists u_3 \bigvee_{\substack{U, U_1, U_2 \in V \\ U \to U_1 U_2 \in P}} \exists w_1 \exists w_2 \exists w_3 \bigvee_{\substack{W, W_1, W_2 \in V \\ W \to W_1 W_2 \in P}}$$

$$\Big(R_{X \to U}(x_1, u_1, u_3, y_4) \wedge R_{U_1 \to W}(u_1, w_1, w_3, u_2)$$

$$\wedge R_{W_1 \to Y_1}(w_1, y_1, x_2, w_2) \wedge R_{W_2 \to Y_2}(w_2, y_2, x_3, w_3)$$

$$\wedge R_{U_2 \to Y_3}(u_2, y_3, x_4, u_3) \Big) \qquad \square$$

We now use the relations $R_{Z \to Z'}$ and the formulas $\varphi_{X \to Y_1, Y_2, Y_3}$ for maintaining context-free path queries on acyclic graphs.

Proof sketch (of Proposition 2.5.6). Let L be an arbitrary context-free language and let $\mathcal{G} = (V, \Sigma, S, P)$ be a grammar for L in Chomsky normal form. We provide a DYNFO-program $\mathcal{P}$ with designated binary query symbol Q that maintains L on acyclic graphs. The input schema is $\{E_\sigma \mid \sigma \in \Sigma\}$ and the auxiliary schema is $\tau_{\text{aux}} = \{R_{X \to Y} \mid X, Y \in V\} \cup \{T\}$. The intention of the auxiliary relation symbols $R_{X \to Y}$ has already been explained above; the relation symbol T shall store the transitive closure of the input graph (where the input graph is the union of all E_σ).

Before showing how to update the relations $R_{X \to Y}$, we state the update formulas for the query relation Q. The update formulas distinguish whether the witness path is of length 0 or of length at least 2. The updated relations $R_{X \to Y}$ are used for the latter case.

$$\phi^Q_{\text{INS}_{E_\sigma}} (u, v; x, y) \stackrel{\text{def}}{=} ([S \to \epsilon \in P] \wedge x = y)$$
$$\vee \exists z_1 \exists z_2 \bigvee_{\substack{U \in V \\ U \to \tau \in P}} \left(\phi^{R_{S \to U}}_{\text{INS}_{E_\sigma}} (u, v; x, z_1, z_2, y) \wedge E_\tau(z_1, z_2) \right)$$

$$\phi^Q_{\text{DEL}_{E_\sigma}} (u, v; x, y) \stackrel{\text{def}}{=} ([S \to \epsilon \in P] \wedge x = y)$$
$$\vee \exists z_1 \exists z_2 \bigvee_{\substack{U \in V \\ U \to \tau \in P}} \left(\phi^{R_{S \to U}}_{\text{DEL}_{E_\sigma}} (u, v; x, z_1, z_2, y) \wedge E_\tau(z_1, z_2) \right)$$

It remains to present update formulas for each $R_{X \to Y}$. For simplicity we identify names of variable and elements.

After inserting a σ-edge (u, v), a tuple (x_1, y_1, x_2, y_2) is contained in $R_{X \to Y}$ if there are two witness paths p_1 and p_2 such that (1) p_1 and p_2 have already been witnesses before the insertion, or (2) only p_1 uses the new σ-edge, or (3) only p_2 uses the new σ-edge, or (4) both p_1 and p_2 use the new σ-edge. In case (2) the path p_1 can be split into a path from x_1 to u, the edge (u, v) and a path from v to y_1. Similarly in the other cases and for p_2. Using the formulas from Lemma 2.5.7 this can be expressed as follows:

$$\phi^{R_{X \to Y}}_{\text{INS}_{E_\sigma}} (u, v; x_1, y_1, x_2, y_2) \stackrel{\text{def}}{=} R_{X \to Y}(x_1, y_1, x_2, y_2) \vee \tag{2.1}$$

$$\bigvee_{\substack{U_1, U_2 \in V \\ U_1 \to \sigma \in P \\ U_2 \to \sigma \in P}} \left(\varphi_{X \to U_1, Y}(x_1, u, v, y_1, x_2, y_2) \right. \tag{2.2}$$

$$\vee \, \varphi_{X \to Y, U_2}(x_1, y_1, x_2, u, v, y_2) \tag{2.3}$$

$$\left. \vee \, \varphi_{X \to U_1, Y, U_2}(x_1, u, v, y_1, x_2, u, v, y_2) \right) \tag{2.4}$$

After deleting a σ-edge (u, v) a tuple (x_1, y_1, x_2, y_2) is in $R_{X \to Y}$ if it still has witness paths p_1 and p_2 from x_1 to y_1 and from x_2 to y_2, respectively. The update formula for $R_{X \to Y}$ verifies that such witness paths exist. Therefore, similar to Example 2.3.2, the formula distinguishes for each $i \in \{1, 2\}$ whether (1) there was

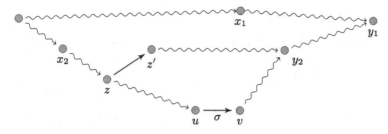

Fig. 2.2 Illustration of the update of $R_{X \to Y}$ after deletion of σ-edge (u, v) in the proof of Proposition 2.5.6. The nodes x_1 and y_1 satisfy Condition (1), whereas nodes x_2 and y_2 satisfy Condition (2).

no path from x_i to y_i via (u, v) before deleting the σ-edge (u, v), or (2) there was a path from x_i to y_i via (u, v). See Fig. 2.2 for an illustration.

In case (1) all paths present from x_i to y_i before the deletion of the σ-edge (u, v) are also present after the deletion. In particular the set of possible witnesses p_i remains the same. For case (2), the update formula has to check that there is still a witness path p_i. Such a path p_i has the options (a) to still use the edge (u, v) but for a $\tau \neq \sigma$, and (b) to not use the edge (u, v) at all.

The update formula for $R_{X \to Y}$ is a disjunction over all those cases for the witnesses for (x_1, y_1) and (x_2, y_2). Instead of presenting formulas for all those cases, we explain the idea for two representative cases. All other cases are analogous.

We first look at the case where (x_1, y_1) satisfies (1), (x_2, y_2) satisfies (2) and there are witness paths p_1 and p_2 where p_2 satisfies (a). The following formula deals with this case:

$$(\neg T(x_1, u) \vee \neg T(v, y_1)) \wedge T(x_2, u) \wedge T(v, y_2)$$
$$\wedge \bigvee_{\substack{\tau \neq \sigma, U_2 \in V \\ U_2 \to \tau \in P}} \left(\varphi_{X \to Y, U_2}(x_1, y_1, x_2, u, v, y_2) \wedge E_\tau(u, v) \right)$$

In the first line the premises for this case are checked, in the second line it is verified that p_2 uses τ-edge (u, v) for $\sigma \neq \tau$.

Now we consider the case where both (x_1, y_1) as well as (x_2, y_2) satisfy (2), and where there are witness paths p_1 and p_2 where p_1 satisfies (a) and p_2 satisfies (b). The existence of such a path p_1 can be verified as above. For verifying the existence of such a path p_2, a path not using (u, v) has to be found. This is achieved by relying on the same technique as for maintaining reachability for acyclic graphs (see Example 2.3.2). The following formula verifies the existence of such p_1 and p_2:

$$T(x_1, u) \wedge T(v, y_1) \wedge T(x_2, u) \wedge T(v, y_2)$$

$$\wedge \exists z \exists z' \bigvee_{\substack{\tau \neq \sigma, U_1, U_2 \in V \\ U_1 \to \tau \in P \\ U_2 \to \tau' \in P}} \Big(\varphi_{X \to U_1, Y, U_2}(x_1, u, v, y_1, x_2, z, z', y_2) \wedge E_\tau(u, v)$$

$$\wedge \big(T(x_2, z) \wedge E_{\tau'}(z, z') \wedge (z \neq u \vee z' \neq v)$$

$$\wedge T(z', y_2) \wedge T(z, u) \wedge \neg T(z', u) \big) \Big)$$

Again, in the first line the premises for this case are checked. In the second line z and z' are chosen with the purpose to find an alternative path p_2 (as in Example 2.3.2), and it is verified that p_1 and p_2 are witness paths. The third and forth lines verify that z and z' yield an alternative path.   □

Finally we exhibit examples of non-context-free languages that can be maintained in restricted settings.

Proposition 2.5.8. *There is a non-context-free path query that can be maintained from scratch in* DYNFO *on acyclic graphs.*

Proof. Let $L \stackrel{\text{def}}{=} \{a^n b^n c^n \mid n \in \mathbb{N}\}$. We provide a DYNFO-program $\mathcal{P} = (P, \text{INIT}, Q)$ that maintains L on acyclic graphs. The input schema τ_{inp} contains a binary relation symbol E_σ for each $\sigma \in \{a, b, c\}$.

We assume that arithmetic is available on the elements that have been used in modifications so far, that is, that there is a linear order relation $<$ as well as its corresponding addition relation $+$ on those elements. In [Ete98], Etessami showed that basic arithmetic relations can be maintained by a DYNFO-program (see also Sect. 3.4). The linear order $<$ can be used to interpret elements of the active domain as numbers, i.e. an element x is interpreted as the number k if x is the kth element with respect to $<$.

For each $\sigma \in \{a, b, c\}$ the program $\mathcal{P}$ has a binary auxiliary relation T_σ and a ternary auxiliary relation D_σ. The intention is as follows. In a given state $\mathcal{S}$, the relation $T_\sigma^{\mathcal{S}}$ shall contain the transitive closure of $E_\sigma^{\mathcal{S}}$; and the relation $D_\sigma^{\mathcal{S}}$ shall contain a tuple (x, y, k) if and only if there is a σ^*-path from x to y of length k.

Already in Example 2.3.2 we have seen how the transitive closure of an acyclic graph can be maintained in DYNFO. Thus the relations T_σ can be easily maintained. Their update formulas can be easily extended to also keep track of the length of paths:

$$\phi_{\text{INS}_{E_\sigma}}^{D_\sigma}(u, v; x, y, k) \overset{\text{def}}{=} D_\sigma(x, y, k) \vee \exists \ell \exists \ell' \big(\ell + \ell' + 1 = k$$
$$\wedge D_\sigma(x, u, \ell) \wedge D_\sigma(v, y, \ell')\big)$$

$$\phi_{\text{DEL}_{E_\sigma}}^{D_\sigma}(u, v; x, y, k) \overset{\text{def}}{=} D_\sigma(x, y, k) \wedge \Big((\neg T_\sigma(x, u) \vee \neg T_\sigma(v, y))$$
$$\vee \exists z \exists z' \exists \ell \exists \ell' \big(\ell + \ell' + 1 = k \wedge D_\sigma(x, z, \ell) \wedge E_\sigma(z, z')$$
$$\wedge (z \neq u \vee z' \neq v) \wedge D_\sigma(z', y, \ell')$$
$$\wedge T_\sigma(z, u) \wedge \neg T_\sigma(z', u))\Big)$$

For updates to $E_{\sigma'}$ for $\sigma' \neq \sigma$, the relations D_σ and T_σ remain unchanged. Finally, whether there is an L-path between to nodes after an update δ can be expressed by the following formulas:

$$\phi_\delta^Q(u, v; x, y) \overset{\text{def}}{=} \exists z \exists z' \exists k \big(\phi_\delta^{D_a}(u, v; x, z, k) \wedge \phi_\delta^{D_b}(u, v; z, z', k) \wedge \phi_\delta^{D_c}(u, v; z', y, k)\big) \qquad \Box$$

Proposition 2.5.9. *There is a non-context-free path query that can be maintained from scratch in* DYNFO *when only insertions are allowed.*

Proof sketch. Consider the language $L \overset{\text{def}}{=} \{a^{n!+n} \mid n \in \mathbb{N}\}$. Observe that L is not context-free (because its Parikh image is not semi-linear). Furthermore L has the property that if there is a path from x to y containing a loop, then there is an L-path from x to y. To see this, let p be a path from x to y containing a loop of length ℓ, and let k be the length of the path p without the loop. Then there is an a^*-path of length $m\ell + k$ between x and y for every m, since the loop can be repeated m many times. Now, choosing $n \overset{\text{def}}{=} k\ell + k$ shows that there is an L-path from x to y since there is an m such that $m\ell + k = (k\ell + k)! + k\ell + k$ (because ℓ divides $(k\ell + k)! + k\ell$).

Thus, in order to maintain L under insertions, it is sufficient to maintain for all nodes x and y auxiliary data that indicates (1) whether there is a path with a loop between x and y, and (2) the lengths of loop-free paths between x and y.

This can be achieved by using the technique used for maintaining $\{a^n b^n c^n \mid n \in \mathbb{N}\}$ in the acyclic case. Hence, again, the dynamic program maintains a linear order $<$, as well as its corresponding addition and multiplication relations on the elements that have been used in modifications so far [Ete98]. Further, the program maintains a relation D which stores all tuples (x, y, k) for which there is an a^*-path from x to y of length k.

This suffices to check condition (1). For checking (2), additionally a unary relation F is maintained, which is supposed to store all elements k such that $k = m! + m$ for some $m \in \mathbb{N}$. This can be easily achieved by extending Etessami's construction.

Now, when an a-edge (u, v) is added, then there is an L-path between x and y if there was such a path before; or there is a node z such that there are a^*-paths from x to z, from z to z and from z to y; or there is an a^*-path from x to y of length k where k is in F. This can be easily expressed by a first-order update formula. $\qquad \Box$

2.6   Outlook and Bibliographic Remarks

In this chapter the basic dynamic complexity framework and the basic dynamic complexity classes have been introduced. We presented examples for the power of dynamic programs and discussed variants of the framework used in the literature. Furthermore several small results for maintaining queries on graph databases have been obtained.

The most promising direction for future work is to conduct a deeper, more systematic study of graph queries. Here, we only looked at very basic graph query languages. Extensions, such as the query language ECRPQ [BLLW12], might be worth studying as well. As an example, the length of paths used in a conjunctive regular path query can be compared in ECRPQ. It is conceivable that such queries can be maintained in DYNFO. This would also settle the open question whether a context-free path query can be maintained in DYNFO when both insertions and deletions are allowed.

As a minimal prerequisite for maintaining such queries, it is necessary to be able to maintain distances in a graph. Extending the result that reachability is in DYNFO in this direction seems not to be trivial, but also not out of reach.

Another possible research direction is motivated from the discussion of the framework. The discussion highlighted that many different settings have been looked at and that some variants actually collapse. In order to be able to transfer results easily between different settings, it would be very convenient to have a systematic overview of how the settings relate to each other. This is, however, probably not easy to achieve.

Bibliographical Remarks

The dynamic complexity framework presented in Sect. 2.2 has originally been introduced by Patnaik and Immerman in [PI94]. In this form it was introduced in joint work with Thomas Schwentick in [ZS13], and reused in [ZS14, Zeu14a]. A variant of the class DYNFO was introduced as DYN- FO in [PI94]; the classes DYNPROP and DYNQF have been introduced in Hesse's thesis [Hes03b]. The examples for those classes are attributed as follows. Example 2.3.2 has been independently presented in [DS95][1] and [PI94]. The technique used in Example 2.3.4 has been introduced in [GMS09], the example itself is from [ZS13]. Example 2.3.7 will also be contained in the full versions of [ZS14, Zeu14a].

With the only exception of Theorems 2.5.1 and 2.5.2 and Proposition 2.5.9, the results for graph queries are solely by the author and have not been published before. Theorems 2.5.1 and 2.5.2 are joint work with Samir Datta, Raghav Kulkarni, Anish Mukherjee and Thomas Schwentick [DKM+15]. Proposition 2.5.9 originated from related discussions with Katja Losemann.

---

[1] In the cited work the result is attributed to earlier work by the same authors from 1993. I was not able to obtain this previous work.

Chapter 3
Relating Small Dynamic Complexity Classes

One of the major goals of descriptive complexity theory is to study the relationship of the expressive power of various logics. The motivation is that results relating the expressive power of logics may help to answer questions like "Is a given query expressible in some logic?" more easily. It may also help to explain why it is hard to express a given query in some logic. Answers to those questions, on the other hand, are highly relevant as they have an immediate impact on the amount of resources necessary to answer a query, due to the close connection between logics and traditional computational complexity classes.

The goal of this chapter is to systematically pursue a similar program for dynamic descriptive complexity classes. We will study dynamic classes from two different perspectives.

First, the relationship between different dynamic complexity classes will be studied. This is interesting for the same reason as studying the relationship of static classes. If two dynamic complexity classes $\text{DYN}\mathcal{C}$ and $\text{DYN}\mathcal{C}'$ (induced by two static complexity classes $\mathcal{C}$ and $\mathcal{C}'$, respectively) — although they seem to be different at first glance — turn out to be equal, then queries that can be maintained in $\text{DYN}\mathcal{C}$ can be maintained in $\text{DYN}\mathcal{C}'$ as well. In particular, when $\mathcal{C}'$ is defined by syntactically restricting $\mathcal{C}$, upper bounds for the more restricted class $\text{DYN}\mathcal{C}'$ can be obtained by showing upper bounds for the less restricted class $\text{DYN}\mathcal{C}$. It also has implications for lower bounds as, under this premise, proving lower bounds for $\text{DYN}\mathcal{C}'$ is as hard as proving lower bounds for $\text{DYN}\mathcal{C}$. In other, more optimistic words, for proving lower bounds for $\text{DYN}\mathcal{C}$ one can focus the attention on $\text{DYN}\mathcal{C}'$.

Our second perspective on dynamic descriptive complexity classes is to see how they relate to classical (static) descriptive complexity classes. In the previous chapter we have seen several examples for queries that can be maintained in a dynamic class $\text{DYN}\mathcal{C}$ but can only be (statically) expressed in a class $\mathcal{C}'$ larger than $\mathcal{C}$. A more generic result is to find examples of classes $\mathcal{C}$ and $\mathcal{C}'$ such that $\mathcal{C}'$ can express more queries than $\mathcal{C}$, but $\mathcal{C}'$ is contained in $\text{DYN}\mathcal{C}$. Such results are interesting, for example, in the context of database query languages, where one can argue that the weak query language $\mathcal{C}$ is actually strong enough when used in a dynamic setting.

© Springer-Verlag GmbH Germany 2017
T. Zeume, *Small Dynamic Complexity Classes*, LNCS 10110
DOI: 10.1007/978-3-662-54314-6_3

Before discussing our goals and results for those two perspectives in detail, we informally introduce the dynamic complexity classes under consideration.

Our main interest is in fragments of DYNFO. Most of the fragments of DYNFO studied in the literature have been obtained from DYNFO by restricting the update programs with respect to three different aspects: the arity of the auxiliary relations, the syntax of the update formulas and the power of the initialization mapping. Here we will focus on studying syntactic restrictions of DYNFO; yet we will also have a short look on restricting the power of the initialization mapping. Dynamic complexity classes with restricted arity will play an important role in Chap. 4.

The exploration of syntactic fragments of DYNFO, such as the one obtained by disallowing quantification in update formulas, was started by Hesse [Hes03b]. Here, further fragments of DYNFO obtained by syntactically restricting first-order update formulas will be studied. Namely, first-order update formulas with restricted quantifier structure and restricted quantifier-free matrix of formulas in prenex normalform will be of interest. Our main attention, however, is on classes of queries maintainable by conjunctive queries and variants thereof. These classes are motivated from database theory and adhere to both restrictions mentioned above.

Conjunctive queries (CQs), that is, in terms of logic, existential first-order queries whose quantifier-free part is a conjunction of atoms, are one of the most investigated query languages. Starting with Chandra and Merlin [CM77], who analyzed conjunctive queries for relational databases, those queries have been studied for almost every emerging new database model. Usually also the extension by unions (UCQs), by negations (CQ⁻s) as well as by both unions and negations (UCQ⁻s or, equivalently, ∃*FO) have been studied. Disallowing also existential quantification yields the less-studied classes PROPCQ, PROPUCQ, PROPCQ⁻ and PROPUCQ⁻, respectively. It is folklore that all those classes are distinct for relational databases, see Fig. 3.1.

Fig. 3.1 Hierarchy of fragments of first-order logic. Solid lines are strict separations.

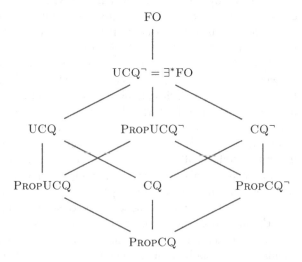

Already Dong and Topor studied conjunctive queries as update mechanism [DT92]. They showed that certain fragments of Datalog can be maintained by unions of conjunctive queries (though under Δ-semantics and under insertions only). Those queries have also been used in [DR97] to maintain several variants of the transitive closure query (under insertions only).

Other fragments of first-order logic obtained by restricting the quantifier prefix of formulas will be of interest as well, an example is the class $\forall^*FO$ of queries definable by universal first-order formulas.

After this short introduction to the fragments under consideration, we will now outline the goals of this chapter. Afterwards we discuss our contributions.

Purpose of this Chapter

The discussion above motivates working towards the following goals.

Goal 3.1. *Obtain a better understanding of the relative expressiveness of small dynamic descriptive complexity classes.*

Goal 3.2. *Exhibit examples of small dynamic descriptive complexity classes that capture (larger) static descriptive complexity classes.*

To the best of our knowledge no (non-trivial) results for the first goal have been obtained so far. A vaguely related result is the characterization of the dynamic class DYNQF by dynamic constant-time concurrent-read, write-only PRAMs due to Hesse [Hes03b]. As for the second goal, only very few such results are known. Dong and Topor showed that under insertions all regular chain Datalog queries can be maintained by unions of conjunctive queries [DT92]. Further, the class of regular languages is characterized by DYNPROP on strings and, on general structures, $\exists^*FO$ is captured by DYNQF [GMS12].

Our focus for those two goals will be on extensions and restrictions of dynamic conjunctive queries in update formulas. For extensions, we add negation and/or disjunction to conjunctive queries, and for restrictions we disallow quantification. We further consider other quantification patterns.

As already stated, the study of conjunctive queries as update language is motivated from query languages for relational databases. In this context a slightly different perspective is interesting as well. In our standard framework, auxiliary relations are re-defined completely after each modification. However, in the context of query re-evaluation in relational databases, it is often convenient to express the new state of an auxiliary relation R in terms of the current relation and some "Delta", that is, by specifying a tuple set R^+ to be added to R and a tuple set R^- to be removed from R. We refer to the former semantics as *absolute semantics* and to the latter as Δ-*semantics*. In the context of dynamic complexity, Δ-semantics has been used already in the pioneering work of Dong and Topor [DT92]. Obviously, the choice of the semantics does not affect the expressiveness of an update language that is closed under Boolean operations. However, some of the query languages considered here, such as conjunctive queries, lack some Boolean closure properties.

Goal 3.3. *Understand the relationship between absolute semantics and Δ-semantics for conjunctive queries and their variants.*

Contributions

For the relationship of the various syntactic fragments of first-order logic in the dynamic complexity framework we obtain a fairly complete picture with respect to both absolute and Δ-semantics. The results are summarized in Fig. 3.2. The notation for classes not mentioned so far will be formally introduced in Sects. 3.1 and 3.2. In general, Δ indicates Δ-semantics, the absence of Δ indicates absolute semantics.

All fragments under consideration have unrestricted arity. Although all the results are stated for arbitrary initialization mappings, they also hold in the setting where queries are maintained from scratch, that is from an initially empty input database and first-order initialized auxiliary data. On the other hand, some proofs do not carry over to the strict setting of Patnaik and Immerman where, in a dynamic class $\text{DYN}\mathcal{C}$, only $\mathcal{C}$ initializations are allowed.

Now, we shortly discuss the results in more detail. The distinctness of the underlying static query classes does not translate into the dynamic setting:

- We show that, in many cases, the addition of the union-operator does not yield additional expressive power in the dynamic setting, for example, $\text{DYNUCQ}^\neg = \text{DYNCQ}^\neg$, $\text{DYNUCQ} = \text{DYNCQ}$, and $\text{DYNPROPUCQ}^\neg = \text{DYNPROPCQ}^\neg$.

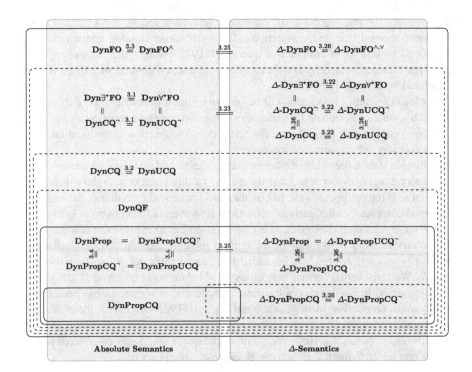

Fig. 3.2 Hierarchy of fragments of DYNFO. Solid lines are strict separations.

- Furthermore, negation often does not increase the expressive power of an update language, e.g. we have DYNPROPUCQ⁻ = DYNPROPUCQ and Δ-DYNCQ⁻ = Δ-DYNCQ.
- Finally, often quantifiers can be replaced by their dual quantifiers, e.g. DYN∃*FO(= DYNUCQ⁻) = DYN∀*FO.

While it remains open whether DYNCQ⁻ = DYNCQ, some of the dynamic classes can be separated:

- By showing that DYNQF, the extension of DYNPROP that allows auxiliary functions, is contained in DYNCQ, we can separate the classes DYNPROP and DYNCQ.
- Dynamic conjunctive queries without negations and quantifiers are strictly weaker than DYNPROP.

As for the relationship between static and dynamic complexity classes we show the following two results:

- Dynamic conjunctive queries extended by negations capture all first-order queries. More generally, the class of first-order queries can be characterized as the class maintainable by non-recursive dynamic DYN∃*FO-programs with a single existential quantifier per update formula.
- When only insertions are allowed, then DYNPROP captures all queries expressible in positive existential first-order logic extended by negated equality atoms. This class contains, in particular, all unions of conjunctive queries.

For the third goal, the main finding is that the difference between absolute and Δ-semantics is much smaller than expected:

- The dynamic classes corresponding to FO, CQ⁻ and PROP yield the same expressive power with respect to absolute and Δ-semantics.
- It turns out that conjunctive queries and conjunctive queries with negation coincide with respect to Δ-semantics, that is, in particular, Δ-DYNCQ = Δ-DYNCQ⁻ and thus, also Δ-DYNCQ = DYNUCQ⁻.

All results from above are about syntactical fragments of DYNFO. An orthogonal result for restricted initialization is obtained as well:

- DYNFO with computation from scratch and DYNFO with built-in arithmetic coincide for domain-independent queries.

As already mentioned, this result is one of the three main steps in the proof that reachability is in DYNFO with computation from scratch [DKM+15].

Parts of this chapter originated in joint work with Samir Datta, Raghav Kulkarni, Anish Mukherjee and Thomas Schwentick. For detailed bibliographic remarks we refer to the end of this chapter.

Outline of this Chapter

All fragments that have not been formally introduced so far will be presented in the next section. In addition the results from the left hand side of Fig. 3.2 will be obtained in that section. Δ-semantics will be introduced and studied in Sect. 3.2; all remaining results depicted in Fig. 3.2 are presented in that section as well. Afterwards, in Sect. 3.3, the relationship of static and dynamic descriptive complexity classes will be studied. In Sect. 3.4, the class DYNFO with computation from scratch is compared to DYNFO with built-in arithmetic. This chapter is concluded by a discussion of possible directions for future work and bibliographical remarks.

3.1   A Hierarchy of Dynamic Classes

In this section we study the relationship between the various syntactic fragments of DYNFO, with a focus on variants of dynamic conjunctive queries.

As mentioned in the introduction above, conjunctive queries are one of the most investigated query languages for relational databases. They correspond to select-project-join queries in the relational algebra and to select-where-from queries in SQL [AHV95]. We define conjunctive queries and unions of conjunctive queries as a subclass of the first-order definable queries:

- CQ is the class of conjunctive queries, that is, queries expressible by first-order formulas of the form $\varphi(\bar{x}) = \exists \bar{y} \psi$ where ψ is a conjunction of atomic formulas.
- UCQ is the class of all unions of conjunctive queries, that is, queries expressible by formulas of the form $\varphi(\bar{x}) = \bigvee_i \exists \bar{y} \psi_i$ where each ψ_i is a conjunction of atomic formulas.

We note that safety of queries is not an issue here: we use queries as update formulas only and we can always assume that, for each required arity, there is an auxiliary "universal" relation containing all tuples of this arity over the active domain which could be used to make queries syntactically safe.

The classes CQ and UCQ can be extended by additionally allowing negated atoms, resulting in CQ$^{\neg}$ and UCQ$^{\neg}$; or they can be restricted by disallowing quantification, resulting in PROPCQ, PROPUCQ, PROPCQ$^{\neg}$ and PROPUCQ$^{\neg}$. It is well known that UCQ$^{\neg}$ and $\exists^*$FO, the class of queries expressible by existential first-order formulas, coincide, but otherwise, all these classes are distinct. Furthermore, other quantification patterns than $\exists^*$ can be considered, for example $\forall^*$ or arbitrary quantification. As usual DYNCQ denotes the class of queries maintainable by dynamic programs that use CQ queries only; similarly for the other classes.

It should be stressed that although the class CQ$^{\neg}$ is usually referred to as conjunctive queries with negations, the negations may only occur directly in front of atoms.

Most of the examples from the previous chapter can actually be maintained by some variant of conjunctive queries. For example, the dynamic program maintaining the transitive closure for acyclic graphs in Example 2.5 is actually a DYNUCQ$^{\neg}$-program. Hence studying those classes is well-motivated.

The main goal of this section is to show that the relationship of all these classes in the dynamic setting is much simpler than in the static setting. Indeed many dynamic classes collapse, as indicated in the left part of Fig. 3.2. The dynamic classes DYNPROPCQ, DYNPROP and DYNCQ can be separated. Whether DYNCQ, DYNCQ⁻ and DYNFO can be separated remains open.

The main results of this section are the following two theorems regarding the second and the third fragment in the left part of Fig. 3.2.

Theorem 3.1.1. *Let Q be a query. Then the following statements are equivalent:*

(a) Q can be maintained in DYNUCQ⁻.
(b) Q can be maintained in DYNCQ⁻.
(c) Q can be maintained in DYN∃*FO.
(d) Q can be maintained in DYN∀*FO.

Theorem 3.1.2. *Let Q be a query. Then the following statements are equivalent:*

(a) Q can be maintained in DYNUCQ.
(b) Q can be maintained in DYNCQ.

Using the same technique as is used for removing unions from dynamic unions of conjunctive queries, a normal form for DYNFO can be obtained. The class DYNFO^ contains all queries maintainable by a program whose update formulas are in prenex normal form where the quantifier-free part is a conjunction of atoms.

Theorem 3.1.3. *Let Q be a query. Then the following statements are equivalent:*

(a) Q can be maintained in DYNFO.
(b) Q can be maintained in DYNFO^.

Further we prove the following result for the quantifier-free variants of dynamic conjunctive queries.

Theorem 3.1.4. *Let Q be a query. Then the following statements are equivalent:*

(a) Q can be maintained in DYNPROP.
(b) Q can be maintained in DYNPROPUCQ⁻.
(c) Q can be maintained in DYNPROPCQ⁻.
(d) Q can be maintained in DYNUCQ.

The four theorems follow from Lemmata 3.1.10, 3.1.11, 3.1.12 and 3.1.14, which will be stated and proved in the following subsections.

Those results are complemented by the following separation theorem.

Theorem 3.1.5. *(a) The class* DYNPROPCQ *is a strict subclass of* DYNPROP.
(b) The class DYNPROP *is a strict subclass of* DYNCQ.

Part (b) follows immediately from the following theorem and the fact that DYNQF can express the equal cardinality query while DYNPROP can not [GMS12]. The proof of part (a) is deferred to Sect. 4.1 in the next chapter.

Theorem 3.1.6. DYNQF *is contained in* DYNCQ.

The rest of this section is structured as follows. Before we turn to the proofs of the theorems, we discuss the proof techniques that will be used. Afterwards we exhibit constructions for removing negations and for switching quantifiers in dynamic programs, that is, e.g., for constructing an ∃*FO-program from an ∀*FO-program. Then we present various ways for eliminating disjunctions from dynamic programs. Finally we present a construction for translating DYNQF-programs into equivalent DYNCQ-programs.

3.1.1 Tools for Collapsing Dynamic Classes

For showing that a class DYN$\mathcal{C}$ of queries is contained in a class DYN$\mathcal{C}'$, it is sufficient to construct, for every dynamic program with update queries from class $\mathcal{C}$, an equivalent dynamic program with update queries from class $\mathcal{C}'$. In cases where $\mathcal{C}' \subset \mathcal{C}$ this can also be seen as constructing a $\mathcal{C}'$-normal form for $\mathcal{C}$-programs.

Most of the proofs for the collapse of two dynamic classes presented here are not very deep. Indeed, most of them use one or more of the following three (easy) techniques.

The *replacement technique* is used to remove subformulas of a certain kind from update formulas and to replace their "meaning" by additional auxiliary relations. In this way, we often can remove negations (by choosing negative literals as subformulas, see the proof of Lemma 3.1.10) and disjunctions (see proof of Lemma 3.1.14) from update formulas.

The *preprocessing technique* is used to convert (more) complicated update formulas into easier update formulas by splitting the computation performed by the complicated update formula into two parts; one of them performed by the initialization mapping and stored in an additional auxiliary relation, the other one performed by the easier update formula using the pre-computed auxiliary relation. Applications of this technique are the removal of unions from dynamic unions of conjunctive queries (see example below) and, in the next section, proving that dynamic conjunctive queries with negations are equally expressive under absolute semantics and Δ-semantics (see Lemma 3.2.8).

Example 3.1.7. We consider the update formula

$$\phi_\delta^R(u; x) = \exists y \big(U(x, y) \lor V(x, u) \big)$$

for a unary relational symbol R. We aim at an equivalent update formula $\psi_\delta^R(u; x)$ without disjunction. The idea is to store a 'disjunction blue print' in a precomputed auxiliary relation T and to use existential quantification to guess which disjunct becomes true.

In this example, we assume that in every state of the dynamic program on every database, both the interpretations of U and V are always non-empty sets. Then, $\phi_\delta^R(u; x)$ can be replaced by

$$\exists y \exists z_1 \exists z_2 \exists z_3 \exists z_4 \big(U(z_1, z_2) \wedge V(z_3, z_4) \wedge T(z_1, z_2, z_3, z_4, x, y, u)\big)$$

where T is an additional auxiliary relation symbol which is interpreted, in every state $\mathcal{S}$, by a 7-ary relation $T^{\mathcal{S}}$ containing all tuples $(a_1, \ldots, a_7)$ with $(a_1, a_2) = (a_5, a_6)$ or $(a_3, a_4) = (a_5, a_7)$. Thus $T^{\mathcal{S}}$ ensures that either the values chosen for z_1, z_2 coincide with the values of x, y or the values of z_3, z_4 coincide with x, u.

Therefore, the initialization mapping initializes T with the result of the query

$$\mathcal{Q}_T(z_1, z_2, z_3, z_4, x, y, u) \stackrel{\text{def}}{=} (z_1, z_2) = (x, y) \vee (z_3, z_4) = (x, u).$$

Observe that this approach fails when U or V are interpreted by empty relations. In order to cover empty relations as well, some extra work needs to be done (see Lemma 3.1.13). ☐

The *squirrel technique* maintains additional auxiliary relations that reflect the state of some auxiliary relation after every possible single modification (or short modification sequence).[1] For example, if a dynamic program contains a relation symbol R then a fresh relation symbol R_{INS} can be used, such that the interpretation of R_{INS} contains the content of R after modification INS (for every possible insertion tuple). Of course, R_{INS} has higher arity than R, as it takes the actual inserted tuple into account. Sample applications of this technique are the removal of quantifiers from *some* update formulas (see the following example and Lemma 3.1.9) and the maintenance of first-order queries in DYNCQ¬ (see Theorem 3.3.1).

Example 3.1.8. Consider the update formula

$$\phi_{\text{INS}}^{Q}(u_1; x) = \exists y \big(Q(x) \vee \neg S(u_1, y)\big)$$

for the query symbol Q of some dynamic program $\mathcal{P}$. Sometimes it will be convenient if the update formulas for the designated query symbol are quantifier-free. In order to obtain a quantifier-free update formula for Q under insertions we maintain the relation $Q_{\text{INS}}(\cdot, \cdot)$ that contains a tuple (a, b) if and only if b would be in Q in the state reached after inserting a. Similarly for S and deletions.

Then the update formula ϕ_{INS}^{Q} can be replaced by the quantifier-free formula $\phi_{\text{INS}}^{Q}(u_1; x) \stackrel{\text{def}}{=} Q_{\text{INS}}(u_1, x)$. The relation Q_{INS} can be updated via

$$\phi_{\text{INS}}^{Q_{\text{INS}}}(u_0; u_1, x) \stackrel{\text{def}}{=} \exists y \big(Q_{\text{INS}}(u_0, x) \vee \neg S_{\text{INS}}(u_0, u_1, y)\big)$$

$$\phi_{\text{DEL}}^{Q_{\text{INS}}}(u_0; u_1, x) \stackrel{\text{def}}{=} \exists y \big(Q_{\text{DEL}}(u_0, x) \vee \neg S_{\text{DEL}}(u_0, u_1, y)\big)$$

and similarly, for the other new auxiliary relations. The new auxiliary relations are initialized accordingly. ☐

---

[1] Squirrels usually make provisions for every possible future, at least in literary fiction (see, e.g., [Pot03]).

We note that, in this example, the application of the technique does not eliminate all quantifiers in the program (in fact, it removes one and introduces two new formulas with quantifiers), but it removes quantification from the update formula for a *particular relation*. Removing quantification from the update formulas of the query relation will turn out to be useful in the proofs of Lemmata 3.1.14, 3.1.11 and 3.2.8.

This concludes the description of the techniques. In the following, as a preparatory step, we generalize the preceding example and show how to remove quantifiers from the update formulas of the query relation for arbitrary DYNFO-programs. For an arbitrary quantifier prefix $\mathbb{Q} \in \{\exists, \forall\}^*$ let $\mathbb{Q}$FO be the class of queries expressible by formulas with quantifier prefix $\mathbb{Q}$. If $\mathbb{Q}$ is a substring of $\mathbb{Q}'$ and $\mathcal{Q}$ is a query in $\mathbb{Q}$FO then trivially $\mathcal{Q}$ is in $\mathbb{Q}'$FO as well.

Lemma 3.1.9. *Let $\mathbb{Q}$ be an arbitrary quantifier prefix. For every* DYN$\mathbb{Q}$FO-*program there is an equivalent* DYN$\mathbb{Q}$FO-*program $\mathcal{P}$ such that the update formulas for the designated query symbol of $\mathcal{P}$ consist of a single atom.*

Proof. We follow the approach from Example 3.1.8 and use the squirrel technique. For ease of presentation we fix the input schema to be $\tau_{\text{inp}} = \{E\}$ where E is a binary relation symbol; the proof can be easily adapted to arbitrary input schemas.

Let $\mathcal{P}$ be a DYN$\mathcal{C}$-program over auxiliary schema τ with designated query symbol Q. We construct an equivalent DYN$\mathcal{C}$ program $\mathcal{P}'$ over schema τ' where τ' contains a designated query symbol Q' and a $(k+2)$-ary relation symbol R_δ for every k-ary $R \in \tau$ and every $\delta \in \{\text{INS}, \text{DEL}\}$.

The idea is that R_δ shall reflect the content of R in the next state, for each possible modification of the kind δ. More precisely, let $G = (E, V)$ be a graph, α a sequence of modifications, $\beta = \delta(\bar{e})$ a modification with $\delta \in \{\text{INS}, \text{DEL}\}$ and $\bar{e} \in V^2$. If $\mathcal{S}$ is the state obtained by $\mathcal{P}$ after applying $\alpha\beta$ to G, i.e. $\mathcal{S} = \mathcal{P}_{\alpha\beta}(\text{INIT}(G))$, and $\mathcal{S}'$ is the state obtained by $\mathcal{P}'$ after applying α to G, i.e. $\mathcal{S}' = \mathcal{P}'_\alpha(\text{INIT}'(G))$, then

$$\bar{a} \in R^{\mathcal{S}} \text{ if and only if } (\bar{e}, \bar{a}) \in R_\delta^{\mathcal{S}'}. \tag{3.1}$$

Thus for every $\delta(\bar{e})$ the relation $R_\delta(\bar{e}, \cdot)$ stores $R(\cdot)$ after application of $\delta(\bar{e})$.

Then the update formula for Q' after a modification δ can be written as follows:

$$\phi_\delta^{Q'}(\bar{u}; \bar{x}) \stackrel{\text{def}}{=} R_\delta(\bar{u}, \bar{x})$$

It remains to explain how to update the relations R_δ. Therefore it will be convenient to assume that the edge relation E is updated by formulas ϕ_{INS}^E and ϕ_{DEL}^E that express the impact of a modification to E, for example, $\phi_{\text{INS}}^E(a, b; x, y) = E(x, y) \vee (a = x \wedge b = y)$.

By $\phi_{\delta_1}^R[\tau \to \tau_{\delta_0}](\bar{u}_0; \bar{u}_1, \bar{x})$ we denote the formula obtained from $\phi_{\delta_1}^R(\bar{u}_1; \bar{x})$ by replacing every atom $S(\bar{z})$ with $S \in \tau$ by $S_{\delta_0}(\bar{u}_0, \bar{z})$. Then the update formula for R_{δ_1} is

$$\phi_{\delta_0}^{R_{\delta_1}}(\bar{u}_0; \bar{u}_1, \bar{x}) \stackrel{\text{def}}{=} \phi_{\delta_1}^R[\tau \to \tau_{\delta_0}](\bar{u}_0; \bar{u}_1, \bar{x}).$$

We observe that all quantifier prefixes of formulas thus obtained have been used by the program $\mathcal{P}$ already.

The initialization mapping of $\mathcal{P}'$ is as follows. The query symbol Q' is initialized like Q in $\mathcal{P}$. For every graph G the relation symbol $R_\delta \in \tau'$ is initialized as

$$\bigcup_{\bar{e} \in V^2} \{\bar{e}\} \times \mathcal{P}_{\delta(\bar{e})}(\text{INIT}(G)) \upharpoonright R_\delta$$

where $\mathcal{P}_{\delta(\bar{e})}(\text{INIT}(G)) \upharpoonright R_\delta$ denotes the relation R_δ in state $\mathcal{P}_{\delta(\bar{e})}(\text{INIT}(G))$.

The correctness of this construction is proved inductively over the length of modification sequences by showing that states of $\mathcal{P}'$ *simulate* states of $\mathcal{P}$ as specified by (3.1).

Therefore, let G be a graph and $\alpha = \alpha_1 \ldots \alpha_i$ a modification sequence with $\alpha_i = \delta_i(\bar{e}_i)$. Further let $\mathcal{S}_i$ and $\mathcal{S}'_i$ be the states obtained by $\mathcal{P}$ and $\mathcal{P}'$, respectively, after application of $\alpha_1 \ldots \alpha_i$.

If α is of length 0 and β is an arbitrary modification with $\beta = \delta(\bar{e})$ then $\mathcal{S} \stackrel{\text{def}}{=} \mathcal{P}_\beta(\mathcal{S}_0)$ and $\mathcal{S}' \stackrel{\text{def}}{=} \mathcal{S}'_0$ satisfy (3.1) due to the definition of the initialization mapping of $\mathcal{P}'$. If α is of length $i \geq 1$ then, by induction hypothesis, the states $\mathcal{S} \stackrel{\text{def}}{=} \mathcal{S}_i = \mathcal{P}_{\alpha_i}(\mathcal{S}_{i-1})$ and $\mathcal{S}' \stackrel{\text{def}}{=} \mathcal{S}'_{i-1}$ satisfy (3.1) that is

$$\bar{a} \in R^{\mathcal{S}} \text{ if and only if } (\bar{e}_i, \bar{a}) \in R^{\mathcal{S}'}_{\delta_i} \tag{3.2}$$

for all relations R and R_{δ_i}.

Now, let $\beta = \delta(\bar{e})$ be an arbitrary modification. Further let $\mathcal{T} \stackrel{\text{def}}{=} \mathcal{P}_\beta(\mathcal{S})$ and $\mathcal{T}' \stackrel{\text{def}}{=} \mathcal{P}'_{\alpha_i}(\mathcal{S}')$. By definition, $\bar{b} \in R^{\mathcal{T}}$ if and only if

$$(R^{\mathcal{S}}, \{\bar{u}_1 \mapsto \bar{e}, \bar{x} \mapsto \bar{b}\}) \models \phi^R_\delta(\bar{u}_1; \bar{x}).$$

Thanks to (3.2) and the definition of $\phi^{R_{\delta_1}}_{\delta_0}$ this is equivalent to

$$(R^{\mathcal{S}'}, \{\bar{u}_0 \mapsto \bar{e}_i, \bar{u}_1 \mapsto \bar{e}, \bar{x} \mapsto \bar{b}\}) \models \phi^R_{\delta_i}[\tau \to \tau_{\delta_0}](\bar{u}_0; \bar{u}_1, \bar{x}).$$

By definition this is equivalent to $(\bar{e}, \bar{b}) \in R^{\mathcal{T}'}$.   □

3.1.2 Eliminating Negations and Inverting Quantifiers

Now we turn towards constructions for removing negations and inverting quantifiers. Both constructions employ the replacement technique. We start by exhibiting negation-free normal forms for DYNFO and for DYNPROP.

Lemma 3.1.10. *(a) Every* DYNFO-*program has an equivalent negation-free* DYNFO-*program.*
(b) Every DYNPROP-*program has an equivalent* DYNPROPUCQ-*program.*

Proof. This lemma is a generalization of Theorem 6.6 from [Hes03b]. Given a dynamic program $\mathcal{P}$, the simple idea is to maintain, for every auxiliary relation R of $\mathcal{P}$, an additional auxiliary relation $\widehat{R}$ for the complement of R.

We make this more precise. In the following we prove (a). As the construction does not introduce quantifiers, it can be used for (b) as well.

Let $\mathcal{P} = (P, \text{INIT}, Q)$ be a DYNFO-program over schema τ. We assume, without loss of generality, that $\mathcal{P}$ is in negation normal form. Further we assume, for ease of presentation, that the input relations have update formulas as well, e.g. if the input database is a graph, then $\phi_{\text{INS}}^E(a, b; x, y) = E(x, y) \vee (a = x \wedge b = y)$ et cetera.

We construct a negation-free DYNFO-program equivalent to $\mathcal{P}$ that uses the schema $\tau \cup \widehat{\tau} \cup \{\widehat{=}\}$ where $\widehat{\tau}$ contains for every relation symbol $R \in \tau$ a fresh relation symbol $\widehat{R}$ of equal arity. Recall that τ includes the input schema and the auxiliary schema. The idea is to maintain in $\widehat{R}^{\mathcal{S}}$ the negation of $R^{\mathcal{S}}$, for all states $\mathcal{S}$. Further $\widehat{=}$ shall always contain the complement of $=$.

In a first step we construct a DYNFO-program $\mathcal{P}' = (P', \text{INIT}', Q)$ in negation normal form over $\tau \cup \widehat{\tau} \cup \{\widehat{=}\}$ that maintains $R^{\mathcal{S}}$ and $\widehat{R}^{\mathcal{S}}$ (but still uses negations). The update formulas for relation symbols $R \in \tau$ are as in $\mathcal{P}$. For every $\widehat{R} \in \widehat{\tau}$ and every modification δ, the update formula $\phi_\delta^{\widehat{R}}(\bar{x}; \bar{y})s$ is the negation normal form[2] of $\neg \phi_\delta^R(\bar{x}; \bar{y})$. The relation $\widehat{=}$ never changes. The initialization mapping INIT' initializes $\widehat{R}$ with the complement of $\text{INIT}(R)$.

From $\mathcal{P}'$ a negation-free DYNFO-program $\mathcal{P}'' = (P'', \text{INIT}', Q)$ can be constructed as follows. An update formula $\phi_\delta^R(\bar{x}; \bar{y})$ for $\mathcal{P}''$ is obtained from the update formula $\phi_\delta^R(\bar{x}; \bar{y})$ for $\mathcal{P}'$ by replacing all negative literals $\neg S$ by $\widehat{S}$. The initialization mapping of $\mathcal{P}''$ is the same as for $\mathcal{P}'$.

The equivalence of $\mathcal{P}$ and $\mathcal{P}''$ can be proved by induction over the length of modification sequences.   □

Now we prove that $\text{DYN}\exists^*\text{FO} = \text{DYN}\forall^*\text{FO}$, and therefore that unions of conjunctive queries with negation coincide with $\text{DYN}\forall^*\text{FO}$ in the dynamic setting. The proof uses the replacement technique to maintain the complements of the auxiliary relations used in the $\text{DYN}\exists^*\text{FO}$-program via $\text{DYN}\forall^*\text{FO}$-formulas. A small complication arises from the fact that the query relation (and not its complement) has to be maintained. This is solved by ensuring that the update formulas of the query relation are atomic.

A slightly more general result can be shown.

Lemma 3.1.11. *Let $\mathbb{Q}$ be an arbitrary quantifier prefix. A query can be maintained in $\text{DYN}\mathbb{Q}\text{FO}$ if and only if it can be maintained in $\text{DYN}\overline{\mathbb{Q}}\text{FO}$.*

Proof. Let $\mathcal{P} = (P, \text{INIT}, Q)$ be an arbitrary dynamic $\text{DYN}\mathbb{Q}\text{FO}$-program over schema τ. By Lemma 3.1.9 we can assume, without loss of generality, that the update formulas of Q are atomic. We construct a dynamic $\text{DYN}\overline{\mathbb{Q}}\text{FO}$-program $\mathcal{P}'$ over schema $\widehat{\tau} \cup \{Q'\}$ where $\widehat{\tau}$ contains a k-ary relation symbol $\widehat{R}$ for every

---

[2]Observe that this fails for the classes DYNCQ⁻ and DYNUCQ⁻.

k-ary $R \in \tau$. The intention is that $\widehat{R}$ is always equal to the complement of R. This is achieved in a similar way as in the proof above.

We denote by $\phi[\tau \rightarrow \widehat{\tau}]$ the formula obtained from ϕ by replacing every atom $S(\bar{z})$ in ϕ by $\neg \widehat{S}(\bar{z})$. Then the update formulas of $\mathcal{P}'$ are obtained as $\phi_\delta^{\widehat{R}} \stackrel{\text{def}}{=} \neg \phi_\delta^R[\tau \rightarrow \widehat{\tau}]$ for every $\widehat{R} \in \widehat{\tau}$. Observe that this formula can be easily transformed into an $\overline{\mathbb{Q}}$FO-formula. Further $\phi_\delta^{Q'} = \neg \phi_\delta^Q$ which is a $\overline{\mathbb{Q}}$FO-formula since ϕ_δ^Q is quantifier-free. The initialization mapping of $\mathcal{P}'$ is straightforward. □

3.1.3 Eliminating Disjunctions

Two different methods are used for removing disjunctions. For removing disjunctions from quantifier-free programs, the replacement technique is employed. For removing disjunctions from DYNUCQ- and DYNUCQ⁻-programs, the preprocessing technique is combined with the replacement technique. The latter technique, employed in a naïve way, can yield programs with larger arity than the original program. After exhibiting the naïve construction, we outline how this increase of arity can be avoided.

We start by giving a disjunction-free normal form for quantifier-free programs.

Lemma 3.1.12. *Every* DYNPROP*-program has an equivalent* DYNPROPCQ⁻*-program.*

Proof. Let $\mathcal{P} = (P, \text{INIT}, Q)$ be a DYNPROP-program over schema τ. We assume, without loss of generality, that τ contains, for every relation symbol R, a relation symbol $\widehat{R}$ and that $\mathcal{P}$ ensures that $\widehat{R}^S$ is the complement of R^S for every state S. This can be achieved by using the same technique as in Lemma 3.1.10. Further we assume that all update formulas of $\mathcal{P}$ are in conjunctive normal form.

The conjunctive DYNPROP-program we are going to construct is over schema $\tau \cup \tau'$ where τ' contains a fresh relation symbol $R_{\neg C}$ for every clause C occurring in some update formula of $\mathcal{P}$. The goal of the construction is to ensure that $R_{\neg C}^S(\bar{z})$ holds if and only if $\neg C(\bar{z})$ is true in state S. Then an update formula $\phi = C_1(\bar{x}_1) \wedge \ldots \wedge C_k(\bar{x}_k)$ with clauses $C_1(\bar{x}_1), \ldots, C_k(\bar{x}_k)$ can be replaced by the conjunctive formula $\neg R_{\neg C_1}(\bar{x}_1) \wedge \ldots \wedge \neg R_{\neg C_k}(\bar{x}_k)$.

In a first step we construct a DYNPROP-program $\mathcal{P}' = (P', \text{INIT}', Q)$ in conjunctive normal form that maintains the relations $R_{\neg C}^S$. To this end, let C be a clause with k variables and let $\bar{z}$ be the k-tuple that contains the variables of C in the order in which they occur. Assume that $C = L_1(\bar{z}_1) \vee \ldots \vee L_\ell(\bar{z}_\ell)$ where $\bar{z}_i \subseteq \bar{z}$ and each L_i is an atom or a negated atom. Thus $\neg C \equiv \neg L_1(\bar{z}_1) \wedge \ldots \wedge \neg L_\ell(\bar{z}_\ell)$. The relation symbol $R_{\neg C}$ is of arity k. For a modification δ the update formula for $R_{\neg C}$ is

$$\phi_\delta^{R_{\neg C}}(\bar{x}; \bar{z}) = \phi_\delta^{X_1}(\bar{x}; \bar{z}_1) \wedge \ldots \wedge \phi_\delta^{X_\ell}(\bar{x}; \bar{z}_\ell)$$

where X_i is the relation symbol R if $L_i = \neg R$ and X_i is $\widehat{R}$ if $L_i = R$. Observe that $\phi_\delta^{R_{\neg C}}(\bar{x}; \bar{z})$ is in conjunctive normal form, because each $\phi_\delta^{X_i}(\bar{x}; \bar{z}_i)$ is in conjunctive normal form; further $\phi_\delta^{R_{\neg C}}(\bar{x}; \bar{z})$ does not use new clauses. The initialization mapping

INIT$'$ extends the initialization mapping INIT to the schema τ' in a natural way. For a clause C and input database $\mathcal{I}$, a tuple $\bar{a}$ is in INIT$'(R_{\neg C})$ if and only if C evaluates to false in INIT$(\mathcal{I})$ for $\bar{a}$.

The second step is to construct from $\mathcal{P}'$ the desired conjunctive DYNPROP-program $\mathcal{P}''$: every clause C in every update formula of $\mathcal{P}'$ is replaced by $\neg R_{\neg C}$. This construction yields a conjunctive program $\mathcal{P}''$. The initialization mapping of $\mathcal{P}''$ is the same as for $\mathcal{P}'$.

We sketch the proof that $\mathcal{P}''$ is equivalent to $\mathcal{P}$. The dynamic program $\mathcal{P}'$ updates relations from τ exactly as program $\mathcal{P}$. By induction over the length of modification sequences, one can prove that $R^{\mathcal{S}}_{\neg C}(\bar{a})$ holds if and only if $\neg C(\bar{a})$ is true in state $\mathcal{S}$ for all tuples $\bar{a}$. Thus corresponding update formulas of $\mathcal{P}$ and $\mathcal{P}''$ always yield the same result.   □

Now we turn to disjunction-free normal forms for DYNUCQ, DYNUCQ$^{\neg}$ and negation-free DYNFO. Observe that the idea of the proof of Lemma 3.1.12 cannot be applied directly since those classes are not closed under negations. Instead we use the idea from Example 3.1.7 and simulate disjunctions by existential quantifiers. As a preparatory step we show how auxiliary relations can be ensured to be non-empty and to not contain all tuples.

Lemma 3.1.13. *Let $k \geq 0$. For every k-ary DYNUCQ-program $\mathcal{P}$ there is a k'-ary DYNUCQ-program $\mathcal{P}'$ with $k' \overset{def}{=} \max\{k, 2\}$ and with query symbol Q' which is equivalent for domains of size at least 2 and satisfies (1) in every possible state all auxiliary relations $\neq Q'$ of $\mathcal{P}'$ are neither empty nor do they contain all tuples, and (2) no update formula uses the relation symbol Q'. Analogously for DYNUCQ$^{\neg}$- and negation-free DYNFO-programs.*

Proof. We present the construction for DYNUCQ-programs. The construction for DYNUCQ$^{\neg}$- and negation-free DYNFO-programs is analogous.

Let $\mathcal{P} = (P, \text{INIT}, Q)$ be an arbitrary DYNUCQ-program over schema τ. For the moment we assume that all auxiliary relations have arity at least 2. Towards the end of this proof we will sketch how to extend the following construction to programs with auxiliary relations with arity less than 2.

We construct a program $\mathcal{P}' = (P', \text{INIT}', Q')$ that is equivalent to $\mathcal{P}$ for domains of size at least 2. The program $\mathcal{P}'$ is over schema $\{Q', A, \bar{A}, B, \bar{B}\} \cup \tau_a \cup \tau_b$ where $A, \bar{A}, B$ and $\bar{B}$ are unary relation symbols and τ_a and τ_b contain a k-ary relation symbol R_a and R_b, respectively, for every k-ary relation symbol $R \in \tau$.

The intuition is as follows. Let a and b be distinct elements of the domain. Every state $\mathcal{S}$ of $\mathcal{P}$ has a corresponding state $\mathcal{S}'$ in $\mathcal{P}'$ which is obtained as follows. The k-ary relation $R^{\mathcal{S}'}_a$ shall contain the tuple $\bar{a} \overset{def}{=} (a, \ldots, a)$ and additionally all tuples from $R^{\mathcal{S}}$ except for the tuple $\bar{a}' \overset{def}{=} (b, a, \ldots, a)$. Similarly $R^{\mathcal{S}'}_b$ shall contain the tuple $\bar{b} \overset{def}{=} (b, \ldots, b)$ and additionally all tuples from $R^{\mathcal{S}}$ except for the tuple $\bar{b}' \overset{def}{=} (a, b, \ldots, b)$. Thus the relations $R^{\mathcal{S}'}_a$ and $R^{\mathcal{S}'}_b$ are exactly as $R^{\mathcal{S}}$, except for the four special tuples $\bar{a}, \bar{a}', \bar{b}$ and $\bar{b}'$. Observe that the tuples $\bar{a}$ and $\bar{a}'$ are in $R^{\mathcal{S}'}_b$ if and only if they are in $R^{\mathcal{S}}$; and the tuples $\bar{b}$ and $\bar{b}'$ are in $R^{\mathcal{S}'}_a$ if and only if they are in $R^{\mathcal{S}}$. The unary relation $A^{\mathcal{S}'}$ contains only the element a, and $\bar{A}^{\mathcal{S}'}$ is the complement of $A^{\mathcal{S}'}$. Similarly for $B^{\mathcal{S}'}$ and $\bar{B}^{\mathcal{S}'}$. Hence all auxiliary relations (except the query relation) are always non-empty and do not contain all tuples.

The initialization mapping INIT' of $\mathcal{P}'$ is obtained from INIT straightforwardly. The update formula $\phi_\delta^{R_a}$ can be defined as

$$\phi_\delta^{R_a}(\bar{u};\bar{x}) \stackrel{\text{def}}{=} \bar{x} = \bar{a} \vee (\psi_\delta^R(\bar{u};\bar{x}) \wedge \bar{x} \neq \bar{a}')$$

where ψ_δ^R is obtained from the update formula ϕ_δ^R of $\mathcal{P}$ by replacing every atom $S(\bar{z})$ by $(\bar{z} \neq \bar{a} \wedge S_a(\bar{z})) \vee (\bar{z} \neq \bar{b} \wedge S_b(\bar{z}))$. Further $\bar{x} = \bar{a}$ is an abbreviation for the formula $\exists y(A(y) \wedge \bar{x} = (y, \ldots, y))$ and $\bar{x} \neq \bar{a}'$ is an abbreviation for $\bar{B}(x_1) \vee \bigvee_{2 \leq i \leq \ell} \bar{A}(x_i)$ (where $\bar{x} = (x_1, \ldots, x_\ell)$). Similarly for $\bar{z} \neq \bar{a}$ and $\bar{z} \neq \bar{b}$.

The update formulas for relation symbols R_b are obtained analogously. The update formula for Q' is as follows:

$$\phi_\delta^{Q'}(\bar{u};\bar{x}) \stackrel{\text{def}}{=} (\bar{x} = \bar{a} \wedge \phi_\delta^{Q_b}(\bar{u};\bar{x})) \vee (\bar{x} = \bar{b} \wedge \phi_\delta^{Q_a}(\bar{u};\bar{x}))$$

Observe that all update formulas are over schema $\{A, \bar{A}, B, \bar{B}\} \cup \tau_a \cup \tau_b$ and in particular do not use Q'. Furthermore all those formulas can be easily translated into a union of conjunctive queries.

It remains to sketch how to deal with programs with auxiliary relations of arity less than 2. In that case, each unary relation R can be simulated by a binary relation R_{bin} with the intention that R_{bin} contains a tuple (a, b) if and only if R (in a corresponding state) contains the tuple a. Similarly for boolean relations. The attentive reader might have noticed that this might also change the arity of the query relation. Yet if a binary version Q_{bin} of the query relation is maintained, then the query relation can be extracted from that relation by a simple UCQ-formula. The formula $\phi_\delta^{Q'}$ can be adapted accordingly.   □

Lemma 3.1.14. *(a) For every* DYNUCQ⁻-*program there is an equivalent* DYNCQ⁻-
program.
(b) For every DYNUCQ-*program there is an equivalent* DYNCQ-*program.*
(c) For every DYNFO-*program there is an equivalent* DYNFO^-*program.*

Proof. We first prove the statements for domains with at least two elements and show how to drop this restriction afterwards. The construction uses the idea from Example 3.1.7. We present the construction for (a) but, as it does not introduce any negation operators it works for (b) as well. For (c) it is sufficient to start from a negation-free DYNFO-program by Lemma 3.1.10; and for those the same construction as for (a) can be used; more precisely, the quantifier prefix $\exists \bar{y}$ used throughout the construction of (a) has to be replaced by the general quantifier-prefix $\exists \bar{y}_1 \forall \bar{y}_2 \ldots \mathbb{Q}\bar{y}_\ell$.

Let $\mathcal{P} = (P, \text{INIT}, Q)$ be a DYNUCQ⁻-program over schema τ. For domains of size at least 2 we can assume, due to Lemma 3.1.13, that all auxiliary relations of $\mathcal{P}$, except for Q, are not empty and do not contain all tuples, and that Q is not used in any update formula. Further, without loss of generality, we assume that the quantifier-free parts of all update formulas of $\mathcal{P}$ are in disjunctive normal form.

We convert $\mathcal{P}$ into an equivalent DYNCQ^--program $\mathcal{P}'$ whose update formulas are in prenex normal form with quantifier-free parts of the form $T(\bar{w}) \wedge \bigwedge_i L_i(\bar{w}_i)$, where L_i, for all i, is an arbitrary literal over τ and the symbols T are fresh auxiliary relation symbols. To this end the program $\mathcal{P}' = (P', \text{INIT}', Q)$ is over schema $\tau' = \tau \cup \tau_T$, where τ_T contains a relation symbol $T_{R,\delta}$ for every relation symbol $R \in \tau$ and every modification δ. The intention is that corresponding states for $\mathcal{P}$ and $\mathcal{P}'$ agree on the relations from τ. The relations $T_{R,\delta}$ will be used as in Example 3.1.7.

Now we construct the update formulas for program $\mathcal{P}'$. Let $R \in \tau$ and let δ be a modification. Further let

$$\phi_\delta^R(\bar{u}; \bar{x}) = \exists \bar{y}\big(C_1(\bar{u}, \bar{x}, \bar{y}) \vee \ldots \vee C_k(\bar{u}, \bar{x}, \bar{y})\big)$$

be the update formula of R with respect to δ in $\mathcal{P}$, where every C_i is a conjunction of literals.

For

$$C_i(\bar{u}, \bar{x}, \bar{y}) = L_i^1(\bar{v}_i^1) \wedge \ldots \wedge L_i^\ell(\bar{v}_i^\ell)$$

we define

$$\widehat{C}_i(\bar{z}_i) \stackrel{\text{def}}{=} L_i^1(\bar{z}_i^1) \wedge \ldots \wedge L_i^\ell(\bar{z}_i^\ell)$$

where all $\bar{z}_i^j$ contain pairwise different, fresh variables and $\bar{z}_i \stackrel{\text{def}}{=} (\bar{z}_i^1, \ldots, \bar{z}_i^\ell)$. We also let $\bar{v}_i \stackrel{\text{def}}{=} (\bar{v}_i^1, \ldots, \bar{v}_i^\ell)$. Further let X be the set of variables appearing in $\bar{u}, \bar{x}, \bar{y}$ and in the tuples $\bar{z}_i$.

The update formula $\psi_\delta^R(\bar{u}; \bar{x})$ for $R \in \tau$ in $\mathcal{P}'$ is as follows:

$$\psi_\delta^R(\bar{u}; \bar{x}) \stackrel{\text{def}}{=} \exists \bar{y} \, \exists \bar{z}_1 \ldots \exists \bar{z}_k \big(\widehat{C}_1(\bar{z}_1) \wedge \ldots \wedge \widehat{C}_k(\bar{z}_k) \wedge T_{R,\delta}(\bar{u}, \bar{x}, \bar{y}, \bar{z}_1, \ldots, \bar{z}_k)\big)$$

The relation $T_{R,\delta}$ is fixed, that is, both update formulas reproduce the current value of $T_{R,\delta}$. The relation contains a tuple $\bar{a}$ if there is an assignment $\pi : X \to D$ with $\bar{a} = \pi(\bar{u}, \bar{x}, \bar{y}, \bar{z}_1, \ldots, \bar{z}_k)$ and $\pi(\bar{z}_i) = \pi(\bar{v}_i)$ for some i. Here, the tuple $\bar{v}_i$ consists of elements from $\bar{u}, \bar{x}$ and $\bar{y}$ as specified by the definition of $\bar{v}_i$ above.

Auxiliary relation symbols $R \in \tau$ are initialized as in $\mathcal{P}$. The relations $T_{R,\delta}$ are initialized as intended by simple quantifier-free formulas (but with a disjunction for selecting i).

We roughly sketch why $\mathcal{P}$ and $\mathcal{P}'$ are equivalent. The proof is by induction over the length of modification sequences. It is sufficient to show that the formulas ϕ_δ^R and ψ_δ^R yield the same result for states S and S', where S' contains, in addition to the relations of S, the relation $T_{R,\delta}$.

If $(S, \bar{a}, \bar{b}) \models \phi_\delta^R(\bar{u}; \bar{x})$ then there is a $\bar{c}$ such that $(S, \bar{a}, \bar{b}, \bar{c}) \models C_i(\bar{u}, \bar{x}, \bar{y})$ for some i. Now, for showing that $(S', \bar{a}, \bar{b}) \models \psi_\delta^R(\bar{u}; \bar{x})$ one can choose $\bar{y}$ in ψ_δ^R as $\bar{c}$ and the values for $\bar{z}_i$ accordingly. This will satisfy $\widehat{C}_i(\bar{z}_i)$ and $T_{R,\delta}$. The values for each $\bar{z}_j$ with $j \neq i$ are chosen such that all literals in $\widehat{C}_j(\bar{z}_j)$ are satisfied, which is possible because all auxiliary relations are neither empty nor do they contain all tuples.

If $(\mathcal{S}', \bar{a}, \bar{b}) \models \psi_\delta^R(\bar{u}; \bar{x})$ then there are tuples $\bar{c}$ and $\bar{d}_1, \ldots, \bar{d}_k$ such that $(\mathcal{S}', \bar{d}_i)$ $\models \widehat{C}_i(\bar{z}_i)$ for some i and $(\mathcal{S}', \bar{a}, \bar{b}, \bar{c}, \bar{d}_1, \ldots \bar{d}_k) \models T_{R,\delta}(\bar{u}, \bar{x}, \bar{y}, \bar{z}_1, \ldots, \bar{z}_k)$. But then, due to the definition of $T_{R,\delta}$, there is a tuple $\bar{c}'$ such that $(\mathcal{S}, \bar{c}') \models C_i(\bar{v}_i)$. Therefore also $(\mathcal{S}, \bar{a}, \bar{b}) \models \phi_\delta^R(\bar{u}; \bar{x})$.

This concludes the proof of (a), (b) and (c) for domains with at least two elements. The restriction on the size of the domains can be dropped as follows. In all three cases the idea is to make a case distinction on the size of the domain in the update formulas of the designated query symbol.

To this end, we first construct a dynamic DYNPROPCQ-program $\mathcal{P}'' = (P'', \text{INIT}'', Q'')$ over schema τ'' with $\tau' \cap \tau'' = \emptyset$ which is equivalent to $\mathcal{P}$ over databases with domains of size one. Then we construct a program $\mathcal{P}'''$ equivalent to $\mathcal{P}$ by combining the programs $\mathcal{P}'$ and $\mathcal{P}''$.

For the construction of $\mathcal{P}''$ we observe that every relation of a database over a single element domain $D = \{a\}$ contains either exactly one tuple, namely $(a, \ldots, a)$, or no tuple at all. Thus every such relation R corresponds to a 0-ary relation R_0 where R_0 is true if and only if $(a, \ldots, a) \in R$. Hence, by Lemma 3.1.15 (see below), there is a DYNPROPCQ-program equivalent to $\mathcal{P}$ for databases with domains of size one.

To combine $\mathcal{P}'$ and $\mathcal{P}''$ we use two different approaches, one for (a) and one for (b) and (c). In both approaches, we assume, by Lemma 3.1.9, that the update formulas for the query relations Q and Q'' of $\mathcal{P}'$ and $\mathcal{P}''$, respectively, consist of single atoms.

First we consider (a). We construct an intermediate program $\tilde{\mathcal{P}} = (\tilde{P}, \widetilde{\text{INIT}}, \tilde{Q})$ over schema $\tilde{\tau} = \{\tilde{Q}, U\} \cup \tau' \cup \tau''$ where U is a fresh 0-ary relation symbol. The intention is that interpretations of symbols in τ' and τ'' are as in $\mathcal{P}'$ and $\mathcal{P}''$, respectively, and that U is interpreted by true if and only if the domain is of size one. The initializations are accordingly.

Thus all update formulas of $\tilde{\mathcal{P}}$ for relation symbols from τ' and τ'' are as in $\mathcal{P}'$ and $\mathcal{P}''$ (and thus disjunction-free). The update formula for U is $\phi_\delta^U \stackrel{\text{def}}{=} U$ and

$$\phi_\delta^{\tilde{Q}} \stackrel{\text{def}}{=} (\phi_\delta^{Q'} \wedge \neg U) \vee (\phi_\delta^{Q''} \wedge U)$$
$$\equiv (\phi_\delta^{Q'} \vee \phi_\delta^{Q''}) \wedge (\neg U \vee \phi_\delta^{Q''}) \wedge (\phi_\delta^{Q'} \vee U).$$

The program $\mathcal{P}'''$ is obtained from $\tilde{\mathcal{P}}$ by removing disjunctions from $\phi_\delta^{\tilde{Q}}$ using the method[3] from the proof of Lemma 3.1.12. For example, the first clause is replaced by $\neg R_{\neg(Q' \vee Q'')}$ where $R_{\neg(Q' \vee Q'')}$ is a fresh auxiliary relation symbol intended to be always interpreted by the result of the query $\neg(\phi_\delta^{Q'} \vee \phi_\delta^{Q''})$. The update formula for $R_{\neg(Q' \vee Q'')}$ after a modification δ is $\neg \phi_\delta^{Q'} \wedge \neg \phi_\delta^{Q''}$; it is disjunction-free since, by our assumption, $\phi_\delta^{Q'}$ and $\phi_\delta^{Q''}$ both consist of a single atom. This concludes the proof of (a).

---

[3] This method cannot be used for DYNCQ and DYNFO^.

The program $\mathcal{P}'''$ for (b) and (c) is over schema $\tau''' = \{Q'''\} \cup \tau' \cup \tau''$. Again all update formulas of $\mathcal{P}'''$ for relation symbols from τ' and τ'' are as in $\mathcal{P}'$ and $\mathcal{P}''$ and $\phi_\delta^{Q'''} \stackrel{\text{def}}{=} \phi_\delta^{Q'} \wedge \phi_\delta^{Q''}$.

The case distinction is delegated to the initialization mapping. Recall that the size of the domain is fixed when the auxiliary relations are initialized. The initialization mapping INIT''' is as follows. If $|D| = 1$ then

$$\text{INIT}'''(R) = \begin{cases} \text{INIT}''(Q'') & \text{for } R = Q''', \\ D^k & \text{for } R \in \tau', \\ \text{INIT}''(R'') & \text{for } R \in \tau'' \end{cases}$$

If $|D| \geq 2$ then

$$\text{INIT}'''(R) = \begin{cases} \text{INIT}'(Q') & \text{for } R = Q''', \\ \text{INIT}'(R') & \text{for } R \in \tau', \\ D^k & \text{for } R \in \tau'' \end{cases}$$

Thus INIT''' selects either $\phi_\delta^{Q'}$ or $\phi_\delta^{Q''}$, depending on the size of the domain. If $|D| = 1$ then $\phi_\delta^{Q'}$ always evaluates to true whereas $\phi_\delta^{Q''}$ yields the same value as in $\mathcal{P}''$, and vice versa for $|D| \geq 2$. As update formulas do not use negation, all relations in the program that are initialized to "true" ($\mathcal{P}'$ or $\mathcal{P}''$) remain "full" throughout a computation.[4] This concludes the proof of (b).   □

It remains to prove that all queries over 0-ary relations can be maintained in DYNPROPCQ. Recall that 0-ary relations can either be true (containing the empty tuple) or false (not containing the empty tuple and thus being empty), thus 0-ary atoms are basically propositional variables. Queries on 0-ary databases are therefore basically families of Boolean functions, one function for each domain size. Such queries are not very interesting from the perspective of databases, but we need to show the following lemma as we used it in the previous proof.

As quantification in queries on 0-ary databases is useless, every FO query can be expressed by a quantifier-free formula and therefore can be maintained in DYNPROP. The following lemma shows that this can be sharpened.

Lemma 3.1.15. *Every query on a 0-ary database can be maintained by a* DYNPROPCQ-*program.*

Proof. Let τ_{inp} be an input schema with 0-ary relation symbols $A_1, \ldots, A_k$. Further let $\mathcal{Q}_1, \ldots, \mathcal{Q}_m$ be an enumeration of all $m \stackrel{\text{def}}{=} 2^{2^k}$ many queries on τ_{inp}. We actually show that all of them can be maintained by one DYNPROPCQ-program $\mathcal{P}$ with auxiliary schema $\tau_{\text{aux}} = \{R_1, \ldots, R_m\}$ maintaining $\mathcal{Q}_i$ in R_i, for every $i \in \{1, \ldots, m\}$.

To this end, let $\varphi_1, \ldots, \varphi_m$ be propositional formulas over τ_{inp} such that φ_i expresses $\mathcal{Q}_i$ and each φ_i is in conjunctive normal form. Without loss of generality, no

---

[4]This cannot be guaranteed for DYNUCQ⁻.

clause contains A_ℓ and $\neg A_\ell$ for any $A_\ell \in \tau_{\text{inp}}$ and any φ_i. As τ_{aux} contains a relation symbol, for every propositional formula over $A_1, \ldots, A_k$, it contains, in particular, an auxiliary relation symbol R_C, for every disjunctive clause over $A_1, \ldots, A_k$.

The update formulas for R_j after changing input relation A_ℓ can be constructed as follows. Let C be the set of clauses of φ_j, i.e. $\varphi_j = \bigwedge_{C \in C} C$. We denote by $C_{A_\ell}^+$, $C_{A_\ell}^-$ and C_{A_ℓ} the subsets of C whose clauses contain A_ℓ, $\neg A_\ell$ and neither A_ℓ nor $\neg A_\ell$, respectively.

If A_ℓ becomes true by a modification then φ_j evaluates to true if all clauses in C_{A_ℓ} and all clauses $C \setminus \{\neg A_\ell\}$ with $C \in C_{A_\ell}^-$ evaluated to true before the modification (clauses in $C_{A_\ell}^+$ will evaluate to true after enabling A_ℓ).

If A_ℓ becomes false by a modification then φ_j evaluates to true if all clauses in C_{A_ℓ} and all clauses $C \setminus \{A_\ell\}$ with $C \in C_{A_\ell}^+$ evaluated to true before the modification (clauses in $C_{A_\ell}^-$ will evaluate to true after disabling A_ℓ).

Therefore the update formulas for R_j after updating A_ℓ can be defined as follows:

$$\phi_{\text{INS}_{A_\ell}}^{R_j} \stackrel{\text{def}}{=} \bigwedge_{C \in C_{A_\ell}} R_C \wedge \bigwedge_{C \in C_{A_\ell}^-} R_{C \setminus \{\neg A_\ell\}}$$

$$\phi_{\text{DEL}_{A_\ell}}^{R_j} \stackrel{\text{def}}{=} \bigwedge_{C \in C_{A_\ell}} R_C \wedge \bigwedge_{C \in C_{A_\ell}^+} R_{C \setminus \{A_\ell\}}$$

The initialization is straightforward. The correctness of this construction can be proved by induction over the length of modification sequences. □

In the proof of Lemma 3.1.14, disjunctions are eliminated by introducing new relation symbols $T_{R,\delta}$. The arity of those relation symbols strongly depends on the number of variable occurrences in a clause. In particular, the constructed disjunction-free program can be of higher arity than the original program. In the rest of this section, we outline how this can be avoided.

The construction for reducing the arity of $T_{R,\delta}$ will require domains whose size depends on the original program. This is formalized as follows. A dynamic program $\mathcal{P}$ *weakly maintains* a query $\mathcal{Q}$, if there is an $n \in \mathbb{N}$ such that $\mathcal{P}$ maintains $\mathcal{Q}$ for every database with a domain of size at least n. We aim at the following theorem.

Theorem 3.1.16. *Every query maintainable in k-ary* DYNUCQ *is weakly maintainable in k'-ary* DYNCQ *where* $k' = \max\{2, k\}$. *Analogously for* DYNUCQ⁻ *and* DYNFO.

The idea is to describe the relations $T_{R,\delta}$ from the proof of Lemma 3.1.14 using conjunctive queries evaluated on a set of binary relations. The challenge is to choose suitable conjunctive queries and binary relations.

A query $\mathcal{Q}$ over schema τ is *described* by a formula φ over schema $\tau \cup \tau'$ if, for every domain D, there is an interpretation $\mathcal{S}_{\tau'}$ of τ' over D such that $\text{ANS}(\mathcal{Q}, \mathcal{S}_\tau) = \text{ANS}(\varphi, (\mathcal{S}_\tau, \mathcal{S}_{\tau'}))$ for all interpretations $\mathcal{S}_\tau$ of τ over D. We need the following weaker notion. A formula φ *weakly describes* $\mathcal{Q}$ if there is an $n \in \mathbb{N}$ such that φ describes

Q for all domains of size at least n. In the rest of this section we are only interested in weak describability.

Each of the relations $T_{R,\delta}$ is defined by a positive quantifier-free formula that uses equality atoms only. Such formulas are called positive quantifier-free =-formulas in the following. Our goal is to weakly describe queries defined by such formulas using conjunctive queries and binary relations; and thus, in particular, the relations $T_{R,\delta}$. We first show how a simple query defined by a disjunction of two equality atoms can be described.

Example 3.1.17. Consider the query

$$Q \overset{\text{def}}{=} \{(a_1, b_1, a_2, b_2) \mid a_1 = b_1 \text{ or } a_2 = b_2\}.$$

Our goal is to weakly describe Q by a conjunctive query C for domains of size at least 6. The query C is a conjunction of three queries C_{12}, C_{34} and C_{56}. The intention of those queries is as follows. Assume that the domain D of a structure S contains the elements $\{1, \ldots, 6\}$. Then C_{12} evaluated on D shall yield the same result as Q, except that all tuples (a_1, b_1, a_2, b_2) where a_1 or a_2 is in $\{1, 2\}$ shall be in the result as well. Thus C_{12} shall weakly describe the following query:

$$Q_{12} \overset{\text{def}}{=} \{(x_1, y_1, x_2, y_2) \mid x_1 = y_1 \text{ or } x_2 = y_2 \text{ or } x_1 \in \{1, 2\} \text{ or } x_2 \in \{1, 2\}\}$$

Similarly C_{34} and C_{56} shall yield the following results:

$$Q_{34} \overset{\text{def}}{=} \{(x_1, y_1, x_2, y_2) \mid x_1 = y_1 \text{ or } x_2 = y_2 \text{ or } x_1 \in \{3, 4\} \text{ or } x_2 \in \{3, 4\}\}$$

$$Q_{56} \overset{\text{def}}{=} \{(x_1, y_1, x_2, y_2) \mid x_1 = y_1 \text{ or } x_2 = y_2 \text{ or } x_1 \in \{5, 6\} \text{ or } x_2 \in \{5, 6\}\}$$

Before showing how to weakly describe the queries Q_{12}, Q_{34} and Q_{56}, we show that they are indeed useful for weakly describing Q. We claim:

$$\text{ANS}(Q, S) = \text{ANS}(Q_{12}, S) \cap \text{ANS}(Q_{34}, S) \cap \text{ANS}(Q_{56}, S)$$

The claim implies that Q is weakly described by $C_{12} \wedge C_{34} \wedge C_{56}$ if C_{12}, C_{34} and C_{56} weakly describe Q_{12}, Q_{34} and Q_{56}, respectively.

We now prove the claim. Obviously every tuple in $\text{ANS}(Q, S)$ is also in the intersection of $\text{ANS}(Q_{12}, S)$, $\text{ANS}(Q_{34}, S)$ and $\text{ANS}(Q_{56}, S)$. Now, let (a_1, b_1, a_2, b_2) be a tuple in $\text{ANS}(Q_{12}, S) \cap \text{ANS}(Q_{34}, S) \cap \text{ANS}(Q_{56}, S)$. Then either $a_1, a_2 \notin \{1, 2\}$ or $a_1, a_2 \notin \{3, 4\}$ or $a_1, a_2 \notin \{5, 6\}$. Without loss of generality $a_1, a_2 \notin \{1, 2\}$, but then $a_1 = b_1$ or $a_2 = b_2$ since $(a_1, b_1, a_2, b_2) \in \text{ANS}(Q_{12}, S)$. This proves the claim.

It remains to exhibit the conjunctive query C_{12}. The queries C_{34} and C_{56} are symmetric. The conjunctive query C_{12} uses schema $\tau' = \{R, S, T\}$ to weakly describe Q_{12} and is defined by

$$\exists z_1 \exists z_2 \Big(T(z_1, z_2) \wedge R(x_1, z_1) \wedge S(z_1, y_1) \wedge R(x_2, z_2) \wedge S(z_2, y_2) \Big)$$

Hence the query graph is as follows:

$$
\begin{array}{ccc}
x_1 & & x_2 \\
R\downarrow & \overset{T}{} & \downarrow R \\
z_1 & \xrightarrow{T} & z_2 \\
S\downarrow & & \downarrow S \\
y_1 & & y_2
\end{array}
$$

We now specify the interpretation $\mathcal{S}'$ of τ' for domain D. The relations $R^{\mathcal{S}'}$, $S^{\mathcal{S}'}$ and $T^{\mathcal{S}'}$ are defined as follows:

$$R^{\mathcal{S}'} \overset{\text{def}}{=} \{(v, v) \mid v \in D \setminus \{1, 2\}\} \cup \{(u, 1) \mid u \in D\} \cup \{(1, 2), (2, 2)\}$$

$$S^{\mathcal{S}'} \overset{\text{def}}{=} \{(v, v) \mid v \in D \setminus \{1, 2\}\} \cup \{(1, u'), (2, u') \mid u' \in D\}$$

$$T^{\mathcal{S}'} \overset{\text{def}}{=} \{(1, v), (v, 1) \mid v \in D \setminus \{1, 2\}\} \cup \{(1, 2), (2, 1)\}$$

Stated differently, the following tuples are contained in $R^{\mathcal{S}'}$, $S^{\mathcal{S}'}$ and $T^{\mathcal{S}'}$:

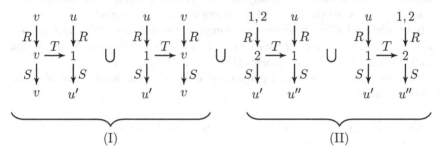

$$
\underbrace{\qquad\qquad\qquad\qquad\qquad\qquad\qquad\qquad}_{\text{(I)}}
\underbrace{\qquad\qquad\qquad\qquad\qquad\qquad\qquad\qquad}_{\text{(II)}}
$$

where $u, u', u'' \in D$ and $v \in D \setminus \{1, 2\}$ and an edge (q, p) labeled by R indicates that $(q, p) \in R^{\mathcal{S}'}$.

Intuitively (I) ensures that exactly the tuples (a_1, b_1, a_2, b_2) satisfying either $a_1 = b_1$ and $a_1 \notin \{1, 2\}$, or $a_2 = b_2$ and $a_2 \notin \{1, 2\}$, are contained in the query result. Condition (II) ensures that exactly the tuples (a_1, b_1, a_2, b_2) with $a_1 \in \{1, 2\}$ or $a_2 \in \{1, 2\}$ are in the query result.

We prove the correctness of this construction. Let (a_1, b_1, a_2, b_2) be a tuple in $\text{ANS}(\mathcal{Q}_{12}, (\mathcal{S}, \mathcal{S}'))$. We show that the assignment that maps (x_1, y_1, x_2, y_2) to (a_1, b_1, a_2, b_2) satisfies $\mathcal{C}_{12}$. If $a_1 \in \{1, 2\}$ then choose z_1 as 2 and z_2 as 1. This choice satisfies the matrix of $\mathcal{C}_{12}$ due to tuples in (II). Similarly for $a_2 \in \{1, 2\}$. If both a_1 and a_2 are not in $\{1, 2\}$ and $a_1 = b_1$ then choose z_1 as a_1 and z_2 as 1. This choice satisfies the matrix of $\mathcal{C}_{12}$ due to tuples in (I). Similarly for $a_2 = b_2$.

Now, let θ be a satisfying assignment of $\mathcal{C}_{12}$ that maps (x_1, y_1, x_2, y_2) to (a_1, b_1, a_2, b_2). We show that (a_1, b_1, a_2, b_2) is in $\text{ANS}(\mathcal{Q}_{12}, (\mathcal{S}, \mathcal{S}'))$. If $a_1 \in \{1, 2\}$ or $a_2 \in \{1, 2\}$ then this follows from the definition of $\mathcal{Q}_{12}$. If both a_1 and a_2 are not in $\{1, 2\}$ then the value 2 is not a witness for z_1 and z_2 for the assignment θ. But then, due to (I), either there is a witness for z_1 which is equal to a_1 and b_1, or there is a witness for z_2 which is equal to a_2 and b_2. Thus either $a_1 = b_1$ or $a_2 = b_2$.   □

The technique from this example can be generalized to weakly describe queries defined by positive quantifier-free =-formulas. The following lemma immediately implies Theorem 3.1.16.

Lemma 3.1.18. *Every positive quantifier-free =-formula can be weakly described by a conjunctive query.*

Proof sketch. Consider an arbitrary positive quantifier-free =-formula which is given, without loss of generality, in conjunctive normal form. It suffices to weakly describe every clause $\bigvee_{i=1}^{k} u_i = v_i$, where some u_i and v_i are possibly the same variable. Such a clause can be rewritten as

$$\exists x_1 \exists y_1 \dots \exists x_k \exists y_k \left(\bigwedge_i (x_i = u_i \wedge y_i = v_i) \wedge \bigvee_{i=1}^{k} x_i = y_i \right)$$

and therefore it is sufficient to weakly describe queries $\mathcal{Q}$ defined by formulas of the form $\bigvee_{i=1}^{k} x_i = y_i$ where all x_i and y_i are pairwise different variables.

In Example 3.1.17 we have seen a technique for weakly describing such queries for $k = 2$. This technique can be extended to arbitrary k. Therefore let us assume that the domain contains the elements $\{1, \dots, 6, c_1, \dots, c_k, d_1, \dots, d_k\}$.

We show how to construct a conjunctive query $\mathcal{C}_{12}$ that weakly describes the following query:

$$\mathcal{Q}_{12} \stackrel{\text{def}}{=} \{(x_1, y_1, \dots, x_k, y_k) \mid x_i = y_i \text{ or } x_i \in \{1, 2\} \text{ for some } i \in \{1, \dots, k\}\}$$

Hence $\mathcal{C}_{12}$ will weakly describe $\mathcal{Q}$ for tuples $(a_1, b_1, \dots, a_k, b_k)$ with $a_i \notin \{1, 2\}$ for all i. Using the same technique as in Example 3.1.17, one can construct conjunctive queries $\mathcal{C}_{34}$ and $\mathcal{C}_{56}$ such that $\mathcal{C}_{12} \wedge \mathcal{C}_{34} \wedge \mathcal{C}_{56}$ weakly describes $\mathcal{Q}$ for all tuples.

The conjunctive query $\mathcal{C}_{12}$ uses schema $\tau' = \{R, S, T_1, \dots, T_k\}$ and is defined by

$$\exists z \exists z_1 \dots \exists z_k \left(\bigwedge_i \big(R(x_i, z_i) \wedge S(z_i, y_i) \big) \wedge \bigwedge_i T_i(z, z_i) \right)$$

and hence the query graph is

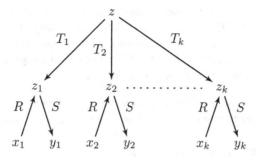

The intention for R and S is as in Example 3.1.17. Recall that in that example the relation T ensured that (1) one z_i was not in $\{1, 2\}$, or (2) one z_i was equal to 2. In the first case $x_i = y_i$ whereas in the second case $x_i \in \{1, 2\}$. The relations T_i are used for the same purpose.

The idea is as follows. For a domain D, the interpretation $\mathcal{S}'$ of τ' is chosen as follows. The relations $T_i^{\mathcal{S}'}$ are such that the variable z can only assume values $\{c_1, \ldots, c_k, d_1, \ldots, d_k\}$ (otherwise $\mathcal{C}_{12}$ will evaluate to false). If the value c_i is assigned to z then this shall encode that z_i is not in $\{1, 2\}$. If the value d_i is assigned to z then this shall encode that z_i is equal to 2.

Now we present the relations. The relations $R^{\mathcal{S}'}$ and $S^{\mathcal{S}'}$ are as in the previous example:

$$R^{\mathcal{S}'} \stackrel{\text{def}}{=} \{(v, v) \mid v \in D \setminus \{1, 2\}\} \cup \{(u, 1) \mid u \in D\} \cup \{(1, 2), (2, 2)\}$$

$$S^{\mathcal{S}'} \stackrel{\text{def}}{=} \{(v, v) \mid v \in D \setminus \{1, 2\}\} \cup \{(1, u), (2, u) \mid u \in D\}$$

The relation T_i for $i \in \{1, \ldots, k\}$ is defined as follows:

$$T_i = \{(c_i, v) \mid v \in D \setminus \{1, 2\}\} \cup \{(d_i, 2)\} \cup \bigcup_{j \neq i} \{(c_j, 1), (d_j, 1)\}$$

The correctness of the construction can be shown as in Example 3.1.17. Exhibiting witnesses for $z, z_1, \ldots z_k$ in order to show that a tuple $(a_1, b_1, \ldots, a_k, b_k)$ from $\text{ANS}(\mathcal{Q}_{12}, (\mathcal{S}, \mathcal{S}'))$ is also in $\text{ANS}(\mathcal{C}_{12}, (\mathcal{S}, \mathcal{S}'))$ is straightforward. Showing that a tuple $(a_1, b_1, \ldots, a_k, b_k)$ is contained in $\text{ANS}(\mathcal{Q}_{12}, (\mathcal{S}, \mathcal{S}'))$ if it satisfies $\mathcal{C}_{12}$ can be shown by a case distinction on the possible values for z.

3.1.4 Simulating Functions by Conjunctive Queries

Finally we show that the class DYNQF is a subclass of DYNCQ. This completes the left hand side of Fig. 3.2.

Thanks to Lemma 3.1.14 it suffices to show that DYNQF is contained in DYNUCQ. The idea of the proof of Theorem 3.1.6 is to simulate auxiliary functions by auxiliary relations with the help of existential quantifiers in a straightforward way. However, some care is necessary in order to remove ITE-conditions and negations. We highlight the idea of the proof in the following example.

Example 3.1.19. Consider a DYNQF-program $\mathcal{P}$ that contains the following update term $t^f_{\text{INS}_E}$ for a unary function f and update formula $\phi^R_{\text{INS}_E}$ for a unary relation R:

$$t^f_{\text{INS}_E}(u, v; x) \overset{\text{def}}{=} f\big(\text{ITE}(R(x), f(x), u)\big)$$

$$\phi^R_{\text{INS}_E}(u, v; x) \overset{\text{def}}{=} \neg R(x) \wedge S\big(f(x), \text{ITE}(\neg R(\text{ITE}(S(u, v), u, x)), f(x), u)\big)$$

As a first step towards the construction of an equivalent DYNCQ-program, we remove negations with the replacement technique by maintaining for every relation T its complement in an auxiliary relation $\widehat{T}$, for example:

$$\phi^R_{\text{INS}_E}(u, v; x) \overset{\text{def}}{=} \widehat{R}(x) \wedge S\big(f(x), \text{ITE}(\widehat{R}(\text{ITE}(S(u, v), u, x)), f(x), u)\big)$$

$$\phi^{\widehat{R}}_{\text{INS}_E}(u, v; x) \overset{\text{def}}{=} R(x) \vee \widehat{S}\big(f(x), \text{ITE}(\widehat{R}(\text{ITE}(S(u, v), u, x)), f(x), u)\big)$$

The crucial step in the construction of an equivalent DYNCQ-program is to simulate the function f by a binary relation R_f with the intention that R_f stores all tuples of the form $(a, f(a))$. Then appearances of f as well as of ITE can be removed. The complement relations obtained in the preprocessing step above are also needed in order to remove ITE-conditions.

The update formula $\phi^{R_f}_{\text{INS}_E}(u, v; x, y)$ for R_f is obtained by 'outsourcing' the computation of the ITE-value:

$$\phi^{R_f}_{\text{INS}_E}(u, v; x, y) \overset{\text{def}}{=} \exists z\Big(R_f(z, y) \wedge \underbrace{\big((R(x) \wedge R_f(x, z)) \vee (\widehat{R}(x) \wedge z = u)\big)}_{z = \text{ITE}(R(x), f(x), u)}\Big)$$

The update formula for R that uses R_f instead of f is obtained similarly:

$$\phi^R_{\text{INS}_E}(u, v; x) \overset{\text{def}}{=} \widehat{R}(x) \wedge \exists z_1 \exists z_2 \exists z_3 \Big(S(z_1, z_2) \wedge R_f(x, z_1)$$

$$\wedge \underbrace{\big((\widehat{R}(z_3) \wedge R_f(x, z_2)) \vee (R(z_3) \wedge z_2 = u)\big)}_{\text{ITE}(\widehat{R}(...), \cdot, \cdot)}$$

$$\wedge \underbrace{\big((S(u, v) \wedge z_3 = u) \vee (\widehat{S}(u, v) \wedge z_3 = x)\big)}_{\text{ITE}(S(...), \cdot, \cdot)}\Big)$$

Observe that only relation symbols from the original DYNQF-program are needed in negated form. The update formula for $\widehat{R}$ is analogous. □

Theorem 3.1.6 (**R**). DYNQF*is contained in* DYNCQ

Proof. Let $\mathcal{P} = (P, \text{INIT}, Q)$ be a dynamic DYNQF-program over schema $\tau = \tau_{\text{rel}} \cup \tau_{\text{fun}}$. We assume, without loss of generality, that $\mathcal{P}$ is in negation normal form. Further we assume, as in Lemma 3.1.10, that the input relations have update formulas as well.

We prove that there is a DYNUCQ-program $\mathcal{P}''$ equivalent to $\mathcal{P}$. Then, by Lemma 3.1.14, there is an equivalent DYNCQ-program.

As a preparation step we construct, from $\mathcal{P}$, a DYNQF-program $\mathcal{P}'$ over schema $\tau' \overset{\text{def}}{=} \tau_{\text{rel}} \cup \widehat{\tau}_{\text{rel}} \cup \{\widehat{=}\} \cup \tau_{\text{fun}}$ where $\widehat{\tau}_{\text{rel}}$ has, for every $R \in \tau$, a relation symbol $\widehat{R}$ intended to contain the complement of R and $\widehat{=}$ contains the complement of the relation $=$. This can be achieved as in the proof of Lemma 3.1.10.

From $\mathcal{P}'$ we construct a DYNUCQ-program $\mathcal{P}''$ over schema $\tau'' \overset{\text{def}}{=} \tau_{\text{rel}} \cup \widehat{\tau}_{\text{rel}} \cup \tau_F$ where τ_F contains a $(k+1)$-ary relation symbol R_f for every k-ary function symbol $f \in \tau_{\text{fun}}$. The intention is that R_f simulates f in the sense that $(\bar{a}, b) \in R_f^{\mathcal{S}'}$ if and only if $f^{\mathcal{S}''}(\bar{a}) = b$ in states $\mathcal{S}'$ and $\mathcal{S}''$ reached in $\mathcal{P}'$ and $\mathcal{P}''$ by the same modification sequence. The initialization of R_f can be obtained easily from the initialization of f.

We say that two states $\mathcal{S}'$ and $\mathcal{S}''$ over τ' and τ'' *correspond*, if (1) the condition $(\bar{a}, b) \in R_f^{\mathcal{S}'}$ if and only if $f^{\mathcal{S}''}(\bar{a}) = b$ is satisfied, and (2) $R^{\mathcal{S}'} = R^{\mathcal{S}''}$ for all $R \in \tau_{\text{rel}} \cup \widehat{\tau}_{\text{rel}}$.

We explain next how to update relations from τ_F. To this end, we will define CQ-formulas $\varphi_t(\bar{x}, z)$ and $\varphi_\phi(\bar{x})$ over τ'', for every update term $t(\bar{x})$ and every update formula $\phi(\bar{x})$ over τ', such that the following conditions are satisfied for all corresponding states $\mathcal{S}', \mathcal{S}''$, all tuples $\bar{a}$ and all elements b:

- $(\mathcal{S}'', \bar{a}, b) \models \varphi_t(\bar{x}, z)$ if and only if $t^{\mathcal{S}'}(\bar{a}) = b$, and
- $(\mathcal{S}'', \bar{a}) \models \varphi_\phi(\bar{x})$ if and only if $(\mathcal{S}', \bar{a}) \models \phi(\bar{x})$

Then the update formulas in $\mathcal{P}''$ after a modification δ can be defined as follows. For every $R_f \in \tau_F$, define the update formula as $\phi_\delta^{R_f} \overset{\text{def}}{=} \varphi_t$ where t is the update term for $f \in \tau_{\text{fun}}$ in $\mathcal{P}'$. For every $R \in \tau_{\text{rel}} \cup \widehat{\tau}_{\text{rel}}$ define the update formula as $\phi_\delta^R \overset{\text{def}}{=} \varphi_\phi$ where ϕ is the update formula of R in $\mathcal{P}'$. An easy induction shows that $\mathcal{P}'$ and $\mathcal{P}''$ yield corresponding states when the same modification sequence is applied. This proves the claim.

It remains to define the CQ-formulas $\varphi_t(\bar{x}, z)$ and $\varphi_\phi(\bar{x})$ for every update term $t(\bar{x})$ and every formula $\phi(\bar{x})$. Those formulas are defined inductively as follows:

(a) If $t(\bar{x}) = y$ for some variable y occurring in $\bar{x}$, then

$$\varphi_t(\bar{x}, z) \overset{\text{def}}{=} y = z.$$

(b) If $t(\bar{x}) = f(t_1(\bar{x}_1), \dots, t_k(\bar{x}_k))$ with $\bar{x}_i \subseteq \bar{x}$, then

$$\varphi_t(\bar{x}, z) \overset{\text{def}}{=} \exists z_1 \dots \exists z_k \left(R_f(z_1, \dots, z_k, z) \wedge \bigwedge_i \varphi_{t_i}(\bar{x}_i, z_i) \right).$$

(c) If $t(\bar{x}) = \text{ITE}(\phi(\bar{y}), t_1(\bar{x}_1), t_2(\bar{x}_2))$ with $\bar{y}, \bar{x}_1, \bar{x}_2 \subseteq \bar{x}$, quantifier-free update formula ϕ and update terms t_1, t_2, then

$$\varphi_t(\bar{x}, z) \stackrel{\text{def}}{=} \big(\varphi_\phi(\bar{y}) \wedge \varphi_{t_1}(\bar{x}_1, z)\big) \vee \big(\varphi_{\neg\phi}(\bar{y}) \wedge \varphi_{t_2}(\bar{x}_2, z)\big).$$

(d) If $\phi(\bar{x})$ contains the maximal update terms $t_1(\bar{x}_1), \ldots, t_k(\bar{x}_k)$ then let

$$\varphi_\phi(\bar{x}) \stackrel{\text{def}}{=} \exists z_1 \ldots \exists z_k \Big(\phi' \wedge \bigwedge_i \varphi_{t_i}(\bar{x}_i, z_i)\Big)$$

where ϕ' is obtained from ϕ by replacing t_i by z_i, transforming the resulting formula into negation normal form and then replacing every literal of the form $\neg R(s_1, \ldots, s_\ell)$ by $\widehat{R}(s_1, \ldots, s_\ell)$. Here, a term t_i is maximal if it is not contained in another update term.

Observe that the formula ϕ in (d) contains only relation symbols from $\tau_{\text{rel}} \cup \widehat{\tau}_{\text{rel}}$, and therefore no relation symbols from τ_{fun} need to be replaced in ϕ'. The correctness of this construction can be proved inductively.   □

3.2 Short Interlude: Δ-Semantics

So far we considered a semantics where the new version of the auxiliary relations is redefined from scratch after each modification. We refer to this as *absolute semantics* in the following.

As already explained in the introduction of this chapter, one usually expects only few auxiliary tuples to change after a modification in the context of view maintenance. Therefore it is common to express the new version of the auxiliary relations in terms of the current relations and some "Delta", that is, a (small) relation R^+ of tuples to be inserted into R and a (small) relation R^- of tuples to be removed from R (with $R^+ \cap R^- = \emptyset$). The updated auxiliary relation R' is then defined by

$$R' \stackrel{\text{def}}{=} (R \cup R^+) \setminus R^-.$$

We refer to this semantics as *Δ-semantics*. This is the semantics usually considered in view maintenance. The intuitive explanations above already reveal that the expressive power of absolute and Δ-semantics can only be different if the underlying update language is not closed under Boolean operations.

Next we formalize Δ-semantics via Δ-update programs which provide formulas defining the relations R^+ and R^-, for every auxiliary relation R.

Definition 3.2.1 (Δ-Update program). *A Δ-update program $\mathcal{P}$ over dynamic schema (τ_{inp}, τ_{aux}) is a set of first-order formulas (called Δ-update formulas in the following) that contains, for every $R \in \tau_{aux}$ and every $\delta \in \{\text{INS}_S, \text{DEL}_S\}$ with $S \in \tau_{inp}$,* *two formulas* $\phi_\delta^{R^+}(\bar{u}; \bar{x})$ *and* $\phi_\delta^{R^-}(\bar{u}; \bar{x})$ *over the schema* τ *where* $\bar{u}$ *and* S *have the same arity,* $\bar{x}$ *and* R *have the same arity, and* $\phi_\delta^{R^+} \wedge \phi_\delta^{R^-}$ *is unsatisfiable.*

The *semantics of* Δ-*update programs* is as follows. For a modification $\delta = \delta(\bar{a})$ and program state $S = (D, \mathcal{I}, \mathcal{A})$ we denote by $P_\delta(S)$ the state $(D, \delta(\mathcal{I}), \mathcal{A}')$, where the relations R' of $\mathcal{A}'$ are defined by

$$R' \overset{\text{def}}{=} \left(R \cup \{\bar{b} \mid S \models \phi_\delta^{R^+}(\bar{a}; \bar{b})\} \right) \setminus \{\bar{b} \mid S \models \phi_\delta^{R^-}(\bar{a}; \bar{b})\}.$$

The effect of a modification sequence on a state, dynamic Δ-programs and so on are defined like their counterparts in absolute semantics except that Δ-update programs are used instead of update programs.

Definition 3.2.2 (Δ-**Dyn**$\mathcal{C}$). *For a class $\mathcal{C}$ of formulas, let Δ-DYN$\mathcal{C}$ be the class of all dynamic queries that can be maintained by dynamic Δ-programs with formulas from $\mathcal{C}$ and arbitrary initialization mapping.*

We note that the definitions above do *not* require that $R^+ \cap R = \emptyset$ or $R^- \subseteq R$, that is, R^+ might contain tuples that are already in R, and R^- might contain tuples that are not in R. While it is conceivable to require that $R^+ \cap R = \emptyset$ and $R^- \subseteq R$ in the definitions, in all proofs below we construct only Δ-update formulas that guarantee these additional properties. As a consequence, for the considered fragments, the expressive power is independent of this difference.

The goal of this section is to prove the remaining results of Fig. 3.2, that is, the collapse results depicted in the right part of the figure and the correspondences between absolute semantics and Δ-semantics.

The main results of this section are the following characterizations of (extensions of) dynamic conjunctive queries with Δ-semantics.

Theorem 3.2.3. *Let $\mathcal{Q}$ be a query. Then the following statements are equivalent:*

(a) $\mathcal{Q}$ can be maintained in Δ-DYNUCQ$^-$.
(b) $\mathcal{Q}$ can be maintained in Δ-DYNUCQ.
(c) $\mathcal{Q}$ can be maintained in Δ-DYNCQ$^-$.
(d) $\mathcal{Q}$ can be maintained in Δ-DYNCQ.
(e) $\mathcal{Q}$ can be maintained in Δ-DYN$\exists^*$FO.
(f) $\mathcal{Q}$ can be maintained in Δ-DYN$\forall^*$FO.

In particular, even more fragments collapse under Δ-semantics. Moreover, there is a tight relationship between absolute and Δ-semantics when conjunctive queries with negations are used as update language.

Theorem 3.2.4. *Let $\mathcal{Q}$ be a query. Then the following statements are equivalent:*

(a) $\mathcal{Q}$ can be maintained in DYNUCQ$^-$.
(b) $\mathcal{Q}$ can be maintained in Δ-DYNUCQ$^-$.

The technique used for removing unions from dynamic unions of conjunctive queries under Δ-semantics can be used to obtain a Δ-DYNFO$^\wedge$ normal form for Δ-DYNFO-programs.

Theorem 3.2.5. *Let Q be a query. Then the following statements are equivalent:*

(a) Q can be maintained in Δ-DYNFO.
(b) Q can be maintained in Δ-DYNFO$^\wedge$.

We state some basic facts about dynamic programs with Δ-semantics before proving those theorems. The following lemma establishes the obvious fact that absolute semantics and Δ-semantics coincide in expressive power for dynamic classes closed under boolean operations. We observe that the proof does not work for (extensions of) conjunctive queries. Later we will see how to extend the result to conjunctive queries.

Lemma 3.2.6. *Let C be some fragment of first-order logic closed under the boolean operations $\vee$, $\wedge$ and $\neg$. Then for every query Q the following are equivalent:*

(a) There is a DYNC-program that maintains Q.
(b) There is a Δ-DYNC-program that maintains Q.

Proof. From a DYNC-update formula ϕ_δ^R, the Δ-DYNC-update formulas are defined as follows:

$$\phi_\delta^{R^+}(\bar{u}; \bar{x}) \stackrel{\text{def}}{=} \phi_\delta^R(\bar{u}; \bar{x}) \wedge \neg R(\bar{x})$$
$$\phi_\delta^{R^-}(\bar{u}; \bar{x}) \stackrel{\text{def}}{=} \neg\phi_\delta^R(\bar{u}; \bar{x}) \wedge R(\bar{x})$$

From Δ-DYNC-update formulas $\phi_\delta^{R^+}$ and $\phi_\delta^{R^+}$, a DYNC-update formula is obtained via

$$\phi_\delta^R(\bar{u}; \bar{x}) \stackrel{\text{def}}{=} \left(R(\bar{x}) \vee \phi_\delta^{R^+}(\bar{u}; \bar{x})\right) \wedge \neg\phi_\delta^{R^-}(\bar{u}; \bar{x}). \qquad \square$$

Removing negations in dynamic programs with Δ-semantics is straightforward using the replacement technique, since the complement $\widehat{R}$ of an auxiliary relation R can be maintained by exchanging the formulas $\phi_\delta^{R^+}$ and $\phi_\delta^{R^-}$. Observe that in contrast to absolute semantics this works for almost any class of queries, even if the class is not closed under complementation.

Lemma 3.2.7. *Let Δ-DYNC be one of the dynamic complexity classes Δ-DYNPROPCQ$^-$, Δ-DYNCQ$^-$, Δ-DYNUCQ$^-$ or Δ-DYN$\mathbb{Q}$FO for arbitrary quantifier prefix $\mathbb{Q}$. If a query Q can be maintained in Δ-DYNC then Q can be maintained in negation-free Δ-DYNC.*

Proof. The idea is again to maintain the complements for auxiliary relations. Given a dynamic Δ-program $\mathcal{P}$ over schema τ we construct a dynamic Δ-program $\mathcal{P}'$ over schema $\tau \cup \widehat{\tau}$ where $\widehat{\tau}$ contains, for every k-ary relation symbol $R \in \tau$, a fresh k-ary relation symbol $\widehat{R}$ with the intention that $\widehat{R}$ always stores the complement of R.

The update formulas for $R \in \tau$ are as in $\mathcal{P}$. For a relation symbol $R \in \tau$ let $\phi_\delta^{R^+}(\bar{u}; \bar{x})$ and $\phi_\delta^{R^-}(\bar{u}; \bar{x})$ be the update formulas of R. Then the update formulas for $\widehat{R}$ can be defined as follows:

$$\phi_\delta^{\widehat{R}^+}(\bar{u}; \bar{x}) = \phi_\delta^{R^-}(\bar{u}; \bar{x})$$

$$\phi_\delta^{\widehat{R}^-}(\bar{u}; \bar{x}) = \phi_\delta^{R^+}(\bar{u}; \bar{x})$$

From $\mathcal{P}'$, a negation-free dynamic Δ-program $\mathcal{P}''$ can be constructed by replacing, for all $R \in \tau$, all occurrences of $\neg R(\bar{x})$ in update formulas of $\mathcal{P}'$ by $\widehat{R}(\bar{x})$. We omit the obvious proof of correctness.   □

We now turn towards proving the main results of this section. We first prove Theorem 3.2.4. Afterwards we use the connection between absolute and Δ-semantics that it establishes, as well as the adaption of Lemma 3.1.14 to Δ-semantics, to prove the characterization of conjunctive queries with Δ-semantics.

The only-if-direction of Theorem 3.2.4 can be generalized to arbitrary quantifier prefixes. It is open whether the if-direction generalizes as well.

Lemma 3.2.8. *Let $\mathbb{Q}$ be an arbitrary quantifier prefix. If a query can be maintained in* DYN$\mathbb{Q}$FO *then it can be maintained in* Δ-DYN$\mathbb{Q}$FO *as well.*

Proof. Let $\mathcal{P} = (P, \text{INIT}, Q)$ be a DYN$\mathbb{Q}$FO-program with schema τ. By Lemma 3.1.9 we can assume, without loss of generality, that the update formulas of Q are atomic. We construct a dynamic Δ-DYN$\mathbb{Q}$FO-program $\mathcal{P}' = (P', \text{INIT}', Q')$.

The main challenge is to design update formulas of the kind $\phi_\delta^{R^-}$ without being able to complement the given update formulas because this would lead to $\overline{\mathbb{Q}}$FO-formulas (additionally, the disjointness requirement for formulas $\phi_\delta^{R^+}$ and $\phi_\delta^{R^-}$ needs to be ensured).

The basic idea is to use two copies of the auxiliary relations, both alternating between empty and useful states, such that one copy is useful for even steps and the other one for odd steps. More precisely, for every auxiliary relation R used by $\mathcal{P}$, the program $\mathcal{P}'$ uses two auxiliary relations R_{even} and R_{odd} with the intention that after an even sequence of modifications R_{even} stores the content of R after the same sequence of modifications while R_{odd} is empty. After an odd sequence of modifications R_{even} is empty while R_{odd} stores the content of R.

Then, for an even modification, the relation R_{even}^+ can be simply expressed as in absolute semantics (using "odd" relations) and R_{even}^- is empty. For an odd modification R_{even}^- can be simply chosen as R_{even} and R_{even}^+ is empty. Similarly for R_{odd}.

In the following we give a precise construction of $\mathcal{P}'$ over schema $\tau_{\text{even}} \cup \tau_{\text{odd}} \cup \{\text{ODD}, Q'\}$ where ODD is a boolean relation symbol, and τ_{even} and τ_{odd} contain, for every k-ary relation symbol $R \in \tau$, a k-ary relation symbol R_{even} and R_{odd}, respectively. The relation ODD is used to store the parity of the number of modifications performed so far.

Let ϕ_δ^R be the update formula of $R \in \tau$ for a modification δ in the dynamic program $\mathcal{P}$. Denote by $\phi_\delta^R[\tau \to \tau_{\text{even}}]$ the formula obtained from ϕ_δ^R by replacing every atom $S(\bar{x})$ with $S \in \tau$ by $S_{\text{even}}(\bar{x})$. Analogously for $\phi_\delta^R[\tau \to \tau_{\text{odd}}]$. Now, the update formulas for R_{odd} and R_{even} are as follows:

$$\phi_\delta^{R_{\text{odd}}^+}(\bar{u}; \bar{x}) \stackrel{\text{def}}{=} \neg \text{ODD} \wedge \phi_\delta^R[\tau \to \tau_{\text{even}}](\bar{u}; \bar{x})$$

$$\phi_\delta^{R_{\text{odd}}^-}(\bar{u}; \bar{x}) \stackrel{\text{def}}{=} \text{ODD} \wedge R_{\text{odd}}(\bar{x})$$

$$\phi_\delta^{R_{\text{even}}^+}(\bar{u}; \bar{x}) \stackrel{\text{def}}{=} \text{ODD} \wedge \phi_\delta^R[\tau \to \tau_{\text{odd}}](\bar{u}; \bar{x})$$

$$\phi_\delta^{R_{\text{even}}^-}(\bar{u}; \bar{x}) \stackrel{\text{def}}{=} \neg \text{ODD} \wedge R_{\text{even}}(\bar{x})$$

Observe that all those formulas can be easily converted into $\mathbb{Q}$FO-formulas. The boolean auxiliary relation ODD can be updated straightforwardly.

Now, since the update formulas of Q in $\mathcal{P}$ are quantifier-free, the relation Q' can be updated with the following quantifier-free update formulas:

$$\phi_\delta^{Q'^+}(\bar{u}; \bar{x}) \stackrel{\text{def}}{=} \phi_\delta^Q(\bar{u}; \bar{x}) \wedge \neg\Big((\text{ODD} \wedge Q_{\text{odd}}(\bar{x})) \vee (\neg\text{ODD} \wedge Q_{\text{even}}(\bar{x}))\Big)$$

$$\phi_\delta^{Q'^-}(\bar{u}; \bar{x}) \stackrel{\text{def}}{=} \neg\phi_\delta^Q(\bar{u}; \bar{x}) \wedge \Big((\text{ODD} \wedge Q_{\text{odd}}(\bar{x})) \vee (\neg\text{ODD} \wedge Q_{\text{even}}(\bar{x}))\Big)$$

The initialization mapping of P' is straightforward. Every $R_{\text{even}} \in \tau_{\text{even}}$ is initialized with $\text{INIT}(R)$. All $R_{\text{odd}} \in \tau_{\text{odd}}$ are initialized with the empty relation. The relation ODD is initialized with $\bot$, and Q' is initialized with $\text{INIT}(Q)$. □

Lemma 3.2.9. *(a) If a query can be maintained in Δ-DYNUCQ⁻ then it can be maintained in DYNUCQ⁻ as well.*

*(b) If a query can be maintained in Δ-DYN∀*FO then it can be maintained in DYN∀*FO as well.*

We note that the first statement could equally be expressed in terms of Δ-DYN∃*FO and DYN∃*FO.

Proof. We only prove (a), the proof of (b) is analogous. Let $\mathcal{P} = (P, \text{INIT}, Q)$ be a dynamic Δ-DYNUCQ⁻-program over schema τ. By Lemma 3.2.7 we can assume, without loss of generality, that the update formulas of $\mathcal{P}$ are negation-free. For ease of presentation we assume that the input schema contains a single binary relation symbol E.

We construct an equivalent DYNUCQ⁻-program $\mathcal{P}'$ using the following idea. Consider some update formulas $\phi_\delta^{R^+}(\bar{u}; \bar{x})$ and $\phi_\delta^{R^-}(\bar{u}; \bar{x})$ of a relation $R \in \tau$ for a modification δ in $\mathcal{P}$. The naïve translation into a DYNFO-update formula $\phi_\delta^R(\bar{u}; \bar{x})$ yields the formula

$$\phi_\delta^R(\bar{u}; \bar{x}) = (R(\bar{x}) \vee \phi_\delta^{R^+}(\bar{u}; \bar{x})) \wedge \neg\phi_\delta^{R^-}(\bar{u}; \bar{x})$$

which is possibly non-UCQ⁻ due to $\neg\phi_\delta^{R^-}(\bar{u}; \bar{x})$. Therefore, $\mathcal{P}'$ maintains a relation R_δ^- that contains all tuples $(\bar{a}, \bar{b})$ such that $\bar{a}$ would be removed from R after applying the modification $\delta(\bar{b})$. Those relations are maintained using the squirrel technique. See the following Example 3.2.10 for a sample construction.

The dynamic program $\mathcal{P}'$ is over schema $\tau \cup \tau_\Delta$ where τ_Δ contains a $(k+2)$-ary relation symbol $R_\delta^- \in \tau$ for every k-ary relation symbol $R \in \tau$ and every modification $\delta \in \{\text{INS}, \text{DEL}\}$ of the input relation E.

The update formula for a relation symbol $R \in \tau$ is

$$\phi_\delta^R(\bar{u}; \bar{x}) \overset{\text{def}}{=} (R(\bar{x}) \vee \phi_\delta^{R^+}(\bar{u}; \bar{x})) \wedge \neg R_\delta^-(\bar{u}, \bar{x}).$$

This formula can be translated into an existential formula in a straightforward manner.

For updating a relation $R_{\delta_1}^-$ after a modification δ_0, the update formula $\phi_{\delta_1}^{R^-}$ for R^- is used. However, since $R_{\delta_1}^-$ shall store tuples that have to be deleted after applying δ_1, the formula $\phi_{\delta_1}^{R^-}$ has to be adapted to use the content of relation symbols $S \in \tau$ after modification δ_0 (instead, as usual, the content from before the modification). For this purpose relation symbols $S \in \tau$ in $\phi_{\delta_1}^{R^-}$ need to be replaced by their update formulas as defined above.

The update formula for $R_{\delta_1}^-$ is

$$\phi_{\delta_0}^{R_{\delta_1}^-}(\bar{u}_0; \bar{u}_1, \bar{x}) \overset{\text{def}}{=} \phi_{\delta_0}^{R_{\delta_1}^-}[\tau \to \phi^\tau](\bar{u}_0; \bar{u}_1, \bar{x})$$

where $\phi_{\delta_0}^{R_{\delta_1}^-}[\tau \to \phi^\tau](\bar{u}_0; \bar{u}_1, \bar{x})$ is obtained from $\phi_{\delta_1}^{R^-}(\bar{u}; \bar{x})$ by replacing every atom $S(\bar{z})$ by $\phi_{\delta_0}^S(\bar{u}_0; \bar{z})$, as constructed above. Since by our initial assumption, $\phi_{\delta_1}^{R^-}$ itself is an UCQ-formula and all update formulas $\phi_{\delta_0}^S$ for $S \in \tau$ are UCQ-formula, the formula $\phi_{\delta_0}^{R_{\delta_1}^-}$ can be easily converted into an UCQ-formula as well.   □

The following example illustrates the construction of Lemma 3.2.9.

Example 3.2.10. Consider the following negation-free Δ-update formulas for a relation symbol R:

$$\phi_{\text{INS}}^{R^+}(u; x) = \exists y (R(y) \wedge S(u, x))$$

$$\phi_{\text{INS}}^{R^-}(u; x) = \exists y (U(x) \vee (R(y) \wedge S(y, u)))$$

$$\phi_{\text{DEL}}^{R^+}(u; x) = \exists y U(y)$$

$$\phi_{\text{DEL}}^{R^-}(u; x) = \exists y \exists z (S(x, z) \wedge S(y, u))$$

Then the construction from the previous Lemma 3.2.9 yields the following update formulas for R and $R_{\delta_1}^-$ which can be easily translated into UCQ$^-$-formulas:

$$\phi_{\text{INS}}^{R}(u; x) = (R(x) \vee \phi_{\text{INS}}^{R+}(u; x)) \wedge \neg R_{\text{INS}}^{-}(u, x)$$

$$\phi_{\text{DEL}}^{R}(u; x) = (R(x) \vee \phi_{\text{DEL}}^{R+}(u; x)) \wedge \neg R_{\text{DEL}}^{-}(u, x)$$

$$\phi_{\text{INS}}^{R_{\text{INS}}^{-}}(u_0; u_1, x) = \exists y \left(\phi_{\text{INS}}^{U}(u_0; x) \vee \left(\phi_{\text{INS}}^{R}(u_0; y) \wedge \phi_{\text{INS}}^{S}(u_0; y, u_1) \right) \right)$$

$$\phi_{\text{DEL}}^{R_{\text{INS}}^{-}}(u_0; u_1, x) = \exists y \left(\phi_{\text{DEL}}^{U}(u_0; x) \right) \vee \left(\phi_{\text{DEL}}^{R}(u_0; y) \wedge \phi_{\text{DEL}}^{S}(u_0; y, u_1) \right)$$

$$\phi_{\text{INS}}^{R_{\text{DEL}}^{-}}(u_0; u_1, x) = \exists y \exists z \left(\phi_{\text{INS}}^{S}(u_0; x, z) \wedge \phi_{\text{INS}}^{S}(u_0; y, u_1) \right)$$

$$\phi_{\text{DEL}}^{R_{\text{DEL}}^{-}}(u_0; u_1, x) = \exists y \exists z \left(\phi_{\text{DEL}}^{S}(u_0; x, z) \wedge \phi_{\text{DEL}}^{S}(u_0; y, u_1) \right) \qquad \Box$$

Lemmas 3.2.8 and 3.2.9 together yield Theorem 3.2.4. We now finally prove Theorem 3.2.3. For this we need the following adaption of Lemma 3.1.14 to Δ-semantics.

Lemma 3.2.11. *(a) For every Δ-DYNUCQ$^{\neg}$-program there is an equivalent Δ-DYNCQ$^{\neg}$-program.*
(b) For every Δ-DYNFO-program there is an equivalent Δ-DYNFO$^{\wedge}$-program.

Proof sketch. The proof uses the idea from the corresponding Lemma 3.1.14 for absolute semantics. We prove (a) only. The construction for (b) is exactly the same.

Let $\mathcal{P}$ be a Δ-DYNUCQ$^{\neg}$-program. As in Lemma 3.1.14 we construct two programs $\mathcal{P}'$ and $\mathcal{P}''$ equivalent to $\mathcal{P}$ for domains of size at least two and domains of size one, respectively. The construction of $\mathcal{P}'$ is exactly the same as the construction for absolute semantics, yet this requires to adapt Lemma 3.1.13 to Δ-semantics. Such an adaption is straightforward. For the construction of $\mathcal{P}''$, Lemma 3.2.12 (see below) is used. A Δ-DYNCQ$^{\neg}$-program $\mathcal{P}'''$ is obtained from $\mathcal{P}'$ and $\mathcal{P}''$ by using a modification of the construction used for the cases (b) and (c) in Lemma 3.1.14.

In order to delegate the case distinction to the initialization mapping, we use an additional 0-ary relation symbol U to ensure that interpretations of relations $R'' \in \tau''$ never change for domains of size a least two and, analogously, interpretations of relations $R' \in \tau'$ never change for domains of size one. To achieve this, U is interpreted by true if and only if the domain is of size at least two and the update formulas of $\mathcal{P}'$ and $\mathcal{P}''$ are slightly modified as follows.

Update formulas $\phi_{\delta}^{R'+}$ and $\phi_{\delta}^{R'-}$ of a relation symbol $R' \in \tau'$ in program $\mathcal{P}'$ are replaced in $\mathcal{P}'''$ by $\phi_{\delta}^{R'+} \wedge U$ and $\phi_{\delta}^{R'-} \wedge U$. Hence the interpretation of R' changes only for domains of size at least two. Similarly, update formulas $\phi_{\delta}^{R''+}$ and $\phi_{\delta}^{R''-}$ of a relation symbol $R'' \in \tau''$ in program $\mathcal{P}''$ are replaced in $\mathcal{P}'''$ by $\phi_{\delta}^{R''+} \wedge \neg U$ and $\phi_{\delta}^{R''-} \wedge \neg U$. Hence the interpretation of R'' changes only for domains of size one.

The initialization of relation symbols from $\tau' \cup \tau'' \cup \{Q'''\}$ is as in Lemma 3.1.14, and U is initialized as true if and only if $|D| = 1$.

Lemma 3.2.12. *Every query on a 0-ary database can be maintained by a Δ-DYNPROPCQ-program.*

Proof. Let τ_{inp} be an input schema with 0-ary relation symbols $A_1, \ldots, A_k$. Further let $Q_1, \ldots, Q_m$ be an enumeration of all $m = 2^{2^k}$ many queries on τ_{inp}. As in

Lemma 3.1.15 we show that all of them can be maintained by one Δ-DYNPROPCQ-program $\mathcal{P}$ with auxiliary schema $\tau_{\text{aux}} = \{R_1, \ldots, R_m\}$ maintaining $\mathcal{Q}_i$ in R_i, for every $i \in \{1, \ldots, m\}$.

Our goal is to re-use the program constructed in Lemma 3.1.15 and the translation

$$\phi_\delta^{R_i^+}(\bar{u}; \bar{x}) = \phi_\delta^{R_i}(\bar{u}; \bar{x}) \wedge \neg R_i(\bar{x})$$

$$\phi_\delta^{R_i^-}(\bar{u}; \bar{x}) = \neg \phi_\delta^{R_i}(\bar{u}; \bar{x}) \wedge R_i(\bar{x})$$

Yet $\neg \phi_\delta^{R_i}$ does not yield a DYNPROPCQ-formulas immediately.

The idea to solve this issue is to use two dynamic programs $\mathcal{P}^\wedge$ and $\mathcal{P}^\vee$ that both maintain all queries $\mathcal{Q}_i$ in their auxiliary relations. The program $\mathcal{P}^\wedge$ will be the program from Lemma 3.1.15 whereas $\mathcal{P}^\vee$ will be a DYNPROP-program whose update formulas are disjunctions of atoms. Then the update formulas of R_i in $\mathcal{P}^\vee$ will be used for defining $\phi_\delta^{R_i^-}$.

We make this more precise. By Lemma 3.1.15 there is a DYNPROPCQ-program $\mathcal{P}^\wedge$ over schema $\tau^\wedge = \{R_1^\wedge, \ldots, R_m^\wedge\}$ that maintains $\mathcal{Q}_i$ in $R_i^\wedge$ with conjunctive quantifier-free update formulas. Analogously a dynamic program $\mathcal{P}^\vee$ over schema $\tau^\vee = \{R_1^\vee, \ldots, R_m^\vee\}$ can be constructed that maintains $\mathcal{Q}_i$ in $R_i^\vee$ with disjunctive quantifier-free update formulas.

Then the update formulas for R_i in $\mathcal{P}$ are constructed as

$$\phi_\delta^{R_i^+} = \phi_\delta^{R_i^\wedge}[\tau^\wedge \to \tau] \wedge \neg R(\bar{x})$$

$$\phi_\delta^{R_i^-} = \neg \phi_\delta^{R_i^\vee}[\tau^\vee \to \tau] \wedge R(\bar{x})$$

where $\phi_\delta^{R_i^\wedge}[\tau^\wedge \to \tau]$ is obtained from $\phi_\delta^{R_i^\wedge}$ by replacing symbols $S^\wedge \in \tau^\wedge$ by $S \in \tau$, and $\phi_\delta^{R_i^\vee}[\tau^\vee \to \tau]$ is obtained from $\phi_\delta^{R_i^\vee}$ by replacing symbols $S^\vee \in \tau^\vee$ by $S \in \tau$.

Those update formulas can be easily written as conjunctions. Negations can be removed by Lemma 3.2.7. $\qquad\square$

Proof (of Theorem 3.2.3). The equivalence of (a) and (b) as well as of (c) and (d) follows from Lemma 3.2.7. Statements (a) and (c) are equivalent by Lemma 3.2.11. Further, (a) and (e) are equivalent by definition. The equivalence of (e) and (f) follows immediately by combining Lemmas 3.2.8 and 3.2.9 with Theorem 3.1.1.

3.3 Relating Dynamic Classes and Static Classes

In this section we are interested in maintaining all queries in some descriptive complexity class using updates from a weaker class. As mentioned already in the introduction of this chapter, only very few examples for results of this kind have been obtained so far. The results most related to our results are that all MSO-queries on strings can be maintained in DYNPROP and that, on general structures, $\exists^*$FO is captured by DYNQF [GMS12]. Here we present two further results of this kind.

The first result characterizes first-order logic by a much weaker dynamic class: all first-order definable queries are maintainable using conjunctive queries with negations as update formalism. More precisely, we characterize first-order queries as the class of queries maintainable by non-recursive UCQ$^{\neg}$-programs and, equivalently, by non-recursive DYN$\exists^1$FO-programs. Here $\exists^1$FO is the class of queries expressible by first-order formulas in prenex normal form with at most one existential quantifier and no universal quantifiers. A *non-recursive dynamic program* is a dynamic program with an acyclic dependency graph (as a directed graph). We refer to Sect. 2.2 for a definition of dependency graphs. For every class $\mathcal{C}$, *non-recursive* DYN$\mathcal{C}$ refers to the set of queries that can be maintained by non-recursive DYN$\mathcal{C}$-programs.

Theorem 3.3.1. *For every query $\mathcal{Q}$ the following statements are equivalent*

(a) $\mathcal{Q}$ can be expressed in FO.
(b) $\mathcal{Q}$ can be maintained in non-recursive DYNFO.
(c) $\mathcal{Q}$ can be maintained in non-recursive DYN$\exists^1$FO.
(d) $\mathcal{Q}$ can be maintained in non-recursive DYN$\forall^1$FO.

With respect to the number of quantifiers in update formulas this result is optimal because the first-order definable alternating reachability query on graphs of bounded diameter cannot be maintained with quantifier-free update formulas [GMS12], but it can be easily defined by a first-order formula. Theorem 3.3.1 should be compared with the related result of [GMS12] that all $\exists^*$FO queries can be maintained in DYNQF.

Combining Theorem 3.3.1 with Theorem 3.1.1 immediately yields the following corollary.

Corollary 3.3.2. *Every first-order query can be maintained in DYNCQ$^{\neg}$.*

The second result for capturing a static class by a weaker dynamic class is that, when restricting modifications to be insertions, queries definable by unions of conjunctive queries with negated equality atoms can be be maintained in DYNPROP. Actually we prove that every property expressible by such a query with k quantifiers can be maintained by a $(k-1)$-ary quantifier-free program under insertions. In Sect. 4.1 we will see that this result is tight with respect to the arity, that is, $(k-2)$-ary quantifier-free programs are not sufficient.

A *positive existential first-order query* over schema τ is a query that can be expressed by a first-order formula of the form $\varphi(\bar{y}) = \exists \bar{x} \psi(\bar{x}, \bar{y})$ where ψ is a quantifier-free formula that contains no negations. *Semi-positive existential first-order queries* may contain literals of the form $z_i \neq z_j$. We observe that the class of positive existential first-order queries coincides with the class of UCQ-queries.

Theorem 3.3.3. *Let $\ell \in \mathbb{N}$. An ℓ-ary query expressible by a semi-positive existential first-order formula with k quantifiers can be maintained under insertions in $(\ell + k - 1)$-ary DYNPROP.*

3.3.1 A Dynamic Characterization of First-Order Logic

In this subsection we prove the characterization of first-order queries as the class of queries maintainable by non-recursive UCQ⁻-programs, that is, we prove Theorem 3.3.1.

The equivalence of (c) and (d) follows from Theorem 3.1.1 and the fact that its proof does not introduce recursion when applied to a non-recursive program. Alternatively, the equivalence to (d) could be stablished by adapting the proof of (a)⇒(c) to a proof of (a)⇒(d). It is obvious that (c) implies (b).

For ease of presentation, we prove the remaining directions (a)⇒(c) and (b)⇒(a) for the input schema $\tau_{inp} = \{E\}$ where E is a binary relation symbol. The proofs can be easily adapted to general (relational) signatures.

First we prove (a)⇒(c). The proof makes use of the following normal form for FO. A formula φ is in *existential prefix form* if it has a prefix over $((\neg \exists)|\exists))^*$ and no quantifier occurs after this prefix (e.g. $\exists x \neg \exists y \neg (E(x,x) \to E(x,y))$ is in existential prefix form with prefix $\exists \neg \exists$). A formula in prefix normal form can be easily translated into existential prefix form by duality of universal and existential quantifiers. The *prefix length* of a formula in existential normal form is the number of existential and $\neg$-symbols in the maximal prefix ending with $\exists$.

The following example outlines the idea of the construction for the proof of (a)⇒(c).

Example 3.3.4. Consider the query Q defined by

$$\varphi = \exists x \forall y \big(E(x,x) \to E(x,y)\big)$$
$$\equiv \exists x \neg \exists y \neg \big(E(x,x) \to E(x,y)\big)$$

We construct a non-recursive dynamic DYN$\exists^1$FO-program $\mathcal{P}$ that maintains Q under deletions only (for simplicity). The construction of $\mathcal{P}$ applies the squirrel technique. It uses a separate auxiliary relation R_ψ for each subformula ψ obtained from φ by stripping off a "quantifier prefix" from the existential prefix form of φ. The relation R_ψ reflects the possible states after a sequence of changes whose length equals the number of stripped off $\neg$- and $\exists$-symbols.

In order to update the query relation after the deletion of an edge, we maintain an auxiliary ternary relation R_1 (here, for simplicity, we write R_1 instead of R_{ψ_1}) that contains the result of the query $\psi_1 \stackrel{\text{def}}{=} \neg \exists y \neg \big(E(x,x) \to E(x,y)\big)$ for every choice a_1 for x and every (possibly deleted) edge $\bar{e}_1$, that is $(a_1, \bar{e}_1) \in R_1$ if and only if

$$(V, E \setminus \{\bar{e}_1\}, \{x \mapsto a_1\}) \models \neg \exists y \neg \big(E(x,x) \to E(x,y)\big).$$

Then we can define $\phi_{\text{DEL}}^Q(\bar{v}_1;) \stackrel{\text{def}}{=} \exists x R_1(x, \bar{v}_1)$ and it only remains to find a way to update the relation R_1. To this end, we maintain a further relation R_2 that contains the result of $\psi_2 \stackrel{\text{def}}{=} \exists y \neg \big(E(x,x) \to E(x,y)\big)$ for every choice a_1 for x and all (possibly deleted) edges $\bar{e}_1, \bar{e}_2$, that is $(a_1, \bar{e}_1, \bar{e}_2) \in R_2$ if and only if

$$(V, E \setminus \{\bar{e}_1, \bar{e}_2\}, \{x \mapsto a_1\}) \models \exists y \neg (E(x, x) \rightarrow E(x, y)).$$

Then $\phi_{\text{DEL}}^{R_1}(\bar{v}_1; x, \bar{v}_2) \stackrel{\text{def}}{=} \neg R_2(x, \bar{v}_1, \bar{v}_2)$ and it remains to update the relation R_2. Therefore we maintain a relation R_3 that contains the result of $\psi_3 = \neg(E(x, x) \rightarrow E(x, y))$ for every choice a_1, a_2 for x, y and all (possibly deleted) edges $\bar{e}_1, \bar{e}_2, \bar{e}_3$. Then

$$\phi_{\text{DEL}}^{R_2}(\bar{v}_1; x, \bar{v}_2, \bar{v}_3) \stackrel{\text{def}}{=} \exists y R_3(x, y, \bar{v}_1, \bar{v}_2, \bar{v}_3)$$

and it remains to update relation R_3 via

$$\phi_{\text{DEL}}^{R_3}(\bar{v}_1; x, y, \bar{v}_2, \bar{v}_3, \bar{v}_4) \stackrel{\text{def}}{=} \neg \big(E'(x, x, \bar{v}_1, \dots, \bar{v}_4) \rightarrow E'(x, y, \bar{v}_1, \dots, \bar{v}_4) \big)$$

where E' is the edge relation obtained from E by deleting $\bar{v}_1, \bar{v}_2, \bar{v}_3$ and $\bar{v}_4$, that is $E'(x, y, \bar{v}_1, \dots, \bar{v}_4)$ can be replaced by

$$E(x, y) \wedge (x, y) \neq \bar{v}_1 \wedge \dots \wedge (x, y) \neq \bar{v}_4.$$

This completes the description of the program $\mathcal{P}$ for φ which is easily seen to be non-recursive.   □

The following definition will be useful in the two remaining proofs of this subsection. For every first-order formula φ with k free variables and every sequence $\delta = \delta_1 \dots \delta_j$ over $\{\text{INS}, \text{DEL}\}$ let $\varphi_{\delta_1 \dots \delta_j}^E$ be a $(k + 2j)$-ary formula such that for every graph $G = (V, E)$, every $\bar{a} \in V^k$ and every instantiation $\alpha = \delta_1(\bar{e}_1) \dots \delta_2(\bar{e}_j)$ of δ with tuples $\bar{e}_1, \dots, \bar{e}_j \in V^2$:

$$\alpha(G) \models \varphi \text{ if and only if } (G, \bar{a}, \bar{e}_1, \dots, \bar{e}_j) \models \varphi_{\delta_1 \dots \delta_j}(\bar{x}, \bar{u}_1, \dots, \bar{u}_j).$$

It is straightforward to construct $\varphi_{\delta_1 \dots \delta_j}^E$. It should be noted that $\varphi_{\delta_1 \dots \delta_j}^E$ can be constructed such that its quantifier-prefix is the same as for φ. In particular, if φ is quantifier-free then $\varphi_{\delta_1 \dots \delta_j}^E$ can be constructed quantifier-free as well. For example, if $\delta = \text{INS DEL}$ and $\varphi(\bar{x}) = \neg E(\bar{x})$ then

$$\varphi_{\text{INS DEL}}^E(\bar{x}, \bar{u}_1, \bar{u}_2) = \neg \big((E(\bar{x}) \vee \bar{x} = \bar{u}_1) \wedge \neg(\bar{x} = \bar{u}_2) \big).$$

Lemma 3.3.5. *If a query is definable in* FO, *then it can be maintained in non-recursive* DYN$\exists^1$FO.

Proof. Inductively over the length of the prefix of a formula φ in existential prefix form, we prove that, for every finite sequence $\delta_1 \dots \delta_j$, the query defined by $\varphi_{\delta_1 \dots \delta_j}$ is maintainable in non-recursive DYN$\exists^1$FO. The claim follows by setting $j = 0$. We construct dynamic programs where the result of the query defined by $\varphi_{\delta_1 \dots \delta_j}$ is stored in the relation $R_{\delta_1 \dots \delta_j}^\varphi$.

For a formula φ with a prefix of length 0 (i.e. a quantifier-free formula), we define

$$\phi_{\delta_0}^{R_{\delta_1\ldots\delta_j}^{\varphi}}(\bar{v}_0; \bar{y}, \bar{v}_1, \ldots, \bar{v}_j) \stackrel{\text{def}}{=} \varphi_{\delta_0\ldots\delta_j}^{E}(\bar{y}, \bar{v}_0, \ldots, \bar{v}_j)$$

where $\varphi_{\delta_0\ldots\delta_j}^{E}$ is as defined above (in the quantifier-free case).

For the induction step, let φ be a formula of prefix length i. By induction hypothesis, every query defined by $\psi_{\delta_1\ldots\delta_j}$ where ψ has prefix length $i-1$, can be maintained in non-recursive $\text{DYN}\exists^1\text{FO}$, for every sequence $\delta_1\ldots\delta_j$ of modifications.

We distinguish the two cases $\varphi(\bar{y}) = \exists x \psi(x, \bar{y})$ and $\varphi(\bar{y}) = \neg\gamma(\bar{y})$. If $\varphi(\bar{y}) = \exists x \psi(x, \bar{y})$ then the dynamic program for φ and $\delta_1\ldots\delta_j$ has auxiliary relations $R_{\delta_0\ldots\delta_j}^{\psi}$ for $\delta_0 \in \{\text{INS}, \text{DEL}\}$ containing the result of the query $\psi_{\delta_0\ldots\delta_j}$. Further,

$$\phi_{\delta_0}^{R_{\delta_1\ldots\delta_j}^{\varphi}}(\bar{v}_0; \bar{y}, \bar{v}_1, \ldots, \bar{v}_j) \stackrel{\text{def}}{=} \exists x R_{\delta_0\ldots\delta_j}^{\psi}(x, \bar{y}, \bar{v}_0, \ldots, \bar{v}_j).$$

If $\varphi(\bar{y}) = \neg\gamma(\bar{y})$ then the dynamic program for φ and $\delta_1\ldots\delta_j$ has auxiliary relations $R_{\delta_0\ldots\delta_j}^{\gamma}$ for $\delta_0 \in \{\text{INS}, \text{DEL}\}$ containing the result of the query $\gamma_{\delta_0\ldots\delta_j}$. Further,

$$\phi_{\delta_0}^{R_{\delta_1\ldots\delta_j}^{\varphi}}(\bar{v}_0; \bar{y}, \bar{v}_1, \ldots, \bar{v}_j) \stackrel{\text{def}}{=} \neg R_{\text{DEL}\,\delta_0\ldots\delta_j}^{\gamma}(\bar{y}, \bar{v}_0, \ldots, \bar{v}_j).$$

This yields a non-recursive $\exists^1\text{FO}$-program, for every $\varphi_{\delta_1\ldots\delta_j}$. □

We now turn towards proving the implication (b)⇒(a) in Theorem 3.3.1. The following notion will be useful. A *topological sorting* of a graph (V, E) is a sequence $v_1, \ldots, v_n$ such that every vertex from V occurs exactly once and $i > j$ for all edges $(v_i, v_j) \in E$. Every acyclic graph has a topological sorting. In particular, if $R_1, \ldots, R_m$ is a topological sorting of the dependency graph of a non-recursive dynamic program $\mathcal{P} = (P, \text{INIT}, Q)$ then update formulas for R_1 do only contain relation symbols from τ_{inp}. Further we can assume, without loss of generality, that $R_m = Q$. We say that R_i is on the ith level of the dependency graph.

Lemma 3.3.6. *If a query can be maintained in non-recursive* DYNFO, *then it can be expressed in* FO.

Proof. Consider a non-recursive dynamic DYNFO-program $\mathcal{P} = (P, \text{INIT}, Q)$ over input schema $\{E\}$.

We start with some intuition. Let R be an auxiliary relation of $\mathcal{P}$ which is (for simplicity) on the first layer of the topological sorting of the dependency graph of $\mathcal{P}$. That is, the update formulas $\phi_{\text{INS}_E}^{R}$ and $\phi_{\text{DEL}_E}^{R}$ of R depend on the input relations only. There is no a priori upper bound on the complexity of the initialization process for R. However, after one modification step the relation is redefined via one of the first-order update formulas $\phi_{\text{INS}_E}^{R}$ or $\phi_{\text{DEL}_E}^{R}$ which only use atoms over the input relations. Similarly, the auxiliary relations on higher levels of the dependency graph depend in a first-order fashion from the input structure after a constant number of modification steps. This is exploited in the proof.

More technically, the proof idea is as follows. For every modification pattern $\delta = \delta_1\ldots\delta_j$ and every auxiliary relation R, a first-order formula φ_{δ}^{R} is constructed that "precomputes" the state of R for every possible modification sequence with the pattern δ. Thanks to non-recursiveness, once δ is longer than the number of auxiliary relations, the formula φ_δ^R can only use relations from the input schema. That is, it is just a first-order formula over τ_{inp}. We get the desired first-order formula for Q by choosing in φ_δ^R a sufficiently long modification sequence δ (by repeatedly inserting and deleting the same tuple).

We make this more precise now. Let Q be a query which can be maintained by a non-recursive DYNFO-program $\mathcal{P} = (P, \text{INIT}, Q)$ over schema $\tau = \tau_{\text{inp}} \cup \tau_{\text{aux}}$. We assume for simplicity that $\tau_{\text{inp}} = \{E\}$, for a binary symbol E. We let $R_0 \stackrel{\text{def}}{=} E$ and assume that the auxiliary relations $R_1, \ldots, R_m$ are enumerated with respect to a topological sorting of the dependency graph of $\mathcal{P}$ with $R_m = Q$.

We define inductively, by i, for every sequence $\delta_1 \ldots \delta_j$ with $j \geq i$, first-order formulas $\varphi_{\delta_1 \ldots \delta_j}^{R_i}(\bar{y}, \bar{x}_1, \ldots, \bar{x}_j)$ over schema $\tau_{\text{inp}} = \{E\}$ such that $\varphi_{\delta_1 \ldots \delta_j}^{R_i}$ defines R_i after modifications $\delta_1(\bar{x}_1) \ldots \delta_j(\bar{x}_j)$. More precisely $\varphi_{\delta_1 \ldots \delta_j}^{R_i}$ will be defined such that for every state $\mathcal{S} = (V, E^{\mathcal{S}}, \mathcal{A}^{\mathcal{S}})$ of $\mathcal{P}$ and every sequence $\delta = \delta_1(\bar{a}_1) \ldots \delta_j(\bar{a}_j)$ of modifications the following holds:

$$\mathcal{P}_\delta(\mathcal{S}) \restriction R_i = \{\bar{b} \mid (V, E) \models \varphi_{\delta_1 \ldots \delta_j}^{R_i}(\bar{b}, \bar{a}_1, \ldots, \bar{a}_j)\} \tag{3.3}$$

Here $\mathcal{P}_\delta(\mathcal{S}) \restriction R_i$ denotes the relation stored in R_i in state $\mathcal{P}_\delta(\mathcal{S})$. For $R_0 = E$ the formula $\varphi_{\delta_1 \ldots \delta_j}^{E}$ is as defined before the previous lemma. For R_i with $i \geq 1$ the formula $\varphi_{\delta_1 \ldots \delta_j}^{R_i}(\bar{y}, \bar{x}_1, \ldots, \bar{x}_j)$ is obtained from the update formula $\phi_{\delta_j}^{R_i}(\bar{x}_j; \bar{y})$ of R_i by substituting all occurrences of $R_{i'}(\bar{z})$ by $\varphi_{\delta_1 \ldots \delta_{j-1}}^{R_{i'}}(\bar{x}_1, \ldots, \bar{x}_{j-1}, \bar{z})$ for all $i' < i$. Using induction over i, one can prove that the formulas $\varphi_{\delta_1 \ldots \delta_j}^{R_i}$ satisfy Eq. 3.3. As $\mathcal{P}$ is non-recursive, each formula $\varphi_{\delta_1 \ldots \delta_j}^{R_i}$ with $j \geq i$ is over schema $\{E\}$.

The first-order formula φ for Q over schema $\tau_{\text{inp}} = \{E\}$ can be constructed as follows. The formula "guesses" a tuple $\bar{a} \in E$, deletes and inserts it m times and applies $\varphi_{(\text{DEL INS})^m}^{R_m}$ to the result (which is identical to the current graph), or (for the case that E is empty) it guesses a tuple $\bar{a} \notin E$, inserts and deletes it m times and applies $\varphi_{(\text{INS DEL})^m}^{R_m}$ to the result.

More precisely, φ for Q is defined by

$$\varphi(\bar{y}) \stackrel{\text{def}}{=} \exists \bar{x} \Big(\big(E(\bar{x}) \wedge \varphi_{(\text{DEL INS})^m}^{R_m}(\bar{y}, \underbrace{\bar{x}, \bar{x}, \ldots, \bar{x}}_{2m-\text{times}}) \big)$$

$$\vee \big(\neg E(\bar{x}) \wedge \varphi_{(\text{INS DEL})^m}^{R_m}(\bar{y}, \underbrace{\bar{x}, \bar{x}, \ldots, \bar{x}}_{2m-\text{times}}) \big) \Big).$$

$\square$

3.3.2 DYNPROP *Captures Semi-positive* ∃*FO *Under Insertions*

In this subsection we prove that, when restricting modifications to be insertions, queries definable by semi-positive existential first-order formulas can be maintained in DYNPROP. Before turning to the proof we give some intuition.

Example 3.3.7. We show how to maintain 3- CLIQUE in binary DYNPROP under insertions. The very simple idea is to use an additional binary auxiliary relation R that stores all edges whose insertion would complete a triangle. Hence a tuple (a, b) is inserted into R as soon as deciding whether there is a 3-clique containing the nodes a and b only depends on those two nodes. More precisely (a, b) is added to R, e.g., if an edge (c, a) is inserted to the input graph and the edge (c, b) is already present (or vice versa).

Thus the update formula for R is

$$\phi^R_{\text{INS}_E}(u, v; x, y) \overset{\text{def}}{=} u \neq v \wedge x \neq y \wedge \Big(\big(E\{u, y\} \wedge v = x\big) \vee \big(E\{u, x\} \wedge v = y\big)$$
$$\vee \big(E\{v, y\} \wedge u = x\big) \vee \big(E\{v, x\} \wedge u = y\big) \Big)$$

where $E\{x, y\}$ is an abbreviation for $E(x, y) \vee E(y, x)$.

The update formula for the query symbol Q is

$$\phi^Q_{\text{INS}_E}(u, v; x, y) = Q \vee R(u, v). \qquad \square$$

The general proof for arbitrary semi-positive existential first-order properties extends the approach from the previous example.

Theorem 3.3.3 (**R**). Let $\ell \in \mathbb{N}$. An ℓ-ary query expressible by a semi-positive existential first-order formula with k quantifiers can be maintained under insertions in $(\ell + k - 1)$-ary DYNPROP.

Proof. For simplicity we restrict the proof to boolean graph queries. The proof easily carries over to arbitrary semi-positive existential queries.

We give the intuition first. Basically a semi-positive existential sentence with k quantifiers can state which (not necessarily induced) subgraphs with k nodes shall occur in a graph. Therefore it is sufficient to construct a dynamic quantifier-free program that maintains whether the input graph contains a subgraph H. Such a program can work as follows. For every induced, proper subgraph $H' = \{u_1, \ldots, u_m\}$ of H, the program maintains an auxiliary relation that stores all tuples $\bar{a} = (a_1, \ldots, a_m)$ such that inserting H' into $\{a_1, \ldots, a_m\}$ (with a_i corresponding to u_i) yields a graph that contains H.

In particular, auxiliary relations have arity at most $k - 1$ (as only proper subgraphs of H have a corresponding auxiliary relation). Furthermore the graph H is contained in the input graph whenever the value of the 0-ary relation corresponding to the empty subgraph of H is true. In the example above, the relation R is the relation for the subgraph of the 3-clique graph that consists of a single edge, and the designated query relation is the 0-ary relation for the empty subgraph.

Those auxiliary relations can be updated as follows. Assume that a tuple $\bar{a} = (a_1, \ldots, a_m)$ is contained in the relation corresponding to H'. If, after the insertion of an edge with end point a_m, every edge from u_m in H' has a corresponding edge from a_m in the graph induced by $\{a_1, \ldots, a_m\}$, then the tuple $\bar{a}' = (a_1, \ldots, a_{m-1})$ has to be inserted into the auxiliary relation for the subgraph $H' \upharpoonright \{u_1, \ldots, u_{m-1}\}$. This is because inserting the graph $H' \upharpoonright \{u_1, \ldots, u_{m-1}\}$ into $\{a_1, \ldots, a_{m-1}\}$ will now yield a graph that contains H. Observe that for those updates no quantifiers are needed.

In the following we make the intuitive idea outlined above more precise. We first show how a quantifier-free dynamic program can maintain whether the input graph contains a certain (not necessarily induced) subgraph. Afterwards we show how to combine the programs for several subgraphs in order to maintain an arbitrary semi-positive existential formula.

For the first step it will be technically easier not to speak about subgraphs H' of H (as in the intuition above) but to work with partitions of H. We introduce this notion as well as other useful notions next. Let H be a graph. A tuple $(\bar{y}, \bar{z})$ is called a *partition* of H if it contains every node of H exactly once. The subgraph of H induced by $\bar{y}$ is denoted by $H \upharpoonright \bar{y}$; the graph obtained from H by removing the edges of $H \upharpoonright \bar{y}$ is denoted by $H_{(\bar{y}, \bar{z})}$.

Now let $G = (V, E)$ and $H = (V', E')$ be graphs, and let $(\bar{y}, \bar{z})$ be an arbitrary partition of H with $|\bar{y}| = \ell$. We say that an ℓ-ary tuple $\bar{a}$ can be extended to $H_{(\bar{y}, \bar{z})}$, if there is a $|\bar{z}|$-tuple $\bar{b}$ such that the mapping π defined by $\pi(\bar{y}, \bar{z}) \stackrel{\text{def}}{=} (\bar{a}, \bar{b})$ maps edges in $H_{(\bar{y}, \bar{z})}$ to edges in G. Intuitively $\bar{a}$ can be extended to $H_{(\bar{y}, \bar{z})}$ when deciding whether H is a subgraph of G, where $\bar{y}$ corresponds to $\bar{a}$, depends only on $\bar{a}$ and not on nodes of G not contained in $\bar{a}$. See Fig. 3.3 for an illustration.

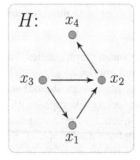 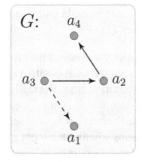

Fig. 3.3 Illustration of the notions used in Theorem 3.3.3. The graph H is the graph defined by the existential semi-positive formula $\exists x_1 \exists x_2 \exists x_3 \exists x_4 \left(\bigwedge_{i \neq j} x_i \neq x_j \wedge E(x_3, x_1) \wedge E(x_1, x_2) \wedge E(x_3, x_2) \wedge E(x_2, x_4) \right)$. Before inserting the edge (a_3, a_1) into G, the tuple (a_1, a_2, a_3) can be extended to $H_{((x_1, x_2, x_3), x_4)}$, but (a_1, a_2) does not extend to $H_{((x_1, x_2), (x_3, x_4))}$. After inserting the edge (a_3, a_1), the tuple (a_1, a_2) can be extended to $H_{((x_1, x_2), (x_3, x_4))}$ as well.

Let $\bar{a} = (a_1, \ldots, a_\ell)$ be a tuple that can be extended to $H_{(\bar{y},\bar{z})}$. Then a node a_i is called *saturated* with respect to a partition $(\bar{y}, \bar{z})$ and $\bar{a}$ if (a_i, a_j) (respectively (a_j, a_i)) is an edge in G whenever (y_i, y_j) (respectively (y_j, y_i)) is an edge in H. A tuple (c, d) is *critical* for a_i with respect to a partition $(\bar{y}, \bar{z})$ and $\bar{a}$ if a_i is not saturated in G but it is saturated in $G + (c, d)$. In Fig. 3.3, the tuple (a_3, a_1) is critical for a_3 with respect to the partition $((x_1, x_2, x_3), x_4)$ and the tuple (a_1, a_2). Observe that therefore the insertion of the edge (a_3, a_1) yields a graph where (a_1, a_2) can be extended to $H_{((x_1,x_2),(x_3,x_4))}$.

We are now ready to construct a DYNPROP-program $\mathcal{P}$ that maintains whether the input graph contains a graph H as (not necessarily induced) subgraph. The program $\mathcal{P}$ has an auxiliary relation $R_{(\bar{y},\bar{z})}$ of arity $|\bar{y}|$ for every partition $(\bar{y}, \bar{z})$ of H with $|\bar{z}| \geq 1$. The intention is that, for a state $\mathcal{S}$ with input graph G, a tuple $\bar{a}$ is in $R^{\mathcal{S}}_{(\bar{y},\bar{z})}$ whenever $\bar{a}$ extends to $H_{(\bar{y},\bar{z})}$ in G. Thus $R_{(\bar{y},\bar{z})}$ corresponds to the auxiliary relation for $H \upharpoonright \bar{y}$ in the intuitive explanation above. The condition $|\bar{z}| \geq 1$ ensures that the auxiliary relations are of arity at most $|H| - 1$.

Before sketching the construction of the update formulas it is illustrative to see what happens when inserting the edge (a_3, a_1) in Fig. 3.3. We observed above that this yields a graph where (a_1, a_2) can be extended to $H_{((x_1,x_2),(x_3,x_4))}$. Therefore (a_1, a_2) should be inserted into the auxiliary relation $R_{((x_1,x_2),(x_3,x_4))}$. However, this update of $R_{((x_1,x_2),(x_3,x_4))}$ can be made without quantifiers since it is sufficient to verify that (a_1, a_2, a_3) is already in $R_{((x_1,x_2,x_3),x_4)}$ and that (a_1, a_3) was critical. This involves the nodes a_1, a_2 and a_3 only.

In general, when an edge e is inserted, the update formulas of $\mathcal{P}$ check for which nodes and partitions the edge is critical; and adapt the auxiliary relations accordingly.

For updating a relation $R_{(\bar{y},\bar{z})}$ with $\bar{y} = (y_1, \ldots, y_\ell)$ and $\bar{z} = (z_1, \ldots, z_{k-\ell})$ the update formula $\phi^R_{\text{INS }E}(u, v; \bar{y})$ has to check whether there is some $R_{(\bar{y}',\bar{z}')}$ with $\bar{y}' = (y_1, \ldots, y_i, z_j, y_{i+1} \ldots, y_\ell)$ and $\bar{z}' = (z_1, \ldots, z_{j-1}, z_{j+1}, \ldots, z_{k-\ell})$ such that the insertion of (u, v) saturates z_j. It is also possible that the insertion of a single edge saturates two nodes, this case is very similar and will not be treated in detail here.

The formula $\phi^R_{\text{INS }E}(u, v; \bar{y})$ is a conjunction of formulas φ_u, φ_v and $\varphi_{u,v}$ responsible for dealing with the cases where u, v and both u and v are being saturated. We only exhibit φ_u:

$$\varphi_u \stackrel{\text{def}}{=} \bigvee_{\substack{\text{For all } (\bar{y}',\bar{z}') \text{ with} \\ \bar{y}'=(y_1,\ldots,y_i,z_j,y_{i+1},\ldots,y_\ell) \\ \bar{z}'=(z_1,\ldots,z_{j-1},z_{j+1},\ldots,z_{k-\ell})}} \Big(R_{(\bar{y}',\bar{z}')}(y_1, \ldots, y_i, u, y_{i+1}, \ldots, y_\ell) \wedge$$

$$\bigwedge_{i'} u \neq y_{i'} \wedge \bigwedge_{(z_j,y_{i'}) \in H \upharpoonright \bar{y}'} E(u, y_{i'}) \wedge \bigwedge_{(y_{i'},z_j) \in H \upharpoonright \bar{y}'} E(y_{i'}, u) \Big)$$

The other formulas are very similar. This completes the construction of $\mathcal{P}$.

It remains to construct a quantifier-free dynamic program for an arbitrary semi-positive existential formula using quantifier-free programs for subgraphs. To this end let $\varphi = \exists \bar{x} \psi(\bar{x})$ be an arbitrary semi-positive existential first-order formula. We show how to translate φ into an equivalent disjunction of formulas φ_i of the form

$$\varphi_i = \exists \bar{x}_i \bigwedge_{y, y' \in \bar{x}_i} \left(y \neq y' \wedge \psi_i(\bar{x}_i) \right)$$

where each ψ_i is a conjunction of atoms over $\{E\}$ and $|\bar{x}_i| \leq |\bar{x}|$.

Observe that the quantifier-free part of each φ_i encodes a subgraph H_i. Hence a graph G satisfies φ if and only if one of the graphs H_i is a subgraph of G. Thus a program maintaining the query defined by φ can be constructed by combining the dynamic programs for all H_i in a straightforward way.

We now sketch how to translate φ into the form stated above. First φ is rewritten as disjunction of conjunctive queries, that is as $\bigvee_i \exists \bar{y}_i \gamma_i(\bar{y}_i)$ where each γ_i is a conjunction of positive literals and literals of the form $x \neq x'$. Afterwards each $\exists \bar{y}_i \gamma_i(\bar{y}_i)$ is rewritten into an equivalent disjunction over all equality types over the variables in $\bar{y}_i$, that is as

$$\bigvee_{\varepsilon} \exists \bar{y}_{i,\varepsilon} \left(\bigwedge_{y, y' \in \bar{y}_{i,\varepsilon}} y \neq y' \wedge \varphi_{i,\varepsilon}(\bar{y}_{i,\varepsilon}) \right)$$

where ε is over all equality types and $\varphi_{i,\varepsilon}$ is a conjunction of atoms over $\{E\}$. $\qquad \square$

3.4 Eliminating Built-In Arithmetic

It is well-known that a query is expressible in $FO(+, \times)$ if and only if it can be evaluated by a DLOGTIME-uniform AC^0-circuit [BIS90]. Here $FO(+, \times)$ denotes the class of queries expressible in first-order logic with built-in linear order as well as its corresponding addition and multiplication; and DLOGTIME-uniform AC^0 refers to the class of queries that can be evaluated by a DLOGTIME-uniform, constant-depth, polynomial-size unbounded fan-in circuit.

This characterization of $FO(+, \times)$ translates immediately to dynamic complexity: a query is maintainable in DYNFO with built-in arithmetic if and only if it can be maintained using DLOGTIME-uniform AC^0 as update mechanism. Here DYNFO *with built-in arithmetic* has distinguished auxiliary relations $<$, $+$ and $\times$ which are initialized, for a domain D of size n, with a linear order on $0, \ldots, n-1$, and its corresponding addition and multiplication relations (where $a + b = n - 1$ if $a + b > n - 1$, and likewise for $\times$).

This begs the question whether built-in arithmetic is necessary for this characterization in the dynamic setting. In this section we show that built-in arithmetic is not needed for domain independent queries.

A query $\mathcal{Q}$ is *domain independent* if ANS($\mathcal{Q}, \mathcal{D}$) and ANS($\mathcal{Q}, \mathcal{D}'$) coincide whenever $\mathcal{D}$ and $\mathcal{D}'$ coincide in all relations and constants (but possibly differ in the underlying domain).

Theorem 3.4.1. *For a domain independent query $\mathcal{Q}$ the following statements are equivalent:*

(a) $\mathcal{Q}$ can be maintained from scratch in DYNFO.
(b) $\mathcal{Q}$ can be maintained in DYNFO *with built-in arithmetic.*

This result does not hold for arbitrary queries. For example, the domain dependent boolean query $\mathcal{Q}_{even}$, which is true for domains of even size and false otherwise, cannot be maintained in DYNFO from scratch. This is because the first-order initialization formulas cannot tell domains of even and odd size apart for large, empty structures. We refer to the second part of Sect. 4.3.2 for a broader discussion of this aspect.

As the reachability query is domain independent, the preceeding theorem implies the following.

Corollary 3.4.2. *If reachability can be maintained in* DYNFO *with built-in arithmetic, then it can be maintained from scratch in* DYNFO *as well.*

Thus for showing that reachability is in DYNFO in the original Patnaik/Immerman framework, that is, with initialization from scratch, it suffices to exhibit a dynamic program with first-order updates that possibly uses arithmetic, or, equivalently, a dynamic program with AC^0-updates. This has been done in [DKM+15] and a short proof overview can be found in Sect. 2.6.

We now turn towards proving Theorem 3.4.1. The *active domain* of a state $\mathcal{S}$ contains all elements that are in a tuple of one of the input relations. An element element a is *touched* by a modification sequence $\alpha = \delta_1, \ldots, \delta_\ell$ if it occurs in some δ_i. For DYNFO-programs that start from scratch we observe that if the application of α yields a state $\mathcal{S}$, then all elements in the active domain of $\mathcal{S}$ have been touched by α.

Already Etessami observed that arithmetic on the active domain can be constructed on the fly when new elements are touched [Ete98]. This is, however, not sufficient for simulating a program $\mathcal{P}$ with built-in arithmetic. Thanks to its built-in arithmetic, $\mathcal{P}$ can maintain complex auxiliary structures even for elements that have not been touched so far. On the other hand, a program $\mathcal{P}'$ starting from scratch can only use elements in a non-trivial way as soon as they have been touched. Indeed, while non-touched elements are already present in the domain before they are touched, it is easy to see that all of them behave similarly since they are all updated by the same first-order formulas. Therefore they cannot be used for storing complex auxiliary data structures. Thus, the challenge for the construction of $\mathcal{P}'$ is to make arithmetic as well as the auxiliary data for an element available as soon as it has been touched.

The construction of $\mathcal{P}'$ uses arithmetic on the elements that have been touched. Therefore we start with a repetition of Etessami's result.

Proposition 3.4.3 [Ete98]. *There is a DYNFO-program that maintains auxiliary relations $\mathcal{D}_t$, $<_t$, $+_t$ and $\times_t$ that represent the elements touched so far, and a linear order as well as its corresponding addition and multiplication relations on those elements.*

Proof idea. The idea is straightforward. When a tuple $\bar{a}$ is modified, so far non-touched elements in $\bar{a}$ are inserted into $\mathcal{D}_t$ and they are appended to the linear order $<_t$ (in the order in which they occur in $\bar{a}$). The relations $+_t$ and $\times_t$ are extended according to their well-known inductive definitions (see, e.g., [Lib04, p. 182]).

We are now ready to sketch the proof of Theorem 3.4.1.

Proof sketch (of Theorem 3.4.1). It suffices to show that (a) implies (b). For a given DYNFO-program $\mathcal{P}$ with built-in arithmetic, we construct an equivalent DYNFO-program $\mathcal{P}'$ that starts from scratch. For simplicity, we assume that $\mathcal{P}$ maintains a graph query, i.e. that it is over input schema $\{E\}$ where E is a binary relation symbol. As stated above, the challenge for the construction of $\mathcal{P}'$ is to make the arithmetic as well as the auxiliary data for an element available as soon as it has been touched.

The basic idea for the construction of $\mathcal{P}'$ is to start simulating $\mathcal{P}$ for m^2 touched elements as soon as m elements have been touched. There will be one such simulation for every m in parallel. For each m, the "m-simulation" starts from an initially empty database and simulates $\mathcal{P}$ for an insertion sequence leading to the current database. The goal is that as soon as $(m-1)^2$ elements have been touched, the m-simulation will be "consistent" with $\mathcal{P}$, that is, both the m-simulation of $\mathcal{P}'$ and $\mathcal{P}$ store the same auxiliary data. Beginning with $(m-1)^2$ touched elements and ending with m^2 touched elements, the program $\mathcal{P}'$ uses the query result of the m-simulation as its overall query result.

The m-simulation is started as soon as the mth element has been touched by a modification sequence. Assume, without loss of generality, that the elements $D_m \overset{\text{def}}{=} \{0, \dots, m-1\}$ have been touched after the mth element has been touched. In order to simulate $\mathcal{P}$ for domains of size m^2, the arithmetic for such domains has to be available. To this end the m-simulation of $\mathcal{P}'$ encodes elements from $\{0, \dots, m^2-1\}$ by tuples from $D_m \times D_m$. Arithmetic on $D_m \times D_m$ can be defined from the arithmetic relations $<_t$, $+_t$ and $\times_t$ on the touched elements D_m via the mapping $\pi : a \mapsto (a_1, a_2)$ where $a = a_1 m + a_2$. Those relations can be maintained due to Proposition 3.4.3. By $\widehat{a}$ we denote the tuple obtained by applying the mapping component-wise to a tuple a.

The actual m-simulation uses a 4-ary relation $\widehat{E}_m$ and, for every k-ary auxiliary relation R of $\mathcal{P}$, a $2k$-ary relation $\widehat{R}_m$. The increase in arity is due to the encoding of elements of $\{0, \dots, m^2-1\}$ by tuples over $\{0, \dots, m\}$. When the mth element is touched, the relation $\widehat{E}_m$ is empty and the relations $\widehat{R}_m$ are initialized according to the initialization formula for R, but adapted to the encoding of elements by tuples. After touching the mth element, every modification $\alpha(e)$ of E induces two steps of modifications to the relation $\widehat{E}_m$:

- The modification $\alpha(\widehat{e})$ is applied to $\widehat{E}_m$.
- Let $e_1, \dots, e_4$ be the four smallest edges present in E such that $\widehat{e}_1, \dots, \widehat{e}_4$ are not in $\widehat{E}_m$. Then $\widehat{e}_1, \dots, \widehat{e}_4$ are inserted into $\widehat{E}_m$.

For every modification of $\widehat{E}_m$, the relations $\widehat{R}_m$ are updated using the corresponding update formulas for R in $\mathcal{P}$, but adapted to the encoding of elements by tuples.

Although m-simulations are run in parallel for many m, all those relations can be stored in a constant number of relations. For example, the relations $\widehat{E}_m$ can be stored in a single 5-ary relation $\widehat{E}$ with m as an additional parameter.

The updates of $\widehat{E}_m$ and $\widehat{R}_m$ are made precise in Algorithm 1. For every modification only a constant number of modifications is induced on $\widehat{E}_m$ and $\widehat{R}_m$. Those can be easily described by a DYNFO-update program.

We shortly describe the correctness of the algorithm. When the mth element has been touched, the input graph contains at most m^2 edges. Thus all edges of the input graph will be present in $\widehat{E}_m$ after at most $\frac{m^2}{4}$ many modifications. On the other hand, at least $\frac{(m-1)^2 - (m+1)}{2}$ insertion steps are necessary in order to touch $(m-1)^2$ elements. Thus, for $m \geq 8$, the relation $\widehat{E}_m$ encodes the current graph when $(m-1)^2$ elements have been touched, and the m-simulation of $\mathcal{P}'$ is consistent with $\mathcal{P}$. The cases $m < 8$ can be hard-coded into the update formulas.

We note that the construction from the proof above does not extend to FOIES, because in FOIES elements are removed from the domain as soon as they are not used in any input relation. While the arithmetical relations can be adapted when elements are removed from the domain, it is not clear how to adapt the other auxiliary relations in general. Thus it remains open whether arithmetic can be simulated for

---

Algorithm 1. Updates for the m-simulation for change operation δ. The set T shall contain all elements that have been touched so far.

1: **if** $m = |T|$ **then**
2:    **for all** $R \in \tau_{\text{aux}}$ **do**
3:        Initialize $\widehat{R}'_m$ according to the initialization formula of R.
4:    **end for**
5: **end if**
6: **if** $m \leq |T| \leq m^2$ after modification $\alpha(e)$ **then**
7:    Apply $\alpha(\widehat{e})$ to $\widehat{E}_m$
8:    **for all** $R \in \tau_{\text{aux}}$ **do**
9:        Apply the update formula for $\alpha(\widehat{e})$ to $\widehat{R}'_m$
10:    **end for**
11:    **for** $i \in \{1, 2, 3, 4\}$ **do**
12:        $f \stackrel{\text{def}}{=}$ "smallest" edge from E such that $\widehat{f}$ is not contained in $\widehat{E}_m$.
13:        Add $\widehat{f}$ to $\widehat{E}_m$
14:        **for all** $R \in \tau_{\text{aux}}$ **do**
15:            Apply the update formula for insertion of $\widehat{f}$ to $\widehat{R}_m$
16:        **end for**
17:    **end for**
18: **end if**
19: **if** $(m-1)^2 < |T| \leq m^2$ **then** $Q' \stackrel{\text{def}}{=}$ decoding of $\widehat{Q}_m$

domain independent queries in the FOIES setting as well. However, for some domain-independent queries this can be achieved in an ad-hoc fashion. An example for this is the reachability query.

3.5 Outlook and Bibliographic Remarks

In this chapter we studied fragments of DYNFO. We have shown that, contrary to the static setting, many fragments collapse in the dynamic world. Further we proved that DYNCQ captures DYNQF which implies that DYNCQ is strictly larger than DYNPROP. Moreover a close connection between absolute semantics and Δ-semantics for conjunctive queries has been established. These results were summarized in Fig. 3.2. In addition, first-order logic and positive existential first-order logic have been related to dynamic complexity classes. Finally, we saw that DYNFO with empty initialization and DYNFO with built-in arithmetic coincide for domain independent queries.

All those results, except for the last one, have been shown for arbitrary initialization mappings. However, they also hold in the setting with first-order definable initialization mappings. Not all of them carry over when the initialization mapping and updates have to be definable in the same class.

Although we obtained a good picture for various small dynamic descriptive complexity classes, many interesting questions remain open.

Several relationships between fragments are still unclear. For example, it is open whether the classes DYNQF, DYNCQ, DYNCQ$^\neg$ and DYNFO can be separated or collapsed. The naïve way for separating two fragments DYN$\mathcal{C} \subseteq$ DYN$\mathcal{C}'$ is to exhibit a query which is contained in DYN$\mathcal{C}'$ but not in DYN$\mathcal{C}$. For this it is necessary to prove a lower bound for DYN$\mathcal{C}$. In the next chapter the currently available techniques for proving lower bounds are presented. Unfortunately separating even the smallest of the above classes, DYNQF, from the largest class DYNFO seems to be out of reach at the moment, at least in the setting with arbitrary initialization.

In addition to untangling the remaining fragments, the dynamic quantifier hierarchy and quantifier alternation hierarchy deserve a closer look. Lemma 3.1.11 shows that in the dynamic setting the Σ_i- and Π_i-fragment of first-order logic coincide. Whether there is a strict Σ_i-hierarchy remains open. Furthermore, the equivalence of $\exists^*$FO with absolute and Δ-semantics does not immediately translate to fragments of FO with alternating quantifiers (although one of the direction does, see Lemma 3.2.8).

A better understanding of the relationship between static and dynamic classes is of interest as well. We believe that the results obtained in [GMS12] and here are only the tip of the iceberg. Pursuing a systematic study, also of dynamic classes larger than DYNFO, looks very promising. The following questions could be another starting point for further studies. We have seen that DYNCQ$^\neg$ captures FO, and that DYNQF captures $\exists^*$FO. Can this gap be closed? What happens in between FO and $\exists^*$FO, respectively, DYNCQ$^\neg$ and DYNQF?

Furthermore capturing first-order logic by dynamic conjunctive queries with negations does not immediately yield performance gains (since a first-order query with k quantifiers is translated to a dynamic DYNCQ$^-$-program of arity at least k). It might be worth to study whether the results obtained here can be a foundation for improving the performance of query maintenance tasks.

Another question, only loosely connected to dynamic complexity, arises from the proof of Theorem 3.1.16. There conjunctive queries and built-in binary relations have been used to describe unions of conjunctive queries. While the expressive power of first-order logic with built-in arithmetic relations has been studied a lot (see, e.g., [Lib04]), studying built-in relations with respect to other aspects might be worthwhile as well.

Bibliographic Remarks

Except for the results in Sects. 3.3.2 and 3.4, all results in this chapter are joint work with Thomas Schwentick.

Almost all those results appeared in [ZS14]; the only exceptions are Lemmas 3.1.10 and 3.1.12, which have been published already in [ZS13], and Theorem 3.1.16, which has not been published before. The proof of Lemma 3.1.14 has been streamlined, including the outsourcing of Lemma 3.1.13.

The result from Sect. 3.3.2 is solely by the author and appeared in [Zeu14a]. The result from Sect. 3.4 is joint work with Samir Datta, Raghav Kulkarni, Anish Mukherjee and Thomas Schwentick [DKM+15].

Chapter 4
Lower Bounds for Dynamic Complexity Classes

In the traditional static setting, several methods for proving inexpressibility results have been developed. For example, Ehrenfeucht-Fraïssé games and locality-based arguments are widely used to establish lower bounds for first-order logic. For a detailed presentation of methods for proving lower bounds for classical logics, we refer the reader to [EF05, Lib04].

For dynamic complexity, the toolset for proving lower bounds is much less developed. One of the reasons is that obtaining lower bounds in the dynamic framework is inherently harder. An a priori hope that lower bound methods for first-order logic can be easily adapted in order to show lower bounds for DYNFO does not withstand a closer inspection. We have already seen that parity and reachability — two standard examples for queries, which are provably not expressible in first-order logic — are contained in DYNFO.

There is also another reason for why proving lower bounds for DYNFO is not easy. As already discussed in Sect. 3.4, Etessami pointed out that DYNFO-programs that start from scratch can construct arithmetic on the active domain [Ete98]. Thus DYNFO contains $FO(+, \times)$ or, equivalently, it contains DLOGTIME-uniform AC^0. However, proving lower bounds is already highly non-trivial for those classes.

Yet some attempts for proving lower bounds for dynamic complexity have been made. The goal of this chapter is to add new lower bound proof techniques to the available toolbox and to present available techniques in an accessible way. Before discussing the goals and contributions of this chapter in detail, we give a short overview of the current state of the art; a more detailed account will be given in subsequent sections.

In fact, there are no general inexpressibility results for DYNFO at all. The lack of results seems to be due to a lack of understanding of the underlying mechanisms of dynamic complexity.

To improve the understanding of dynamic complexity, and to gain insights in how lower bound methods could look like, fragments of DYNFO have been studied. We have already encountered most of those fragments in Chap. 3. In the following

© Springer-Verlag GmbH Germany 2017
T. Zeume, *Small Dynamic Complexity Classes*, LNCS 10110
DOI: 10.1007/978-3-662-54314-6_4

we shortly discuss lower bound results for fragments obtained by restricting the arity of the auxiliary relations, by restricting the syntax of the update formulas and by restricting the power of the initialization mapping.

The study of bounded arity auxiliary relations was started by Dong and Su (see, for example, [DS98]). They showed that unary auxiliary relations are not sufficient to maintain the reachability query and several other queries with first-order updates. Further an arity hierarchy for auxiliary relations was established. However, to separate level $k - 1$ from higher levels, queries of arity k on databases of arity $6k + 1$ were used[1]. A strict hierarchy has not yet been established for queries on graphs. In [DLW03] it was shown that unary auxiliary relations are not sufficient to maintain reachability for update formulas of any logic with certain locality properties. The proofs use the "static" weakness of local logics and do not fully exploit the dynamic setting, as they only require modification sequences of constant length.

As for fragments with restricted syntax of update formulas, mostly the quantifier-free fragment DYNPROP has been studied. Some inexpressibility results for DYNPROP have been shown by Gelade, Marquardt and Schwentick in [GMS12]. The alternating reachability query (on graphs with ∧- and ∨-nodes) is not maintainable in DYNPROP. Furthermore, on strings, DYNPROP exactly captures the regular languages (as Boolean queries on strings); in particular, non-regular languages cannot be maintained in DYNPROP. There is still no proof that reachability on general graphs cannot be maintained in DYNPROP.

All results mentioned so far are independent from the power of the initialization mapping, that is, the bounds hold even if the initialization mapping is arbitrary. Lower bounds for DYNFO with a logical initialization mapping have been obtained bei Grädel and Siebertz in [GS12]. They show that equal cardinality of two unary relations as well as the tree isomorphism problem cannot be maintained in DYNFO if the auxiliary data is initialized by any logical formalism.

After this short presentation of the state of the art, we will now outline the goals of this chapter. Afterwards we discuss our contributions.

Purpose of this Chapter

The first goal of this chapter is straightforward.

Goal 4.1. *Develop new methods for proving dynamic lower bounds and use them to obtain new lower bounds.*

In order to achieve this goal, it is essential to know the techniques that are currently available. Unfortunately the lower bound results discussed above are distributed over many different publications. Sometimes a particular lower bound is one of the main results of an article; sometimes it is hidden away in a theorem which is stated along the lines of the general theme of an article. In many cases, techniques are used in an adhoc fashion in order to prove a particular lower bound.

---

[1] This result has been obtained in the FOIES-framework, where the query relation is not counted as auxiliary relation. In our framework, where the query relation is counted as auxiliary relation, the query used by Dong and Su does not separate $(k - 1)$-ary DYNFO from k-ary DYNFO. In Sect. 4.3.1 we adapt their result to our setting.

This motivates the following goal, aimed at making the available lower bound techniques better accessible to more researchers.

Goal 4.2. *Present essential proof techniques for lower bounds for dynamic complexity in an accessible way.*

Contributions

In this chapter we present the main methods — including methods from the literature as well as new methods — for proving lower bounds for dynamic complexity classes. The methods are sorted by the dynamic complexity classes to which they can be applied; we cover methods for DYNPROP, DYNQF and DYNFO.

The main method for proving lower bounds for DYNPROP is the Substructure Lemma; a variant of which was introduced in [GMS12]. For proving lower bounds using this lemma, one has to find well-behaved isomorphic structures. The challenge is to find such structures. We present how well-known combinatorial tools can be applied to solve this task; two of those tools have not been used in this context before. Using the Substructure Lemma in conjunction with these combinatorial tools we prove several new lower bounds:

- Reachability and k-clique ($k \geq 2$) cannot be maintained in DYNPROP with invariant initialization.
- Reachability and k-clique ($k \geq 3$) cannot be maintained in binary DYNPROP with arbitrary built-in relations (and arbitrary initialization).
- Under insertions, $(k + 2)$-clique cannot be maintained in k-ary DYNPROP with arbitrary built-in relations (and arbitrary initialization).

For DYNQF a generalization of the Substructure Lemma is the main method for proving lower bounds. Here we present a stronger variant of this lemma than the one that has been introduced in [GMS12]. We show how combinatorial tools can be applied to show lower bounds for DYNQF. The following new lower bounds are obtained, some of them extend results from above:

- Reachability and k-clique ($k \geq 2$) cannot be maintained in DYNQF with invariant initialization.
- Reachability cannot be maintained in unary DYNQF (with arbitrary initialization).
- Under insertions, the $(k + 2)$-clique cannot be maintained in k-ary DYNPROP extended by unary auxiliary functions (and with arbitrary initialization).

For DYNFO we present a unified view that captures most lower bounds obtained in prior work. Most of those bounds rely on static lower bounds as well as static lower bound techniques for proving lower bounds for DYNFO. We reprove some of the bounds from this unified point of view. Furthermore we present two approaches for proving lower bounds for DYNFO with restricted initialization settings. The lower bounds obtained by using those approaches are not very strong, yet we hope that they can be used to prove better lower bounds in the future.

Orthogonally to our contributions on methods for proving lower bounds, we exhibit arity hierarchy results. The arity hierarchy for the FOIES-framework obtained by Dong and Su in [DS98] does not immediately transfer to our framework as the query relation is not counted as an auxiliary relation in their framework and they use a k-ary query relation to separate $(k-1)$-ary FOIES from k-ary FOIES. We adapt their proof and show how to separate arity $k - 1$ from arity k by a boolean query. Thereby we also obtain an arity hierarchy for first-order update programs in our framework. Whether DYNFO and FOIES have an arity hierarchy for graph queries remains open. For DYNPROP we show that there is an arity hierarchy upto arity 3 for graph queries; and that there is an infinite arity hierarchy for graph queries if only insertions are allowed.

Parts of this chapter originated in joint work with Thomas Schwentick and Nils Vortmeier, and discussions with Samir Datta. For detailed bibliographic remarks we refer to the end of this chapter.

Outline of this Chapter

The methods for proving lower bounds presented in this chapter are ordered by the expressivity of the dynamic complexity classes to which the methods can be applied. In Sects. 4.1 and 4.2, lower bound methods and results for DYNPROP and DYNQF, respectively, are presented. In Sect. 4.3 we present lower bound techniques for DYNFO. The arity hierarchy for DYNPROP is discussed in Subsect. 4.1.3; the arity hierarchy for DYNFO is discussed in Subsect. 4.3.1.

We conclude this chapter with a discussion of possible directions for future work and bibliographical remarks.

4.1 Quantifier-Free Update Programs

Lower bounds are hard to prove even for the quantifier-free fragment. However, it is known that non-regular languages as well as the alternating reachability query cannot be maintained without quantifiers [GMS12]. From those lower bounds several further lower bounds can be easily derived. For example, since the language $\{a^n b^n \mid n \in \mathbb{N}\}$ is not in DYNPROP, the equal cardinality query for two unary input relations and the isomorphism query cannot be maintained in the quantifier-free fragment as well. Further, the use of very restricted graphs in the proof that the alternating reachability query is not in DYNPROP, implies that there is an $\exists^* \forall^* \exists^*$FO-definable query that cannot be maintained without quantifiers either.

Yet, in general, it is still a difficult task to prove lower bounds for the quantifier-free fragment. We are not at the point where we can, when given a query, apply a set of tools in order to prove that the query cannot be maintained in DYNPROP.

The main tool used to obtain lower bounds for quantifier-free dynamic programs is the Substructure Lemma. It was introduced in [GMS12, Lemma 1], though in a slightly different form then we will present here. To prove that a query $\mathcal{Q}$ is not in DYNPROP with the Substructure Lemma, one basically has to find two structures $\mathcal{S}$ and $\mathcal{T}$ with two isomorphic substructures $\mathcal{A}$ and $\mathcal{B}$, respectively, such that applying two corresponding modification sequences α and β to $\mathcal{A}$ and $\mathcal{B}$ yields one structure

S' in Q and one structure T' not in Q. The challenge is to find such structures S and T with suitable isomorphic substructures.

Here, we present three techniques for finding such structures. The first technique is a simple counting argument that relies on the fact that there are only finitely many atomic types for a fixed schema. It was already used in [GMS12] to show that alternating reachability cannot be maintained in DYNPROP. The second and third technique are more elaborated. The second uses Ramsey's Theorem and Higman's Lemma in order to find structures with isomorphic substructures to which the Substructure Lemma can be applied. The third techniques combines upper and lower bounds for Ramsey numbers in order to exhibit suitable structures.

All three techniques will be used to obtain new lower bounds for the quantifier-free fragment. Two queries will be studied in detail with respect to their maintainability in DYNPROP, namely the reachability query and the k-clique query. Both queries are very important queries.

Reachability in directed graphs is the most intensely investigated problem in dynamic complexity (and also much studied in dynamic algorithms and other dynamic contexts). It is one of the simplest inherently recursive queries and thus serves as a kind of drosophila in the study of the dynamic maintainability of recursive queries by non-recursive means. We refer to the introduction chapter for a more detailed discussion of previous work on the reachability query. A recent result places reachability in DYNFO [DKM+15], yet it is very unlikely that it can also be maintained in DYNPROP.

The other query to be studied in detail is the k-clique query: given a graph G, does G contain k pairwise connected nodes? Since k-clique can be easily expressed in existential first-order logic, it can be trivially maintained by a first-order update program. This makes the query an ideal candidate query for getting a better understanding of the quantifier-free fragment.

For both queries, reachability and k-clique, lower bounds are obtained for different variants of the quantifier-free fragment in this subsection. Both invariant initialization and arbitrary initialization are studied.

It turns out that invariant initialization is not very powerful in the quantifier-free fragment. Yet this initialization setting is a simple test bed to get acquainted with the Substructure Lemma. The following result is proved with the Substructure Lemma and the counting technique.

Theorem 4.1.1. s-t-REACH *cannot be maintained in* DYNPROP *with invariant initialization.*

From this lower bound we obtain, via a reduction, that also k-clique ($k \geq 2$) and k-colorability ($k \geq 1$) cannot be maintained in this setting.

Proving lower bounds for arbitrary initialization is much more intricate. We obtain two different lower bounds.

As stated already in the introduction of this chapter, the proof that s-t-REACH is not in unary DYNFO in [DS98] uses constant-length modification sequences, and is mainly an application of a locality-based static lower bound for monadic second order logic. This technique does not seem to generalize to binary DYNFO. We prove the first unmaintainability result for s-t-REACH with respect to binary auxiliary relations.

Theorem 4.1.2. s-t-REACH *cannot be maintained in binary* DYNPROP, *even with arbitrary built-in relations.*

The proof uses the Substructure Lemma on isomorphic substructures obtained by employing a Ramsey-like argument and Higman's Lemma.

This result is weaker than the result of Dong and Su in terms of the logic (quantifier-free vs. general first-order) but it is stronger with respect to the information content of the auxiliary data (binary relations vs. unary relations). Whether reachability can be maintained with quantifier-free update formulas remains open. Again lower bounds for k-clique ($k \geq 3$) and k-colorability ($k \geq 2$) follow via a reduction. Furthermore, the shallowness of the graphs used in the proof of the lower bound is used to establish a strict hierarchy for unary, binary and ternary DYNPROP on graph queries.

For k-clique we also obtain another lower bound. We have already seen that k-clique can be maintained in $(k-1)$-ary DYNPROP under insertions (see Theorem 3.3.3 in Sect. 3.3). Here we complement this result and obtain the following characterization. The lower bound is proved using the Substructure Lemma and both upper and lower bounds for Ramsey numbers.

Theorem 4.1.3. *When only edge insertions are allowed then* k-CLIQUE ($k \geq 3$) *can be maintained in* $(k-1)$-*ary* DYNPROP, *but it cannot be maintained in* $(k-2)$-*ary* DYNPROP, *even with arbitrary built-in relations.*

The lower bound provided by the theorem is interesting in two ways. First, it exhibits, for every k, a query in $\exists^k$FO that cannot be maintained in $(k-2)$-ary DYNPROP, even when only insertions are allowed. We believe that finding simple queries that cannot be maintained will advance the understanding of dynamic complexity. Second, the lower bound establishes the first arity hierarchy for graph queries, although for a weak fragment of DYNFO and for insertions only. Using the same proof technique, we also exhibit a $\exists^*\forall^*$FO-definable query that cannot be maintained in DYNPROP (with arbitrary arity); this improves a result from [GMS12].

Using the lower bounds described above, we obtain the following arity separations.

Theorem 4.1.4. *(a) Unary, binary and ternary* DYNPROP *form a strict arity hierarchy on graphs.*
(b) Under insertions, DYNPROP *has a strict arity hierarchy on graphs.*

As stated above, reachability and 3-clique cannot be maintained in binary DYNPROP. However, we were not able to prove that reachability and 3-clique cannot be maintained in DYNPROP with auxiliary relations of arbitrary arity. A natural question is, whether lower bounds for arbitrary arity can be proved for syntactic fragments of DYNPROP. In Sect. 3.1 we have seen that queries maintainable in DYNPROP can already be maintained in DYNPROPCQ⁻ and DYNPROPUCQ. Hence proving lower bounds for those fragments is not easier than proving lower bounds for DYNPROP itself. We prove the following lower bounds for the next smaller class DYNPROPCQ.

Theorem 4.1.5. NONEMPTYSET, s-t-REACH *and* 3-CLIQUE *cannot be maintained in* DYNPROPCQ.

In Example 2.3.4 we have seen that NONEMPTYSET can be maintained in DYNPROP, and therefore Theorem 4.1.5 implies that DYNPROPCQ is a strict subclass of DYNPROP. This proves the first part of Theorem 3.1.5.

The rest of this section is structured as follows. In the next subsection, the Substructure Lemma is introduced. The following Subsect. 4.1.2 is devoted to the presentation of the three techniques for finding suitable substructures; each of them is used to prove one of the first three theorems from above. At the end of that subsection, the combinatorial tools underlying the second and third technique will be proved. In the following Subsect. 4.1.3 we exhibit the arity separations for DYNPROP. We conclude this section with lower bounds for DYNPROPCQ.

4.1.1 The Substructure Lemma

In this subsection we introduce the Substructure Lemma. Currently this is the major tool for proving quantifier-free lower bounds. The form of the Substructure Lemma presented here is a slight variation of Lemma 1 from [GMS12].

The intuition of the Substructure Lemma is as follows. When updating an auxiliary tuple $\bar{c}$ after an insertion or deletion of a tuple $\bar{d}$, a quantifier-free update formula has access to $\bar{c}$, $\bar{d}$, and the constants only. Thus, if a sequence of modifications changes only tuples from a substructure $\mathcal{A}$ of $\mathcal{S}$, then the auxiliary data of $\mathcal{A}$ is not affected by information outside $\mathcal{A}$. In particular, two isomorphic substructures $\mathcal{A}$ and $\mathcal{B}$ remain isomorphic, when corresponding modifications are applied to them.

We formalize the notion of corresponding modifications as follows. Let π be an isomorphism from a structure $\mathcal{A}$ to a structure $\mathcal{B}$. Two modifications $\delta(\bar{a})$ on $\mathcal{A}$ and $\delta'(\bar{b})$ on $\mathcal{B}$ are said to be π-*respecting* if $\delta = \delta'$ and $\bar{b} = \pi(\bar{a})$. Two sequences $\alpha = \delta_1 \cdots \delta_m$ and $\beta = \delta'_1 \cdots \delta'_m$ of modifications respect π if δ_i and δ'_i are π-respecting for every $i \leq m$. Recall that $P_\alpha(\mathcal{S})$ denotes the state obtained by executing the dynamic program $\mathcal{P}$ for the modification sequence α from state $\mathcal{S}$.

Lemma 4.1.6 (Substructure Lemma [GMS12]**).** *Let* $\mathcal{P}$ *be a* DYNPROP-*program and let* $\mathcal{S}$ *and* $\mathcal{T}$ *be states of* $\mathcal{P}$ *with domains* S *and* T. *Further let* $A \subseteq S$ *and* $B \subseteq T$ *such that* $\mathcal{S} \upharpoonright A$ *and* $\mathcal{T} \upharpoonright B$ *are isomorphic via* π. *Then* $P_\alpha(\mathcal{S}) \upharpoonright A$ *and* $P_\beta(\mathcal{T}) \upharpoonright B$ *are isomorphic via* π *for all* π-*respecting modification sequences* α, β *on* A *and* B.

The Substructure Lemma is illustrated for a single modification in Fig. 4.1.

Proof. The lemma can be shown by induction on the length of the modification sequences. To this end, it is sufficient to prove the claim for a pair of π-respecting modifications $\delta(\bar{a})$ and $\delta(\bar{b})$ on A and B. We abbreviate $\mathcal{S} \upharpoonright A$ and $\mathcal{T} \upharpoonright B$ by $\mathcal{A}$ and $\mathcal{B}$, respectively.

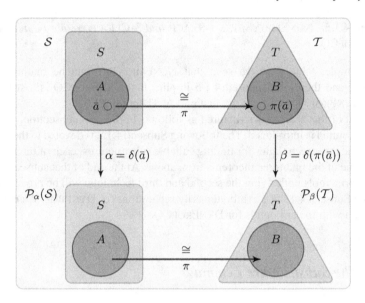

Fig. 4.1 The statement of the Substructure Lemma.

Since π is an isomorphism from $\mathcal{A}$ to $\mathcal{B}$, we know that $R^{\mathcal{A}}(\bar{d})$ holds if and only if $R^{\mathcal{B}}(\pi(\bar{d}))$ holds, for every m-tuple $\bar{d}$ over A and every relation symbol $R \in \tau$. Therefore, $\varphi(\bar{x})$ evaluates to true in $\mathcal{A}$ under $\bar{d}$ if and only if it does so in $\mathcal{B}$ under $\pi(\bar{d}')$, for every quantifier-free formula $\varphi(\bar{x})$ over schema τ. Thus all update formulas from $\mathcal{P}$ yield the same result for corresponding tuples $\bar{d}$ and $\pi(\bar{d})$ from A and B, respectively. Hence $P_{\delta(\bar{a})}(\mathcal{S}) \restriction A$ is isomorphic to $P_{\delta(\pi(\bar{a}))}(\mathcal{S}) \restriction B$. This proves the claim.   □

The following corollary is implied by Lemma 4.1.6, since the 0-ary auxiliary relations of two isomorphic structures coincide.

Corollary 4.1.7. *Let $\mathcal{P}$ be a* DYNPROP-*program with designated Boolean query symbol Q, and let $\mathcal{S}$ and $\mathcal{T}$ be states of $\mathcal{P}$ with domains S and T. Further let $A \subseteq S$ and $B \subseteq T$ such that $\mathcal{S} \restriction A$ and $\mathcal{T} \restriction B$ are isomorphic via π. Then Q has the same value in $P_\alpha(\mathcal{S})$ and $P_\beta(\mathcal{T})$ for all π-respecting sequences α, β of modifications on A and B.*

The Substructure Lemma can be applied along the following lines to prove that a (graph) query $\mathcal{Q}$ cannot be maintained in a setting with quantifier-free updates. Towards a contradiction, assume that there is a quantifier-free program $\mathcal{P} = (P, \text{INIT}, Q)$ that maintains $\mathcal{Q}$. Then, find

- two states $\mathcal{S}$ and $\mathcal{T}$ reachable by $\mathcal{P}$ with current graphs $G_{\mathcal{S}}$ and $G_{\mathcal{T}}$ (here reachable means that $\mathcal{S} = P_\alpha(\mathcal{S}_{\text{INIT}}(G))$ for some graph G and modification sequence α, and likewise for $\mathcal{T}$);
- substructures $\mathcal{S} \restriction A$ and $\mathcal{T}' \restriction B$ of $\mathcal{S}$ and $\mathcal{T}$ isomorphic via π; and

- two π-respecting modification sequences α and β on A and B such that $\alpha(G_S)$ is in Q and $\beta(G_T)$ is not in Q.

This yields the desired contradiction, since Q has the same value in $P_\alpha(S)$ and $P_\beta(T)$ by the Substructure Lemma.

4.1.2 Applications of the Substructure Lemma

The Substructure Lemma can be applied for different settings and different queries. In all cases the critical part is to find suitable isomorphic substructures. In the following, we present three techniques to obtain such substructures. We start with a simple counting argument and then proceed to more advanced techniques that require Higman's Lemma, a Ramsey-like theorem as well as upper and lower bounds for Ramsey numbers.

Using Counting

For proving that the alternating reachability query is not in DYNPROP, the finiteness of the set of atomic types for fixed schemas was used in [GMS12] in order to exhibit isomorphic substructures suitable for applying the Substructure Lemma. Here we give another example of this technique.

Our goal is to prove lower bounds for quantifier-free dynamic programs with invariant initialization. Recall that an initialization mapping INIT is invariant if it maps isomorphic databases to isomorphic auxiliary data, that is if $\pi(\text{INIT}(\mathcal{D})) = \text{INIT}(\pi(\mathcal{D}))$ for every database $\mathcal{D}$ and permutation π of the domain.

First-order logic, second-order logic and other logics considered in computer science can only define queries, i.e. mappings that are invariant under permutations. Therefore the results on invariant initializations to be presented here apply to all initialization mappings defined in those logics.

The following proposition restates Theorem 4.1.1 more precisely.

Proposition 4.1.8. s-t-REACH *cannot be maintained in* DYNPROP *with invariant initialization. This holds even for 1-layered s-t-graphs.*

Proof. Towards a contradiction, assume that the dynamic program (P, INIT, Q) with schema $\tau = \tau_{\text{inp}} \cup \tau_{\text{aux}}$ and invariant initialization mapping INIT maintains the s-t-reachability query for 1-layered s-t-graphs. Let n be the number of atomic types of tuples of arity up to m for $\tau_{\text{aux}} \cup \{E\}$ where m is the highest arity of relation symbols in $\tau_{\text{aux}} \cup \{E\}$.

We consider the 1-layered s-t-graphs $G_i = (V_i, E_i)$, for every i from $1, \ldots, n+1$, with $V_i = \{s, t\} \cup A_i$ where $A_i = \{a_0, \ldots, a_i\}$ and $E = \{s\} \times A_i \cup A_i \times \{t\}$. Further, we let $S_i = (V_i, E_i, \mathcal{A}_i)$ be the state obtained by applying INIT to G_i.

Our goal is to find S_k and S_ℓ with $k < \ell$ such that S_k is isomorphic to $S_\ell \restriction V_k$ (see Fig. 4.2 for an illustration). Then, by the Substructure Lemma, the program $\mathcal{P}$ computes the same query result for the following modification sequences:

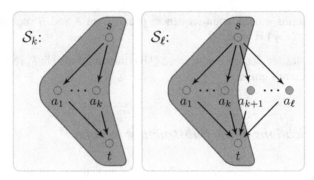

Fig. 4.2 The structures $\mathcal{S}_k$ and $\mathcal{S}_\ell$ from the proof of Proposition 4.1.8. The isomorphic substructures are highlighted in blue. (Color figure online)

(β_1) Delete edges $(s, a_0), \ldots, (s, a_k)$ from $\mathcal{S}_k$.
(β_2) Delete edges $(s, a_0), \ldots, (s, a_k)$ from $\mathcal{S}_\ell$.

However, applying the modification sequence β_1 yields a graph where t is reachable from s, whereas by β_2 a graph is obtained where t is not reachable from s, a contradiction.

Thus it remains to find such states $\mathcal{S}_k$ and $\mathcal{S}_\ell$. A tuple is *diverse*, if all components are pairwise different. For arbitrary $m' \le m$, diverse tuples $\bar{a}, \bar{b} \in A^{m'}$ and $i \le n$, we observe that $G_i \simeq_{id[\bar{a}, \bar{b}]} G_i$ where $id[\bar{a}, \bar{b}]$ is the bijection that maps a_i to b_i, b_i to a_i and every other element from S to itself. Therefore $\mathcal{S}_i \simeq_{id[\bar{a}, \bar{b}]} \mathcal{S}_i$ by the invariance of INIT. Thus $\langle \mathcal{S}_i, \bar{a} \rangle = \langle \mathcal{S}_i, \bar{b} \rangle$, and therefore all diverse m' tuples are of the same atomic type in $\mathcal{S}_i$.

Since n is the number of types up to arity m, there are two states $\mathcal{S}_k$ and $\mathcal{S}_\ell$ such that, for every $m' \le m$, all diverse m'-tuples are of the same atomic type in $\mathcal{S}_k$ and $\mathcal{S}_\ell$. But then $\mathcal{S}_k \simeq \mathcal{S}_\ell \restriction V_k$.   □

The proof of the previous result does not extend to DYNFO, since reachability in graphs of depth three is expressible even in (static) predicate logic. The proof fails, because the Substructure Lemma does not hold for DYNFO-programs.

Lower bounds for the dynamic variants of the k-CLIQUE and k-COL problems (where k is fixed) can be established via reductions to the dynamic s-t-reachability query for shallow graphs.

Corollary 4.1.9. *k-CLIQUE, for $k \ge 2$, and k-COL, for $k \ge 1$, cannot be maintained in DYNPROP with invariant initialization.*

The corollary will be proved in a more general form in Sect. 4.2.

Using Higman's Lemma and Ramsey's Theorem

The search for isomorphic substructures in the lower bound proof of Theorem 4.1.1 relied on a simple counting argument. For proving more powerful lower bounds, stronger tools are required. Next we will present two tools for finding suitable sub-structures for the Substructure Lemma: Higman's Lemma and a Ramsey-like theorem. Afterwards we will see how to use those two tools for proving lower bounds for binary DYNPROP with arbitrary initialization for reachability, k-clique and k-colorability.

We present the variant of Higman's Lemma first. Let Σ be an alphabet. A *subsequence* of a word $v \in \Sigma^*$ is a word obtained from v by deleting letters. Formally, a word $u \in \Sigma^*$ is a subsequence of v, in symbols $u \sqsubseteq v$, if $u = u_1 \dots u_k$ and $v = v_0 u_1 v_1 \dots v_{k-1} u_k v_k$ for some words $u_1, \dots, u_k \in \Sigma^*$ and $v_0, \dots, v_k \in \Sigma^*$.

Theorem 4.1.10 (Higman's Lemma). *For every infinite sequence $(w_i)_{i \in \mathbb{N}}$ of words over an alphabet Σ there are ℓ and k such that $\ell < k$ and $w_\ell \sqsubseteq w_k$.*

We will actually make use of the following stronger result, see e.g. [SS11, Proposition 2.5, p. 3] for a proof. Both results will be referred to as Higman's Lemma.

Theorem 4.1.11. *For every alphabet of size c and function $g : \mathbb{N} \to \mathbb{N}$ there is a natural number $H(c)$ such that in every sequence $(w_i)_{1 \le i \le H(c)}$ of $H(c)$ many words with $|w_i| \le g(i)$ there are ℓ and k with $\ell < k$ and $w_\ell \sqsubseteq w_k$.*

Now we present a Ramsey-like theorem. The classical theorem of Ramsey is about colored (hyper)graphs. As we are mainly interested in structures here, we use a Ramsey-like theorem for structures. Before stating the theorem, we need to introduce some notions. Let τ be a k-ary schema, let S be a τ-structure over domain D and let $\prec$ be a linear order on D. An $\prec$-*ordered τ-clique* of S is a subset $D' \subseteq D$ such that all $\prec$-ordered k-tuples $\bar{a}$ over D' have the same atomic τ-type in S. We also say that such a D' is $\prec$-*homogeneous*. Recall that the atomic type of a tuple $\bar{a}$ includes information on how $\bar{a}$ relates to the constants of the structure, and therefore all tuples over a τ-clique relate in the same way to constants as well.

We are now ready to state the variant of Ramsey's theorem needed in our proofs. It will be proved towards the end of this subsection.

Theorem 4.1.12 (Ramsey's Theorem for Structures). *Let τ be a schema and let ℓ be a positive integer. Then there is a number n such that every $\prec$-ordered τ-structure with at least n elements contains an $\prec$-ordered τ-clique of size ℓ.*

The smallest such number n is called Ramsey number for τ and ℓ. It is denoted by $R(\ell; \tau)$.

We use those two tools to prove lower bounds for the maintainability of the s-t-reachability query. Recall that the extension of DYNPROP by arbitrary built-in relations is denoted by DYNPROP* (cf. Sect. 2.4). We prove the following proposition which is slightly stronger than Theorem 4.1.2.

Proposition 4.1.13. s-t-REACH *cannot be maintained in binary* DYNPROP*, *even for 2-layered s-t-graphs.*

The result for 2-layered s-t-graphs will later help us to show that binary DYNPROP* does not capture ternary DYNPROP. The actual separation shows that the lower bound technique for binary DYNPROP does not immediately transfer to ternary DYNPROP (or ternary DYNPROP*). At the moment we do not know whether it is possible to adapt the technique to full DYNPROP.

Before proving Proposition 4.1.13, we show the following corresponding result for unary DYNPROP* whose proof uses the same techniques in a simpler setting. We remark that the same proof can be used to show that the query NONEMPTYLIST from Example 2.3.4 cannot be maintained in unary DYNPROP* either.

Proposition 4.1.14. s-t-REACH *cannot be maintained in unary* DYNPROP*, *not even for* 1-*layered* s-t-*graphs.*

Proof. Towards a contradiction, assume that $\mathcal{P} = (P, \text{INIT}, Q)$ is a dynamic program over schema $\tau = (\tau_{\text{inp}}, \tau_{\text{aux}}, \tau_{\text{bi}})$ with unary schema τ_{aux} that maintains the s-t-reachability query for 1-layered s-t-graphs. Let n' be sufficiently large with respect to τ and n be sufficiently large with respect to n'; explicit numbers are given at the end of the proof. Further let m be the highest arity of a relation symbol from τ_{bi}.

Let $G = (V, E)$ be a 1-layered s-t-graph such that $V = \{s, t\} \cup A$ with $n = |A|$ and $E = \emptyset$. Further let $\mathcal{S} = (V, E, \mathcal{A}, \mathcal{B})$ be the state obtained by applying INIT to G.

First, we identify a subset of A on which the built-in relations are homogeneous. By Ramsey's Theorem for structures and because $n = |A|$ is sufficiently large with respect to n' there is a set $A' \subseteq A$ of size n' and an order $\prec$ on A' such that all $\prec$-ordered m-tuples over A' are of equal atomic τ_{bi}-type. Recall that the atomic type information of a tuple $\bar{a}$ also includes the relationship of $\bar{a}$ to the constants s and t.

Let $\mathcal{S}' \stackrel{\text{def}}{=} (V, E', \mathcal{A}', \mathcal{B})$ be the state of $\mathcal{P}$ that is reached from $\mathcal{S}$ after application of the following modifications to G (in some arbitrary order):

(α) For every node $a \in A'$, insert edges (s, a) and (a, t).

We observe that the built-in data has not changed, but the auxiliary data might have changed.

Let $a_1 \prec \ldots \prec a_{n'}$ be an enumeration of the elements of A'. For every $i \in \{1, \ldots, n'\}$, we define α_i to be the modification sequence that deletes the edges $(s, a_{n'}), (s, a_{n'-1}), \ldots, (s, a_{i+1})$, in this order. Let $\mathcal{S}'_i$ be the state reached by applying α_i to $\mathcal{S}'$. Thus, in state $\mathcal{S}'_i$ only nodes $a_1, \ldots, a_i$ have edges to node s. For every i, we construct a word w_i of length i that has a letter for every node $a_1, \ldots, a_i$ and captures all relevant information about those nodes in $\mathcal{S}'_i$. The words w_i are over the set of all unary types of τ_{aux}. More precisely, the jth letter σ_i^j of w_i is the unary atomic τ_{aux}-type of a_j in $\mathcal{S}'_i$. We recall that the unary atomic type of a_j captures all information about the tuple (s, a_j, t).

Since $n' = |A'|$ was chosen sufficiently large with respect to τ, it follows by Higman's Lemma that there are k and ℓ such that $k < \ell$ and $w_k \sqsubseteq w_\ell$, that is, $w_k = \sigma_k^1 \sigma_k^2 \ldots \sigma_k^k = \sigma_\ell^{i_1} \sigma_\ell^{i_2} \ldots \sigma_\ell^{i_k}$ for suitable numbers $i_1 < \ldots < i_k$.

We argue that the structures $\mathcal{S}'_k \restriction \{s, t, a_1, \ldots, a_k\}$ and $\mathcal{S}'_\ell \restriction \{s, t, a_{i_1}, \ldots, a_{i_k}\}$ are isomorphic via the mapping π with $\pi(a_j) = a_{i_j}$ for all j, $\pi(s) = s$ and $\pi(t) = t$. By definition of A' and because built-in relations do not change, the mapping π

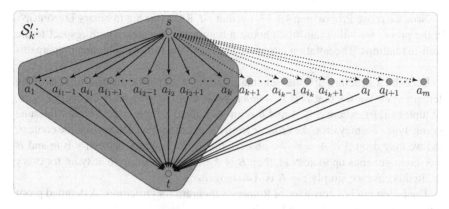

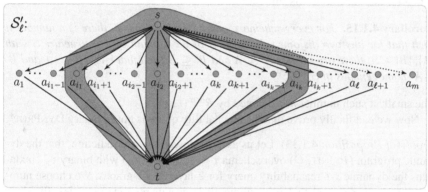

Fig. 4.3 The structures $\mathcal{S}'_k$ and $\mathcal{S}'_\ell$ from the proof of Proposition 4.1.14. Deleted edges are dotted. The isomorphic substructures are highlighted in blue. (Color figure online)

preserves τ_{bi}. The schema τ_{aux} is preserved since a_j and a_{i_j} are of equal unary atomic type, by the definition of w_k and w_ℓ. Thus π is indeed an isomorphism. We refer to Fig. 4.3 for an illustration.

Therefore, by Corollary 4.1.7, the program $\mathcal{P}$ computes the same query result for the following π-respecting modification sequences β_1 and β_2:

(β_1) Delete edges $(s, a_1), \ldots, (s, a_k)$ from $\mathcal{S}'_k$.
(β_2) Delete edges $(s, a_{i_1}), \ldots, (s, a_{i_k})$ from $\mathcal{S}'_\ell$.

However, applying the modification sequence β_1 yields a graph where t is not reachable from s, whereas by β_2 a graph is obtained where t is reachable from s since $k < \ell$, the desired contradiction.

We now specify the numbers n and n' that were chosen in the beginning of the proof. In order to apply Higman's Lemma, the set A' needs to be of size at least $n' \stackrel{\text{def}}{=} H(|n''|)$ where n'' is the number of unary atomic types of τ and H is the function from Higman's Lemma. Therefore, the set A has to be of size $n \stackrel{\text{def}}{=} R(\tau; n')$. $\square$

Now we prove Proposition 4.1.13, i.e. that s-t-REACH is not in binary DYNPROP*. In the proof, we will again first choose a homogeneous subset with respect to the built-in relations. The notation introduced next and the following lemma prepare this step.

Let S be a structure of some schema τ and let A and B be disjoint subsets of the domain of S. We say that B is A-$\prec$-homogeneous up to arity m, if for every $\ell \leq m$, all tuples $(a, \bar{b})$, where $a \in A$ and $\bar{b}$ is an $\prec$-ordered ℓ-tuple over B, have the same atomic type. We may drop the order $\prec$ from the notation if it is clear from the context, and we may drop A if $A = \emptyset$. We observe that if the maximal arity of τ is m and B is A-homogeneous up to arity m, then B is A-homogeneous up to arity m' for every m'. In this case we simply say B is A-*homogeneous*.

The following is a corollary of Ramsey's theorem for structures. A detailed proof is deferred to the end of this subsection.

Corollary 4.1.15. *For every schema τ and natural number ℓ, there is a number n such that for any two disjoint subsets A, B of the domain of a τ-structure S with $|A|, |B| \geq n$, there are subsets $A' \subseteq A$ and $B' \subseteq B$ such that $|A'|, |B'| = \ell$ and B' is A'-homogeneous in S.*

The smallest such number n is denoted by $R^{\mathrm{hom}}(\ell; \tau)$.

Now we can finally prove that the reachability query is not in binary DYNPROP*.

Proof (of Proposition 4.1.13). Let us assume, towards a contradiction, that the dynamic program (P, INIT, Q) over schema $\tau = (\tau_{\mathrm{inp}}, \tau_{\mathrm{aux}}, \tau_{\mathrm{bi}})$ with binary τ_{aux} maintains the dynamic s-t-reachability query for 2-layered s-t-graphs. We choose numbers n, n_1, n_2 and n_3 such that n_3 is sufficiently large with respect to τ, n_2 is sufficiently large with respect to n_3, n_2 is sufficiently large with respect to n_1 and n is sufficiently large with respect to n_1; again, explicit numbers are given at the end of the proof.

Let $G = (V, E)$ be a 2-layered s-t-graph with layers A and B, where A and B are both of size n and $E = \{(b, t) \mid b \in B\}$. Further, let $S = (V, E, \mathcal{A}, \mathcal{B})$ be the state obtained by applying INIT to G.

We will first choose homogeneous subsets. By Corollary 4.1.15 and because n is sufficiently large, there are subsets A_1 and B_1 such that $|A_1| = |B_1| = n_1$ and B_1 is A_1-$\prec$-homogeneous in S, for some order $\prec$. Next, let A_2 and B_2 be arbitrarily chosen subsets of A_1 and B_1, respectively, of size $|B_2| = n_2$ and $|A_2| = 2^{|B_2|}$. We note that B_2 is still A_2-homogeneous. In particular, B_2 is still A_2-homogeneous with respect to schema τ_{bi}. We associate with every subset $X \subseteq B_2$ a unique vertex a_X from A_2 in an arbitrary fashion.

Now, we define the modification sequence α as follows.

(α) For every subset X of B_2 and every $b \in X$ insert an edge (a_X, b), in some arbitrarily chosen order.

Let $S' \stackrel{\mathrm{def}}{=} (V, E', \mathcal{A}', \mathcal{B})$ be the state of $\mathcal{P}$ after applying α to S, i.e. $S' = P_\alpha(S)$. We observe that the built-in data has not changed, but the auxiliary data might have changed. In particular, B_2 is not necessarily A_2-homogeneous with respect to schema τ_{aux} in state S'.

Our plan is to exhibit two sets X, X' such that $X \subsetneq X' \subseteq B_2$ such that the restriction of $\mathcal{S}'$ to $\{s, t, a_{X'}\} \cup X'$ contains an isomorphic copy of $\mathcal{S}'$ restricted to $\{s, t, a_X\} \cup X$. Then the Substructure Lemma will easily give us a contradiction.

By Ramsey's theorem and because $|B_2|$ is sufficiently large with respect to n_2, there is a subset $B_3 \subseteq B_2$ of size n_3 such that B_3 is $\prec$-homogeneous in $\mathcal{S}'$ with respect to τ. Let $b_1 \prec \ldots \prec b_{n_3}$ be an enumeration of the elements of B_3 and let $X_i \stackrel{\text{def}}{=} \{b_1, \ldots, b_i\}$, for every $i \in \{1, \ldots, n_3\}$.

Let $\mathcal{S}'_i$ denote the restriction of $\mathcal{S}'$ to $X_i \cup \{s, t, a_{X_i}\}$. For every i, we construct a word w_i of length i that has a letter for every node in X_i and captures all relevant information about those nodes in $\mathcal{S}'_i$. More precisely, $w_i \stackrel{\text{def}}{=} \sigma_i^1 \cdots \sigma_i^i$, where for every i and j, σ_i^j is the binary atomic type of (a_{X_i}, b_j).

Since B_3 is sufficiently large with respect to τ_{aux}, it follows, by Higman's Lemma that there are k and ℓ such that $k < \ell$ and $w_k \sqsubseteq w_\ell$, that is $w_k = \sigma_k^1 \sigma_k^2 \ldots \sigma_k^k = \sigma_\ell^{i_1} \sigma_\ell^{i_2} \ldots \sigma_\ell^{i_k}$ for suitable numbers $i_1 < \ldots < i_k$. Let $\bar{b} \stackrel{\text{def}}{=} (b_1, \ldots, b_k)$ and $\bar{b}' \stackrel{\text{def}}{=} (b_{i_1}, \ldots, b_{i_k})$. Further, let $\mathcal{T}_k \stackrel{\text{def}}{=} \mathcal{S}'_k \upharpoonright T_k$ where $T_k = \{s, t, a_{X_k}\} \cup \bar{b}$, and let $\mathcal{T}_\ell \stackrel{\text{def}}{=} \mathcal{S}'_\ell \upharpoonright T_\ell$ where $T_\ell \stackrel{\text{def}}{=} \{s, t, a_{X_\ell}\} \cup \bar{b}'$. We refer to Fig. 4.4 for an illustration of the substructures $\mathcal{T}_k$ and $\mathcal{T}_\ell$ of $\mathcal{S}'$.

We show that $\mathcal{T}_k \simeq_\pi \mathcal{T}_\ell$, where π is the isomorphism that maps s and t to themselves, a_{X_k} to a_{X_ℓ} and b_j to b_{i_j} for every $j \in \{1, \ldots, k\}$. We argue that π fulfills the requirements of an isomorphism, for every relation symbol R from $\tau_{\text{inp}} \cup \tau_{\text{bi}} \cup \tau_{\text{aux}}$:

- For the input relation E this is obvious. In $\mathcal{S}'$ there are no edges from s to nodes in A_2 and all nodes from B_2 have an edge to t. Further X_ℓ is connected to all nodes in $\bar{b}$ and X_k is connected to all nodes in $\bar{b}'$.
- For $R \in \tau_{\text{bi}}$, the requirement follows because B_2 is A_2-homogeneous for schema τ_{bi}.
- For $R \in \tau_{\text{aux}}$ of arity 2 and two 2-tuples $\bar{c}$ and $\pi(\bar{c})$ we distinguish two cases. First, if $\bar{c}$ and $\pi(\bar{c})$ contain elements from B_3 only, then $\bar{c} \in R^{\mathcal{T}_k}$ if and only if $\pi(\bar{c}) \in R^{\mathcal{T}_\ell}$ because B_3 is homogeneous in $\mathcal{S}'$. Second, if $\bar{c}$ contains s, t or A_{X_ℓ}, then $\bar{c} \in R^{\mathcal{T}_k}$ if and only if $\pi(\bar{c}) \in R^{\mathcal{T}_\ell}$ because of the construction of w_k and w_ℓ.

Thus, by the Substructure Lemma, application of the following two modification sequences to $\mathcal{S}'$ results in the same query result:

(β_1) Deleting edges $(a_{X_k}, b_1), \ldots, (a_{X_k}, b_k)$ and adding an edge (s, a_{X_k}).

(β_2) Deleting edges $(a_{X_\ell}, b_{i_1}), \ldots, (a_{X_\ell}, b_{i_k})$ and adding an edge (s, a_{X_ℓ}).

However, applying β_1 yields a graph in which t is not reachable from s, whereas by applying β_2 a graph is obtained in which t is reachable from s. This is the desired contradiction.

It remains to specify the sizes of the sets. To apply Higman's Lemma, $|B_3|$ has to be of size at least $n_3 \stackrel{\text{def}}{=} H(m)$ where m is the number of binary atomic types over τ_{aux}. Hence, for applying Ramsey's theorem, $|B_2|$ has to be of size $n_2 \stackrel{\text{def}}{=} R(\tau; n_3)$. Thus it is sufficient if $|B_1|$ and $|A_1|$ contain $n_1 \stackrel{\text{def}}{=} 2^{n_2}$ elements. Therefore, by Corollary 4.1.15, the sets A and B can be chosen of size $n \stackrel{\text{def}}{=} R^{\text{hom}}(n_1; \tau)$. $\qquad\square$

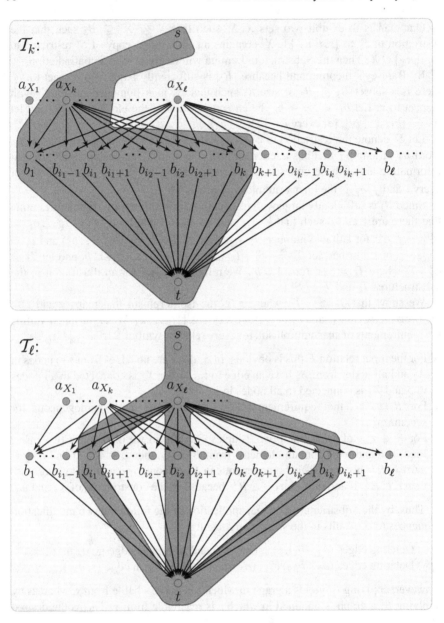

Fig. 4.4 The structure $\mathcal{S}'$ from the proof of Proposition 4.1.13 with highlighted isomorphic substructures $\mathcal{T}_k$ and $\mathcal{T}_\ell$.

Lower bounds for binary DYNPROP for the k-clique query and the k-colorability query (where k is fixed) can be established via reductions to the dynamic s-t-reachability query for shallow graphs.

Corollary 4.1.16. *k-CLIQUE, for $k \geq 3$, and k-COL, for $k \geq 2$, cannot be maintained in binary DYNPROP*.*

Proof. We prove that 3-CLIQUE cannot be maintained in binary DYNPROP. Afterwards we sketch the proof for k-CLIQUE, for arbitrary $k \geq 3$. The graphs used in the proof have a k-clique if and only if they are not $(k-1)$-colorable. Hence the lower bound for $k-1$-COL is immediately implied by the lower bound for k-CLIQUE.

For proving the lower bound for k-CLIQUE, we show that from a binary DYNPROP-program $\mathcal{P}'$ for the query 3-CLIQUE one can construct a dynamic program $\mathcal{P}$ that maintains the s-t-reachability query for 2-layered s-t-graphs. As the latter does not exist thanks to Proposition 4.1.13, we can conclude that the former does not exist either.

The reduction is very simple. For a 2-layered graph $G = (\{s, t\} \cup A \cup B, E)$, let G' be the graph obtained from G by identifying s and t. Clearly, G has a path from s to t if and only if G' has a 3-clique. See Fig. 4.5 for an illustration.

The dynamic program $\mathcal{P}$ uses the same auxiliary schema as $\mathcal{P}'$, the same initialization mapping and the same built-in schema relations. However, edges (u, t) in E are interpreted as if they were edges (u, s) in E'. More precisely, the update formulas of $\mathcal{P}$ are obtained from those in $\mathcal{P}'$ by replacing every atomic formula $E'(x, y)$ with $(y = s \wedge E(x, t)) \vee (y \neq s \wedge E(x, y))$. Obviously, $\mathcal{P}$ is a dynamic program for s-t-reachability for 2-layered s-t-graphs if $\mathcal{P}'$ is a dynamic program for 3-CLIQUE, as desired.

For arbitrary k, the construction is similar. The idea is that $\mathcal{P}$ simulates on a graph G the behavior of $\mathcal{P}'$ on $G \otimes K_{k-3}$, that is, the graph that results from G by adding a $(k-3)$-clique and completely connecting it with every node of G. Interestingly, the update formulas of $\mathcal{P}$ are exactly as in the previous reduction to 3-CLIQUE, as the "virtual" additional $k-3$ nodes are never involved in changes of the graph. However, INIT is not the same as $\text{INIT}'(G)$ but rather the projection of $\text{INIT}'(G \otimes K_{k-3})$ to the nodes of G. □

Using Bounds on Ramsey Numbers

The third technique for obtaining suitable substructures for an application of the Substructure Lemma is based on upper and lower bounds for Ramsey numbers. More precisely, the technique exploits a disparity between upper bounds for Ramsey numbers in k-ary structures and lower bounds for Ramsey numbers in $(k+1)$-dimensional hypergraphs. We will apply the technique to show that the k-clique query cannot be maintained in $(k-2)$-ary DYNPROP, even when only insertions are allowed.

We introduce hypergraphs first. A k-*hypergraph* G is a pair (V, E) where V is a set and E is a subset of $[V]^k$. If $E = [V]^k$ then G is called *complete*. An r-*coloring* col of G is a mapping that assigns to every edge in E a color from $\{1, \ldots, r\}$. A

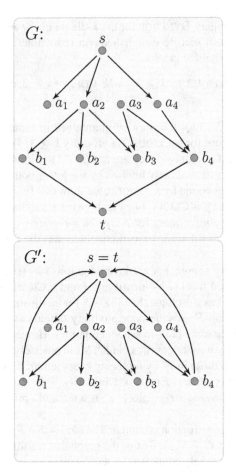

Fig. 4.5 The construction from Proposition 4.1.13. The s-t-paths (s, a_2, b_1, t) and (s, a_4, b_4, t) in G correspond to the cliques $\{s, a_2, b_1\}$ and $\{s, a_4, b_4\}$ in G'.

r-colored k-hypergraph is a pair (G, col) where G is a k-hypergraph and *col* is a *r*-coloring of G. If the name of the r-coloring is not important we also say G is *r-colored*.

The following lemma formalizes the above-mentioned disparity. While the first condition guarantees the existence of a Ramsey clique of size $f(|A|)$ in k-ary structures over A, the second condition states that there is a 2-coloring of the complete $(k + 1)$-hypergraph over A that does not contain a Ramsey clique of size $f(|A|)$. This disparity is the key to the lower bound proof.

Lemma 4.1.17. *Let $k \in \mathbb{N}$ be arbitrary and τ a k-ary schema. Then there is a function $f : \mathbb{N} \to \mathbb{N}$ and an $n \in \mathbb{N}$ such that for every domain A larger than n the following conditions are satisfied:*

(S1) *For every τ-structure S over A and every linear order $\prec$ on A there is a subset A' of A of size $|A'| \geq f(|A|)$ such that all $\prec$-ordered k-tuples over A' have the same atomic type in S.*

(S2) *The set $[A]^{k+1}$ of all $(k + 1)$-hyperedges over A can be partitioned into two sets B and B' such that for every set $A' \subseteq A$ of size $|A'| \geq f(|A|)$ there are $(k + 1)$-hyperedges $b, b' \subseteq A'$ with $b \in B$ and $b' \in B'$.*

The proof of the lemma uses upper and lower bounds for Ramsey numbers. It is deferred to the end of this subsection.

We now apply the lemma to obtain the lower bound for the k-clique query.

Proposition 4.1.18. *Under insertions, $(k + 2)$-CLIQUE $(k \geq 1)$ cannot be maintained in k-ary DYNPROP*.*

Proof. To keep the idea clear we prove the statement for DYNPROP (without built-in relations) first. Afterwards we will sketch how to extend the proof to DYNPROP*.

Towards a contradiction assume that there is a k-ary DYNPROP-program $\mathcal{P}$ over schema τ that maintains $(k + 2)$-CLIQUE. Let n and f be as in Lemma 4.1.17. For a set A larger than n let $\prec$ be an arbitrary order on A and let $D \stackrel{\text{def}}{=} A \uplus C$ be a domain with $C \stackrel{\text{def}}{=} [A]^{k+1}$. Further let B, B' be the partition of $[A]^{k+1}$ guaranteed to exist by (S2) in Lemma 4.1.17.

We consider a state S over domain D where the input graph G contains the following edges:

$$\{(b, b_1), (b, b_2), \ldots, (b, b_{k+1}) \mid b = \{b_1, b_2, \ldots, b_{k+1}\} \in B\}$$

See Fig. 4.6 for an illustration.

By Condition (S1) there is a subset $A' \subseteq A$ of size $|A'| \geq f(|D|)$ such that all ordered k-tuples over A' have the same atomic τ-type in S. Then by (S2) there are $(k + 1)$-hyperedges $b, b' \subseteq A'$ with $b \in B$ and $b' \in B'$. Without loss of generality $b = \{b_1, b_2, \ldots, b_{k+1}\}$ with $b_1 \prec \ldots \prec b_{k+1}$ and $b' = \{b'_1, b'_2, \ldots, b'_{k+1}\}$

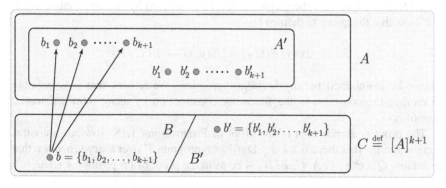

Fig. 4.6 The construction from the proof that $(k + 2)$-clique cannot be maintained in k-ary DYNPROP.

with $b'_1 \prec \ldots \prec b'_{k+1}$. By construction of the graph G, all elements in b are connected to the node $b \in C$ while there is no node in C connected to all elements of b'. Thus applying the modification sequences

(α) Insert the edges (b_i, b_j) in lexicographic order with respect to $\prec$.
(β) Insert the edges (b'_i, b'_j) in lexicographic order with respect to $\prec$.

yields one graph with a $(k + 2)$-clique and one graph without a $(k + 2)$-clique, respectively. However, by the Substructure Lemma, the program $\mathcal{P}$ yields the same result since the substructures induced by $\bar{b} = (b_1, \ldots, b_{k+1})$ and $\bar{b}' = (b'_1, \ldots, b'_{k+1})$ are isomorphic. This is the desired contradiction.

For extending the proof to DYNPROP*, a preprocessing step similar to the one in Proposition 4.1.14 can be used. The idea is to make the domain D from above homogeneous with respect to the built-in schema τ_{bi} before the actual construction. Then applying the same construction to this homogeneous domain yields the lower bound.

To this end, instead of starting from the domain $D \stackrel{\mathrm{def}}{=} A \uplus C$, one starts from a much larger domain D'. Using Ramsey's Theorem for structures, a τ_{bi}-homogeneous subset of D' of size $|D|$ can be found. This homogeneous subset can be used as the domain to start from.   □

The proof technique from the previous theorem can also be applied to improve upon a result by Gelade et al. [GMS12]. They provided a lower bound for the alternating reachability problem. The use of very restricted graphs in their proof implies that there is a $\exists^*\forall^*\exists^*$FO-definable query that cannot be maintained in DYNPROP. We show that there is a first-order property expressible by a formula with only one quantifier alternation which cannot be maintained in DYNPROP. It remains open whether there is a $\exists^*$FO- or $\forall^*$FO-property that is not maintainable in DYNPROP.

Proposition 4.1.19. *There is an $\exists^*\forall^*$FO-definable query which cannot be maintained by a DYNPROP*-program.*

Proof. We prove the statement only for DYNPROP; the proof can be easily adapted for DYNPROP*. Consider the graph schema $\{E\}$ extended by two constants s and t. We show that the query $\mathcal{Q}$ defined by

$$\varphi \stackrel{\mathrm{def}}{=} \exists x \forall y \big(E(s, x) \wedge (E(y, t) \to E(x, y)) \big)$$

cannot be maintained by any DYNPROP-program. We remark that it is possible to remove the constants in the following construction by using more existential quantifiers.

The proof is an adaption of the proof of Proposition 4.1.18. Towards a contradiction assume that there is a k-ary DYNPROP-program $\mathcal{P}$ over k-ary schema τ that maintains $\mathcal{Q}$. Let n, f, A, C, B, B', $\prec$ be as in the proof of Proposition 4.1.18.

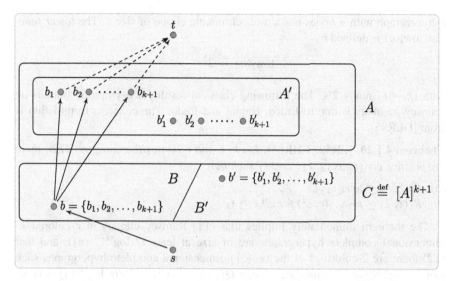

Fig. 4.7 The construction from the proof that the $\exists^*\forall^*$FO-definable query $\varphi \stackrel{\text{def}}{=} \exists x \forall y \big(E(s, x) \wedge (E(y, t) \to E(x, y))\big)$ cannot be maintained in DYNPROP. The edges inserted by the modification sequence α are dashed.

We consider a state $\mathcal{S}$ over domain D where the input graph G contains, as before, the edges

$$\{(b, b_1), (b, b_2), \ldots, (b, b_{k+1}) \mid b = \{b_1, b_2, \ldots, b_{k+1}\} \in B\}$$

and, additionally, the edges

$$\{(s, b) \mid b = \{b_1, b_2, \ldots, b_{k+1}\} \in B\}$$

We refer to Fig. 4.7 for an illustration. By Lemma 4.1.17, we can find tuples $b = \{b_1, b_2, \ldots, b_{k+1}\}$ with $b_1 \prec \ldots \prec b_{k+1}$ and $b' = \{b'_1, b'_2, \ldots, b'_{k+1}\}$ with $b'_1 \prec \ldots \prec b'_{k+1}$ such that (s, t, b) and (s, t, b') have the same atomic τ-type in $\mathcal{S}$.

However, applying the modification sequences

(α) Insert the edges (b_i, t) in lexicographic order with respect to $\prec$.
(β) Insert the edges (b'_i, t) in lexicographic order with respect to $\prec$.

yields one graph that satisfies φ and one graph that does not. However, by the Substructure Lemma, the program $\mathcal{P}$ yields the same result. This is the desired contradiction. $\qquad\square$

Proofs of the Combinatorial Tools

It remains to prove the Ramsey-like theorems used in the previous subsections. We recapitulate some useful notions and results first.

The *k-dimensional Ramsey* number for r colors and clique-size ℓ, denoted by $R_k(\ell; r)$, is the smallest number n such that every r-coloring of a complete

k-hypergraph with n nodes has a monochromatic clique of size ℓ. The *tower function* $\text{tow}_k(n)$ is defined by

$$\text{tow}_k(n) \overset{\text{def}}{=} 2^{2^{\cdot^{\cdot^{\cdot^{2^n}}}}}$$

with $(k-1)$ many 2's. The following classical result for asymptotic bounds on Ramsey numbers is due to Erdős, Hajnal and Rado. The concrete formulation is from [DLR95].

Theorem 4.1.20 [ER52, EHR65]. *Let k, ℓ and r be positive integers. Then there are positive constants c_k, $c_{k,r}$ and ℓ_k such that*

(a) $R_k(\ell; r) \leq \text{tow}_k(c_{k,r}\ell)$
(b) $R_k(\ell; 2) \geq \text{tow}_{k-1}(c_k\ell^2)$ *for all $\ell \geq \ell_k$*

The theorem immediately implies that (T1) Ramsey cliques in r-colored k-dimensional complete hypergraphs are of size at least $\Omega(\log^{(k-1)}(n))$; and that (T2) there are 2-colorings of the $(k+1)$-dimensional complete hypergraphs such that monochromatic cliques are of size $O((\log^{(k-1)}(n))^{\frac{1}{2}})$. Here $\log^{(k)}(n)$ denotes $\log(\log(\ldots(\log n)\ldots))$ with k many log's. The conditions (T1) and (T2) are formalized and proved in the following corollary.

Corollary 4.1.21. *Let k and r be integers. There are functions $g \in \Omega(\log^{(k-1)}(n))$ and $h \in O(\sqrt{\log^{(k-2)}(n)})$ such that:*

(a) *Every r-colored complete k-hypergraph with n nodes contains a monochromatic clique of size $g(n)$.*
(b) *The complete k-hypergraph with n nodes can be 2-colored such that every monochromatic clique is of size at most $h(n)$.*

Proof. The corollary follows immediately from Theorem 4.1.20. Define g and h by

$$g(n) \overset{\text{def}}{=} \left\lfloor \frac{1}{c_{k,r}} \log^{(k-1)}(n) \right\rfloor \text{ and } h(n) \overset{\text{def}}{=} \left\lceil \sqrt{\frac{1}{c_k} \log^{(k-2)}(n)} \right\rceil + 1$$

where the constants $c_{k,r}$ and c_k are as in Theorem 4.1.20.

For proving (a), consider an arbitrary hypergraph G with n nodes, and an arbitrary r-coloring of G. Then, by Theorem 4.1.20(a), there is a monochromatic clique of size ℓ where ℓ is the maximal number such that $\text{tow}_k(\ell c_{k,r}) \leq n$. The number ℓ is exactly $g(n)$.

For proving (b), consider again an arbitrary hypergraph G with n nodes. By Theorem 4.1.20(b), there is a 2-coloring without a monochromatic clique of size ℓ where ℓ is the minimal number such that $n < \text{tow}_{k-1}(\ell^2 c_k)$. Thus the largest monochromatic clique of G is of size at most $h(n)$. $\square$

The upper bound from the Theorem 4.1.20 can be generalized to Ramsey numbers for structures as follows. Recall that, for a schema τ and a positive integer ℓ, the smallest number n such that every $\prec$-ordered τ-structure with at least n elements contains an $\prec$-ordered τ-clique of size ℓ is called Ramsey number for τ and ℓ; denoted by $R(\ell; \tau)$.

Theorem 4.1.22. *Let τ be a schema with maximal arity k and let ℓ be a positive integer. Then there is a constant c such that $R(\ell; \tau) \leq tow_k(\ell c)$.*

Proof. The proof of Observation 1' in [GMS12, p. 11] yields this bound. For the sake of completeness we repeat the full construction.

Consider the schema τ and let Γ be the set of all k-ary atomic types for τ. Let S be a τ-structure over domain D of size $tow_k(\ell c)$ where $c = |\Gamma|$. Further let $\prec$ be an arbitrary order on D. Define a coloring col of the complete k-dimensional hypergraph over domain D with colors Γ as follows. An edge $\{e_1, \ldots, e_k\}$ with $e_1 \prec \ldots \prec e_k$ is colored by the atomic type $\langle S, e_1, \ldots, e_k \rangle$. Recall that the atomic type of a tuple $\bar{a}$ includes information about $\bar{a}$ as well as the constants of the structure. By Theorem 4.1.20 there is an induced monochromatic sub-k-hypergraph with domain $D' \subseteq D$ with $|D'| \geq \ell$. By the definition of the coloring col, two $\prec$-ordered k-tuples over D' have the same atomic type and therefore D' is a $\prec$-ordered τ-clique in S as well. $\square$

The previous theorem immediately implies Theorem 4.1.12. Furthermore it implies that Ramsey cliques in k-ary structures are of size at least $\Omega(\log^{(k-1)}(n))$. The proof is analogous to the proof of Corollary 4.1.21.

Corollary 4.1.23. *Let τ be a schema with maximal arity k. There is a function $g \in \Omega(\log^{(k-1)}(n))$ such that every τ-structure with n elements contains an ordered τ-clique of size $g(n)$.*

In the rest of this section we prove Corollary 4.1.15 and Lemma 4.1.17. For the sake of convenience we also repeat the statements.

Corollary 4.1.15 (R). *For every schema τ and natural number ℓ, there is a number n such that for any two disjoint subsets A, B of the domain of a τ-structure S with $|A|, |B| \geq n$, there are subsets $A' \subseteq A$ and $B' \subseteq B$ such that $|A'|, |B'| = \ell$ and B' is A'-homogeneous in S.*

Proof. Let τ be a schema with maximal arity k. Choose n' to be a large number with respect to τ and ℓ; and let n be a large number with respect to n'; explicit numbers can be found at the end of the proof. In particular n is large with respect to the number of constant symbols in τ. Further let A and B be disjoint subsets of the domain of a τ-structure S with $|A|, |B| > n$. Since n is large with respect to the number of constants in S, we assume, without loss of generality, that neither A nor B contains a constant.

Fix a n'-tuple $\bar{a} = (a_1, \ldots, a_{n'})$ of A. Further let $\prec$ be an arbitrary order on B. Because $|B|$ is large with respect to n', ℓ and τ, and by Ramsey's theorem on structures (treating $a_1, \ldots, a_{n'}$ as constants), there is a subset B' of B of size ℓ such that the atomic type of $(\bar{a}, \bar{b})$ in S is the same, for all $\prec$-ordered k-tuples $\bar{b}$ over B'.

Since n' is large with respect to τ and because there is only a bounded number of $(k+1)$-ary atomic τ-types, there is an increasing sequence $i_1, \ldots, i_\ell$ such that the atomic τ-types of tuples $(a_{i_j}, \bar{b})$ are equal, for all $\prec$-ordered k-tuples $\bar{b}$ over B'

and $j \in \{1, \ldots, \ell\}$. We choose $A' \overset{\text{def}}{=} \{a_{i_1}, \ldots, a_{i_\ell}\}$. Then B' is A'-homogeneous up to arity k and therefore A'-homogeneous.

It remains to give explicit numbers. For the sequence $i_1, \ldots, i_\ell$ to exist in $1, \ldots, n'$, the number n' has to be at least $(\ell - 1)K + 1$ where K is the number of $(k + 1)$-ary atomic τ-types. Thus n has to be of size at least $R(\tau; n') + c$ where c is the number of constants in τ. $\square$

Lemma 4.1.17 **(R).** *Let $k \in \mathbb{N}$ be arbitrary and τ a k-ary schema. Then there is a function $f : \mathbb{N} \to \mathbb{N}$ and an $n \in \mathbb{N}$ such that for every domain A larger than n the following conditions are satisfied:*

(S1) For every τ-structure S over A and every linear order $\prec$ on A there is a subset A' of A of size $|A'| \geq f(|A|)$ such that all $\prec$-ordered k-tuples over A' have the same atomic type in S.

(S2) The set $[A]^{k+1}$ of all $(k + 1)$-hyperedges over A can be partitioned into two sets B and B' such that for every set $A' \subseteq A$ of size $|A'| \geq f(|A|)$ there are $(k + 1)$-hyperedges $b, b' \subseteq A'$ with $b \in B$ and $b' \in B'$.

Proof. Let $k \in \mathbb{N}$ be arbitrary and let τ be a k-ary schema τ. Choose $f \overset{\text{def}}{=} g$ where $g \in \Omega(\log^{(k-1)}(n))$ is the function from Corollary 4.1.23. We show that there is an n such that f satisfies the conditions (S1) and (S2) for all domains larger than n.

Let $h \in O(\sqrt{\log^{(k-1)}(n)})$ be the function guaranteed to exist for $k + 1$ by Corollary 4.1.21(b). Then $h \in o(f)$, and therefore there is an n such that $f(n') > h(n')$ for all $n' > n$. Hence for every domain larger than n condition (S1) is satisfied for f due to Corollary 4.1.23 and condition (S2) is satisfied due to Corollary 4.1.21. $\square$

4.1.3 An Arity Hierarchy for Quantifier-Free Programs

In this subsection we use the lower bound results from the previous section to obtain a strict hierarchy between unary, binary and ternary DYNPROP for graph queries, and a strict arity hierarchy for all arities under insertions.

Theorem 4.1.4 **(R).**

(a) Unary, binary and ternary DYNPROP form a strict arity hierarchy on graphs.
(b) Under insertions, DYNPROP has a strict arity hierarchy on graphs.

Furthermore, boolean queries are used for the separations. The second part of the theorem follows immediately from Theorem 3.3.3 and Proposition 4.1.18. For separating unary, binary and ternary DYNPROP, we use the following queries obtained by analyzing the proofs of Propositions 4.1.14 and 4.1.13:

> *Problem: s- t- TwoPATH*
> *Input: An s-t-graph $G = (V, E)$.*
> *Question: Is there a path of length two from s to t?*

Problem: s-TWOPATH

   Input: A graph $G = (V, E)$ with one distinguished node $s \in V$.
   Question: Is there a path of length two starting from s?

Proposition 4.1.24. s-t-TWOPATH *is in binary* DYNPROP, *but not in unary* DYNPROP*.

Proof sketch. That s-t-TWOPATH is not in unary DYNPROP* follows immediately from Proposition 4.1.14 as such a program would also maintain the dynamic s-t-reachability query for 1-layered graphs.

   In order to prove that s-t-TWOPATH is in binary DYNPROP, we sketch a DYNPROP-program (P, INIT, Q) whose auxiliary schema contains unary relation symbols IN, OUT, FIRST, and LAST and a binary relation symbol LIST. The idea is to store, in a program state $\mathcal{S}$, a list of all nodes a such that (s, a, t) is a path in $E^{\mathcal{S}}$. The relation IN$^{\mathcal{S}}$ contains all nodes with an incoming edge from s, and OUT$^{\mathcal{S}}$ contains all nodes with an outgoing edge to t. The relations FIRST$^{\mathcal{S}}$, LAST$^{\mathcal{S}}$, LIST$^{\mathcal{S}}$ maintain the actual list, similarly to Example 2.3.4. The current query bit is maintained in $Q^{\mathcal{S}}$.

   For a given instance of s-t-TWOPATH the initialization mapping initializes the auxiliary relations accordingly.

Insertion of (a, b) into E. We note that edges (a, b) where $a \neq s$ and $b \neq t$ can be ignored, as they cannot contribute to any path of length 2 from s to t. Furthermore, paths of length 2 involving only nodes s and t can be easily handled by DYNPROP formulas, and therefore will be ignored as well.

   If $a = s$ and $b \neq t$, then b is inserted into IN, otherwise if $a \neq s$ and $b = t$ then a is inserted into OUT. Afterwards a or b is inserted into LIST, if it is now contained in both IN and OUT. In that case the query bit is set true.

   Formally:

$$\phi_{\text{INS}_E}^{\text{IN}}(a, b; x) = \text{IN}(x) \vee (x = b \wedge a = s \wedge b \neq s \wedge b \neq t)$$

$$\phi_{\text{INS}_E}^{\text{OUT}}(a, b; x) = \text{OUT}(x) \vee (x = a \wedge a \neq s \wedge a \neq t \wedge b = t)$$

$$\phi_{\text{INS}_E}^{\text{FIRST}}(a, b; x) = \text{FIRST}(x) \vee (\neg Q \wedge \varphi_n(x))$$

$$\phi_{\text{INS}_E}^{\text{LAST}}(a, b; x) = (\text{LAST}(x) \wedge \neg\varphi_n(a) \wedge \neg\varphi_n(b)) \vee \varphi_n(x)$$

$$\phi_{\text{INS}_E}^{\text{LIST}}(a, b; x, y) = (\text{LIST}(x, y) \wedge \neg\varphi_n(a) \wedge \neg\varphi_n(b)) \vee (\text{LAST}(x) \wedge \varphi_n(y))$$

$$\phi_{\text{INS}_E}^{Q}(a, b) = Q \vee \varphi_n(a) \vee \varphi_n(b)$$

Here, $\varphi_n(x)$ is an abbreviation for

$$\phi_{\text{INS}_E}^{\text{IN}}(a, b; x) \wedge \phi_{\text{INS}_E}^{\text{OUT}}(a, b; x) \wedge (\neg\text{IN}(x) \vee \neg\text{OUT}(x))$$

expressing that x is becoming newly inserted into LIST.

Deletion of (a, b) from E. First, if $a = s$, then b is removed from IN. Further if $b = t$ then a is removed from OUT. Afterwards a or b is removed from LIST, if it has been removed from IN or OUT. If LIST is empty now, then the query bit is set to false. The precise formulas are along the lines of the formulas of Example 2.3.4. □

Proposition 4.1.25. s-TWOPATH *is in ternary* DYNPROP, *but not in binary* DYNPROP*.

Proof sketch. For proving that s-TWOPATH is not in binary DYNPROP*, assume to the contrary that there is a binary DYNPROP*-program $\mathcal{P} = (P, \text{INIT}, Q)$ for s-TWOPATH. With the help of $\mathcal{P}$ one can, for the graphs from the proof of Proposition 4.1.13, maintain whether there is a path from s to some node of B. However, this yields a correct answer for s-t-REACH for those graphs, since in the proof all nodes of B have an edge to t.

In order to prove that s-TWOPATH is in ternary DYNPROP, we sketch a DYNPROP-program (P, INIT, Q) whose auxiliary schema contains unary relation symbols IN, OUT, FIRST_1, LAST_1 and EMPTY_1, binary relation symbols LIST_1, FIRST_2, LAST_2 and EMPTY_2, and a ternary relation symbol LIST_2. The idea is that in a state $\mathcal{S}$, the binary relation $\text{LIST}_1^{\mathcal{S}}$ contains a list of all nodes a on a path (s, a, b) in $E^{\mathcal{S}}$, for some node b. The relation $\text{IN}^{\mathcal{S}}$ contains all nodes with an incoming edge from s, and $\text{OUT}^{\mathcal{S}}$ contains all nodes with an outgoing edge. In order to update $\text{OUT}^{\mathcal{S}}$, the projection $\text{LIST}_2^{\mathcal{S}}(a, \cdot, \cdot)$ of the ternary relation $\text{LIST}_2^{\mathcal{S}}$ stores a list of nodes b with $(a, b) \in E^{\mathcal{S}}$, for every node a. The lists $\text{LIST}_1^{\mathcal{S}}$ and $\text{LIST}_2^{\mathcal{S}}(a, \cdot, \cdot)$ are maintained by using the technique from Example 2.3.4 and by using the auxiliary relations stored in $\text{FIRST}_1^{\mathcal{S}}$, $\text{LAST}_1^{\mathcal{S}}$, $\text{EMPTY}_1^{\mathcal{S}}$, $\text{FIRST}_2^{\mathcal{S}}$, $\text{LAST}_2^{\mathcal{S}}$ and $\text{EMPTY}_2^{\mathcal{S}}$. The current query bit is maintained in $Q^{\mathcal{S}}$.

For a given instance of s-TWOPATH the initialization mapping initializes the auxiliary relations accordingly.

Insertion of (a, b) **into** E. First, if $a = s$ then b is inserted into IN. Otherwise, a is inserted into OUT and b is inserted into $\text{LIST}_2(a, \cdot, \cdot)$. Afterwards a or b is inserted into LIST_1, if it is now contained in both IN and OUT. If one of them is inserted, then the query bit is set true.

Deletion of (a, b) **from** E. First, if $a = s$ then b is removed from IN. Otherwise, b is removed from $\text{LIST}_2(a, \cdot, \cdot)$ and if $\text{LIST}_2(a, \cdot, \cdot)$ is empty afterwards, then a is removed from OUT. Afterwards a or b is removed from LIST_1, if it has been removed from IN or OUT. The query bit is set to false, if the list LIST_1 is empty now.   □

4.1.4 Fragments of Quantifier-Free Programs

In the previous sections we have seen that the reachability query and the 3-clique query cannot be maintained in binary DYNPROP. However, a lower bound for arbitrary initialization appears to be non-trivial. Here we pursue the natural question, whether lower bounds for syntactic fragments of DYNPROP with no arity restriction can be proved. We aim at the following theorem.

Theorem 4.1.5 **(R)**. NONEMPTYSET, s-t-REACH and 3-CLIQUE cannot be maintained in DYNPROPCQ.

As NONEMPTYSET can be maintained in DYNPROP (see Example 2.3.4), it follows that DYNPROPCQ is a strict subclass of DYNPROP. To prove Theorem 4.1.5, we first show that the query NONEMPTYSET from Example 2.3.4 cannot be maintained in this fragment. Afterwards we sketch how to adapt this proof for the reachability query and the 3-clique query.

For technical reasons, the proof assumes a DYNPROPCQ-program in which no atom contains any variable more than once. We first illustrate by an example how this restriction can be achieved.

Example 4.1.26. We consider the following DYNPROPCQ-program, where, for simplicity, only update formulas for insertions are specified.

$$\phi_{\text{INS}}^R(u; x, y) = S(x, y) \wedge R(x, x)$$
$$\phi_{\text{INS}}^S(u; x, y) = S(x, y)$$

An equivalent DYNPROPCQ-program in which all update formulas only contain atoms with distinct variables can be obtained by replacing $R(x, x)$ by $R'(x)$ where R' is a fresh unary relation symbol. It then has to be ensured, that $R'(x) \equiv R(x, x)$. This can be achieved by updating R' with the update formula for R, in which x and y are unified.

$$\phi_{\text{INS}}^R(u; x, y) = S(x, y) \wedge R'(x)$$
$$\phi_{\text{INS}}^S(u; x, y) = S(x, y)$$
$$\phi_{\text{INS}}^{R'}(u; x) = S(x, x) \wedge R'(x)$$

Finally we apply the same construction to the atom $S(x, x)$ in $\phi_{\text{INS}}^{R'}$:

$$\phi_{\text{INS}}^R(u; x, y) = S(x, y) \wedge R'(x)$$
$$\phi_{\text{INS}}^S(u; x, y) = S(x, y)$$
$$\phi_{\text{INS}}^{R'}(u; x) = S'(x) \wedge R'(x)$$
$$\phi_{\text{INS}}^{S'}(u; x) = S'(x)$$

$\square$

The process of Example 4.1.26 necessarily terminates since there is only a finite number of equality types for the variables of each of the atoms occurring in an update formula. An *equality type* ρ over a set of variables $X = \{x_1, \ldots, x_n\}$ is an equivalence relation on X.

Lemma 4.1.27. *For every* DYNPROPCQ-*program with unary input schema there is an equivalent* DYNPROPCQ-*program in which no atom in any update formula contains a variable more than once.*

Proof sketch. For a given DYNPROPCQ-program $\mathcal{P}$ over schema τ, construct an equivalent DYNPROPCQ-program $\mathcal{P}'$ over schema τ' where τ' contains, for every k-ary relation symbol $R \in \tau$ and every equality type ρ over k variables $x_1, \ldots, x_k$, a relation symbol R^ρ of arity k' where k' is the number of equivalence classes of ρ.

The intention is that $(\mathcal{S}, \Theta) \models R(\bar{x})$, for a state $\mathcal{S}$ and variable assignment Θ satisfying ρ, if and only if $(\mathcal{S}, \Theta^\rho) \models R^\rho(\bar{y})$, where Θ^ρ maps every variable y_i to the value of the i-th equivalence class of ρ under Θ. This can be ensured along the lines of Example 4.1.27.   □

We prove Theorem 4.1.5 in a slightly more general setting. A modification α is *honest* with respect to a given state if it does not insert a tuple already present in the input database and does not delete a tuple which is not present in the database. A query is in h-DYN$\mathcal{C}$ if it can be maintained with $\mathcal{C}$ update programs for all sequences of honest modifications. It is easy to see that for a class $\mathcal{C}$ closed under boolean operations, the classes DYN$\mathcal{C}$ and h-DYN$\mathcal{C}$ coincide. However for weak classes such as DYNPROPCQ the restriction to honest modifications might make a difference, since update formulas cannot explicitly test (at least not in a straightforward way) whether a modification is honest. Nevertheless, all our proofs work for both kinds of types of modifications.

Proposition 4.1.28. NONEMPTYSET *can neither be maintained in* DYNPROPCQ *nor in* h-DYNPROPCQ.

Proof. Towards a contradiction, we assume that there is a h-DynPropCQ-program $\mathcal{P} = (P, \text{INIT}, Q)$ over schema τ that maintains NONEMPTYSET, i.e. the query defined by $\exists x U(x)$. Further, we assume, by Lemma 4.1.27, that no variable occurs more than once in any atom of an update formula of $\mathcal{P}$.

The notions of a (deletion) dependency graph will be convenient for the proof. Recall that the dependency graph of a dynamic program $\mathcal{P}$ has vertex set $V = \tau$ and an edge (R, R') if the relation symbol R' occurs in one of the update formulas for R. In the deletion dependency graph only update formulas for deletions are used. The *deletion depth* of a relation R is defined as the length of the shortest path from Q to R in the deletion dependency graph.

We start with a simple observation. Let $R(u)$ be a relation atom in the formula ϕ^Q_{DEL} for the 0-ary query relation Q, that is:

$$\phi^Q_{\text{DEL}}(u) \stackrel{\text{def}}{=} \ldots \wedge R(u) \wedge \ldots$$

Further let $\mathcal{S}$ be a state in which the relation U contains two elements $a \neq b$. Then, necessarily, $R^{\mathcal{S}}$ contains a and b, as otherwise deletion of a or b would make Q false (since $R(u)$ evaluates to false for a or b) without U becoming empty. This observation can be generalized: if a relation R has "distance k" from Q in the deletion dependency graph and U contains at least $k + 1$ elements, then R must contain all *diverse* tuples over U, that is, tuples that consist of pairwise distinct elements from U. Note that the empty tuple is always diverse.

We prove this observation next, afterwards we look at how the statement of the lemma follows. Using our assumption on non-repeating variables, it is easy to see that the arity of relations of deletion depth k is at most k (at most one plus the arity of the updated relation).

We prove by induction on k that, for each relation R of deletion depth k, and every state S in which U contains at least $k+1$ elements, R has to contain all diverse tuples over U.

For $k = 0$ this is obvious as Q needs to contain the empty tuple if U is non-empty.

For $k > 0$, let S be a state such that U^S contains at least $k + 1$ elements. Further let R be some arbitrary relation symbol of deletion depth k. Then $R(\bar{x})$ occurs in the update formula $\phi^{R'}_{\text{DEL}}(u; \bar{y})$ of some relation symbol R' of deletion depth $k - 1$ for some $\bar{x} = (x_1, \ldots, x_\ell)$, with $\bar{x} \subseteq \{u\} \cup \bar{y}$. By the above, $\ell \leq k$ and $\bar{y}$ contains at most $k - 1$ variables. We assume, without loss of generality, that the arity of R is k.

Towards a contradiction, let us assume that there is a diverse k-tuple $\bar{a} = (a_1, \ldots, a_k)$ over U^S that is not in R^S. Let $\Theta : \{x_1, \ldots, x_\ell\} \to U^S$ be the assignment with $\Theta(x_i) = a_i$ and let $\hat{\Theta}$ be some extension of Θ to an injective assignment of $\{u\} \cup \bar{y}$ to elements from U^S (such an assignment exists because $|\{u\} \cup \bar{y}| \leq k < |U|$). Then $\phi^{R'}_{\text{DEL}}(u; \bar{y})$ evaluates to false in state S under $\hat{\Theta}$ (since $\bar{a} \notin R^S$ by assumption). Thus, deleting $\hat{\Theta}(u)$ from U^S yields a state S' with $\hat{\Theta}(\bar{y}) \notin R'^{S'}$. However, $U^{S'}$ still contains at least k elements and therefore, by induction hypothesis, the relation $R'^{S'}$ contains every diverse tuple over $U^{S'}$ and thus, in particular, $\hat{\Theta}(\bar{y})$, the desired contradiction from the assumption that $\bar{a} \notin R^S$.

Now we can complete the proof of Proposition 4.1.29. Let S be a state in which the set U contains $m+1$ elements, where m is the maximum (finite) deletion depth of any relation symbol in $\mathcal{P}$. By the claim above, all relations whose symbols are reachable from Q in the deletion dependency graph of $\mathcal{P}$ contain all diverse tuples over U^S. Thus, all relation atoms over tuples from U^S evaluate to true. It is easy to show by induction on the length of modification sequences that this property (applied to $U^{S'}$) holds for all states S' that can be obtained from S by deleting elements from U^S. In particular, it holds for any such state in which $U^{S'}$ contains only one element a. But then, $\phi^Q_{\text{DEL}}(a)$ evaluates to true in S' and thus Q remains true after deletion of a, the desired contradiction to the assumed correctness of $\mathcal{P}$. $\qquad\square$

Proposition 4.1.29. s-t-REACH *and* 3-CLIQUE *can neither be maintained in* DYNPROPCQ *nor in* h-DYNPROPCQ.

Proof. Towards a contradiction assume that there is a DYNPROPCQ-program $\mathcal{P}$ for s-t-REACH over schema τ. We show that a DYNPROPCQ-program $\mathcal{P}'$ can be constructed from $\mathcal{P}$ such that $\mathcal{P}'$ maintains NONEMPTYSET under deletions. As the proof of the preceding lemma shows that NONEMPTYSET cannot be maintained in DYNPROPCQ even if elements are deleted from U only, this is the desired contradiction.

The intuition behind the construction of $\mathcal{P}'$ is as follows. For sets $U \subseteq A$, the 1-layered graph G with nodes $\{s, t\} \cup A$ and edges $\{(s, a) \mid a \in U\} \cup \{(a, t) \mid a \in A\}$ naturally corresponds to the instance I of NONEMPTYSET over domain A with set U.

The deletion of an element a from U in I corresponds to the deletion of the edge (s, a) from G. Using this correspondence, the program $\mathcal{P}'$ essentially maintains the same auxiliary relations as $\mathcal{P}$. When a is deleted from U then $\mathcal{P}'$ simulates $\mathcal{P}$ after the deletion of (s, a).

A complication arises from the fact that NONEMPTYSET does not have constants s and t. Therefore the program $\mathcal{P}'$ encodes the relationship of s and t to elements from A by using additional auxiliary relations. More precisely, for every k-ary relation symbol $R \in \tau$ and every tuple $\rho = (\rho_1, \ldots, \rho_k)$ over $\{\bullet, s, t\}$, the program $\mathcal{P}'$ has a fresh ℓ-ary relation symbol R^ρ where ℓ is the number of ρ_i's with $\rho_i = \bullet$. The intention is as follows. Let $i_1 < \ldots < i_\ell$ such that $\rho_{i_j} = \bullet$. With every ℓ-tuple $\bar{u} = (y_1, \ldots, y_\ell)$ of variables we associate the tuple $\bar{u}^\rho = (u_1^\rho, \ldots, u_k^\rho)$ of terms from $\{s, t, y_1, \ldots, y_\ell\}$, where (1) $u_i^\rho = s$ if $\rho_i = s$, (2) $u_i^\rho = t$ if $\rho_i = t$, and (3) $u_{i_j}^\rho = y_j$, for $j \in \{1, \ldots, \ell\}$. Analogously, we define $\bar{a}^\rho$ for tuples $\bar{a} = (a_1, \ldots, a_\ell)$ over A. Then $\mathcal{P}'$ ensures that $\bar{a} \in R^\rho$ in some state if and only if $\bar{a}^\rho \in R$ in the corresponding state of $\mathcal{P}$.

Update formulas $\phi_{\text{DELU}}^{R^\rho}(v; x_1, \ldots, x_\ell)$ of $\mathcal{P}'$ are obtained from update formulas $\phi_{\text{DELE}}^R(u, v; x_1, \ldots, x_k)$ of $\mathcal{P}$ in two steps. First, from ϕ_{DELE}^R a formula ϕ' is constructed by (syntactically) replacing every occurrence of x_i by x_i^ρ and replacing every occurrence of u by s. Then $\phi_{\text{DELU}}^{R^\rho}$ is obtained from ϕ' by replacing every atom $T(\bar{w})$ in ϕ_{DELE}^R by $T^\rho(\bar{y})$, for the unique tuple $\bar{y}$ of variables and the unique tuple ρ, for which $\bar{y}^\rho = \bar{w}$.

Now, $\mathcal{P}'$ yields the same query result after deletion of elements $a_1, \ldots, a_m$ as $\mathcal{P}$ after deletion of edges $(s, a_1), \ldots, (s, a_m)$. Hence the program $\mathcal{P}'$ maintains NONEMPTYSET under deletions. This is a contradiction.

The proof that 3-CLIQUE cannot be maintained neither in DYNPROPCQ nor in h-DYNPROPCQ is the same, except that G additionally has an edge (s, t). Here, one can assume without loss of generality that the constants s and t are available. □

The preceding propositions immediately imply Theorem 4.1.5.

4.2 Quantifier-Free Update Programs with Functions

In quantifier-free update programs with merely auxiliary relations only the modified and updated tuple as well as the constants can be accessed while updating an auxiliary tuple. Since lower bounds for first-order update programs — where arbitrary elements can be accessed in updates — seem to be out of reach for the moment, it seems natural to look for lower bounds for extensions of quantifier-free update programs that allow for accessing more elements in some restricted way.

For this reason DYNQF, the extension of quantifier-free programs by auxiliary functions will be studied in this section. Recall that auxiliary functions may access, besides the elements of the modified and updated tuples, functional values of those tuples. Thus auxiliary functions allow access to more elements but in a restricted way, and therefore are a good candidate for trying to prove better lower bounds.

Our main tool for proving lower bounds for DYNQF is a generalization of the Substructure Lemma from the previous section. A restricted generalization of this kind was proposed already in [GMS12, Lemma 4], though only for DYNPROP extended by a successor and a predecessor function. Here, we introduce a Substructure Lemma for DYNQF with arbitrary auxiliary functions.

For DYNPROP the Substructure Lemma requires to exhibit two isomorphic substructures. For DYNQF this is not sufficient anymore, as tuples outside such a substructure can possibly be accessed using the auxiliary functions. Therefore the Substructure Lemma for DYNQF requires to exhibit isomorphic substructures that, additionally, have similar neighborhoods. Isomorphic substructures with similar neighborhoods can be obtained via the basic techniques we have seen before. We will use the counting technique, Ramsey's Theorem and bounds on Ramsey numbers in order to obtain lower bounds for DYNQF. Yet, the constructions from the previous section need to be adapted.

Again, we look for lower bounds for DYNQF with respect to both invariant initialization and arbitrary initialization.

The result from the previous section for invariant initialization can be generalized in a straight-forward fashion to the following theorem.

Theorem 4.2.1. s-t-REACH *cannot be maintained in* DYNQF *with invariant initialization.*

A reduction yields lower bounds for k-clique ($k \geq 2$) and k-colorability ($k \geq 1$) as well.

For arbitrary initialization we are only able to prove lower bounds for unary auxiliary functions. So far there has been only one lower bound for dynamic classes with auxiliary functions: alternating reachability was shown to be not maintainable in DYNPROP in the presence of a successor and a predecessor function [GMS12]. Here, we prove further lower bounds for unary DYNQF with arbitrary unary auxiliary functions.

Theorem 4.2.2. s-t-REACH *cannot be maintained in unary* DYNQF.

Theorem 4.2.3. *Under insertions, k-CLIQUE ($k \geq 3$) cannot be maintained in $(k-2)$-ary* DYNPROP *with unary auxiliary functions.*

The first result is obtained using Ramsey's theorem; the second by using bounds on Ramsey numbers.

Currently the barrier for proving lower bounds for natural queries is DYNQF with unary functions. Towards the end of this section we will argue why proving bounds for binary auxiliary functions likely requires new techniques. To this end we show that binary DYNQF can maintain every boolean graph property when the domain is large with respect to the actually used domain.

The rest of this section is structured as follows. In the next subsection, the generalization of the Substructure Lemma for DYNQF is presented. Then, one subsection is devoted to prove the main theorems above; the subsection is structured according to the technique used for obtaining isomorphic substructures with similar neighborhoods. The last part of this section argues why the current techniques are not sufficient for proving lower bounds for binary DYNQF.

4.2.1 A Generalization of the Substructure Lemma

The main tool for proving lower bounds for DYNQF is a generalization of the Substructure Lemma. A restricted variant of this lemma was already used in [GMS12].

As discussed already in the introduction above, when a modification changes a tuple from a substructure $\mathcal{A}$ of a structure $\mathcal{S}$, then the update of the auxiliary data of $\mathcal{A}$ can depend on elements obtained from applying functions to elements from the domain of $\mathcal{A}$. All elements that can be obtained by update terms of a fixed depth from the domain of $\mathcal{A}$ will be called the neighborhood of $\mathcal{A}$. The Substructure Lemma for DYNQF requires two isomorphic substructures whose neighborhoods behave very similarly. Before presenting the precise statement of the Substructure Lemma for DYNQF, we will formalize the notions of neighborhood and similarity.

We start by defining neighborhoods. The *nesting depth* $d(t)$ of an update term t is its nesting depth with respect to function symbols: If t is a variable, then $d(t) = 0$; if t is of the form $f(t_1, \ldots, t_k)$ then $d(t) = \max\{d(t_1), \ldots, d(t_k)\} + 1$; and if t is of the form $\text{ITE}(\phi, t_1, t_2)$ then $d(t) = \max\{d(\phi), d(t_1), d(t_2)\}$. The nesting depth $d(\phi)$ of ϕ is the maximal nesting depth of all update terms occurring in ϕ. The *nesting depth of* $\mathcal{P}$ is the maximal nesting depth of an update term occurring in $\mathcal{P}$.

For a schema τ, let TERMS_τ^m be the set of terms of nesting depth at most m with function symbols from τ. Informally, the m-neighborhood of a set A is the set of all elements that can be obtained by applying a term of nesting depth at most m to a tuple of elements from A. We formalize this as follows.

Let $t_1, \ldots, t_\ell$ be the lexicographic enumeration of TERMS_τ^m with respect to some fixed order of the function symbols. Let the *m-neighborhood tuple* $\bar{\mathcal{N}}_\mathcal{S}^m(a)$ of an element a in $\mathcal{S}$ be the tuple $(a, t_1(a), \ldots, t_\ell(a))$. The *$m$-neighborhood* $\mathcal{N}_\mathcal{S}^m(a)$ of a is the set of all elements occurring in $\bar{\mathcal{N}}_\mathcal{S}^m(a)$. The m-neighborhood $\mathcal{N}_\mathcal{S}^m(A)$ of a set A is the union of all neighborhoods of elements $a \in A$. The neighborhood of a tuple can be defined analogously.

Two subsets $A \subseteq \mathcal{S}$, $B \subseteq \mathcal{T}$ are *m-similar*, if there is a bijection $\pi : \mathcal{N}_\mathcal{S}^m(A) \to \mathcal{N}_\mathcal{T}^m(B)$ such that

- the restriction of π to A is a bijection of A and B,
- π preserves τ_{rel} over $\mathcal{N}_\mathcal{S}^m(A)$, and
- π satisfies $\pi(t^\mathcal{S}(\bar{a})) = t^\mathcal{T}(\pi(\bar{a}))$ for all $t \in \text{TERMS}_\tau^m$ and $\bar{a}$ over A.

We write $A \approx_m^{\pi, \mathcal{S}, \mathcal{T}} B$ to indicate that A and B are m-similar via π in $\mathcal{S}$ and $\mathcal{T}$. The structures $\mathcal{S}$ and $\mathcal{T}$ are dropped from this notation if they are clear from the context, and π is dropped if the name is not important. We also write $(a_1, \ldots, a_p) \approx_m^{\mathcal{S}, \mathcal{T}} (b_1, \ldots, b_p)$ to indicate that $\{a_1, \ldots, a_p\} \approx_m^{\pi, \mathcal{S}, \mathcal{T}} \{b_1, \ldots, b_p\}$ via the isomorphism π that maps a_i to b_i, for every $i \in \{1, \ldots, p\}$. Note that if

$A \approx_0 B$, then $S \upharpoonright A$ and $T \upharpoonright B$ are τ_{rel}-isomorphic by the first and second property of similar subsets.

The relation $\approx_m^{\pi,S,T}$ is an equivalence relation on tuples. Its equivalence classes are called similarity types.

We now state the Substructure Lemma for DYNQF formally.

Lemma 4.2.4 (Substructure Lemma for DYNQF). *Let $\mathcal{P}$ be a DYNQF program and let ℓ be some number. There is a number $m \in \mathbb{N}$ such that for all states S and T of $\mathcal{P}$ with domains S and T; and all subsets A and B of S and T the following holds. If $A \approx_m^{\pi,S,T} B$, then $A \approx_0^{\pi,P_\alpha(S),P_\beta(T)} B$, for all π-respecting modification sequences α and β on A and B of length at most ℓ.*

Proof. The lemma follows by an induction over the length ℓ of the modification sequence. For $\ell = 0$ there is nothing to prove. The induction step follows easily using Claim (C) below.

Let k be the nesting depth of $\mathcal{P}$, and let $\delta(\bar{a})$ and $\delta(\bar{b})$ be two π-respecting modifications on A and B, respectively, i.e. $\bar{b} = \pi(\bar{a})$. Further let $S' \stackrel{\text{def}}{=} P_{\delta(\bar{a})}(S)$ and $T' \stackrel{\text{def}}{=} P_{\delta(\bar{b})}(T)$. We prove the following claims for arbitrary $r \in \mathbb{N}$:

(A) If $A \approx_{r+k}^{\pi,S,T} B$, then for all $\bar{c}$ over $\mathcal{N}_S^r(A)$:

  (i) $\bar{c} \in R^{S'}$ if and only if $\pi(\bar{c}) \in R^{T'}$ for all relation symbols $R \in \tau$.
  (ii) $f^{S'}(\bar{c}) \in \mathcal{N}_S^{r+k}(A)$ and $\pi(f^{S'}(\bar{c})) = f^{T'}(\pi(\bar{c}))$ for all function symbols $f \in \tau$.

(B) If $A \approx_{r \cdot k}^{\pi,S,T} B$, then $t^{S'}(\bar{c}) \in \mathcal{N}_S^{r \cdot k}(A)$ and $\pi(t^{S'}(\bar{c})) = t^{T'}(\pi(\bar{c}))$ for all terms $t \in \text{TERMS}_\tau^r$ and $\bar{c}$ over S.
(C) If $A \approx_{r \cdot k + k}^{\pi,S,T} B$, then $A \approx_r^{\pi,S',T'} B$.

We prove Claim (A) first. We recall that $\bar{c} \in R^{S'}$ if and only if $S \models \phi_\delta^R(\bar{a}; \bar{c})$, and that $f^{S'}(\bar{c})$ is $[\![t_\delta^f(\bar{x}; \bar{y})]\!]_{(S,\gamma)}$, where γ maps $(\bar{x}, \bar{y})$ to $(\bar{a}, \bar{c})$. Since $\bar{a}$ and $\bar{c}$ are tuples over $\mathcal{N}_S^r(A)$ it is sufficient to prove, for every tuple $\bar{d}$ over $\mathcal{N}_S^r(A)$, that (i) $\varphi(\bar{d})$ holds in S if and only if $\varphi(\pi(\bar{d}))$ holds in T, for every quantifier-free formula φ with nesting depth at most k, and that (ii) $\pi([\![t]\!]_{(S,\bar{d})}) = [\![t]\!]_{(T,\pi(\bar{d}))}$, for every update term t with nesting depth at most k. Here, we use $\bar{d}$ to denote the variable assignment mapping the free variables of t to the components of $\bar{d}$.

The proof is by induction on k. We start with the base case. If $k = 0$, terms and update terms do not use any function symbols and therefore, (i) and (ii) hold trivially, because π witnesses the $(r + k)$-similarity of A and B in S and T.

For the induction step, we consider update terms and update formulas with nesting depth $k' \in \{1, \ldots, k\}$. If an update term t with $d(t) = k'$ is of the form $f(\bar{s})$ with $\bar{s} = (s_1, \ldots, s_n)$, then, by induction hypothesis, $\pi([\![s_i]\!]_{(S,\bar{e}_i)}) = [\![s_i]\!]_{(T,\pi(\bar{e}_i))}$ and $s_i^S(\bar{e}_i) \in \mathcal{N}_S^{r+k'-1}(A)$ for every i and tuple $\bar{e}_i$ consisting of elements from $\bar{d}$. Thus, $\pi([\![f(\bar{s})]\!]_{(S,\bar{d})}) = [\![f(\bar{s})]\!]_{(T,\pi(\bar{d}))}$ because A and B are $(r + k)$-similar and $k' \leq k$. The other cases are analogous. This concludes the proof of Claim (A).

Claim (B) can be proved by an induction over the nesting depth of t. The induction step uses Claim (A ii).

For Claim (C) we have to prove that π is witnessing the r-similarity of A and B in $\mathcal{S}'$ and $\mathcal{T}'$. The first property of similarity is trivial. For the second property let $\bar{c}$ be an arbitrary m-tuple over $\mathcal{N}_A^r(\mathcal{S}')$ and R some m-ary relation symbol. Then $\bar{c} = (\llbracket t_1 \rrbracket_{(\mathcal{S}', \bar{c}_1)}, \ldots, \llbracket t_n \rrbracket_{(\mathcal{S}', \bar{c}_n)})$ with $\bar{c}_i$ over A and $t_i \in \text{TERMS}_\tau^r$. Thus $\bar{c}$ is a tuple over $\mathcal{N}_A^{r \cdot k}(\mathcal{S})$, by Claim (B), and therefore $R^{\mathcal{S}'}(\bar{c})$ if and only if $R^{\mathcal{T}'}(\pi(\bar{c}))$, by Claim (A). The third property follows from Claim (B).   □

The Substructure Lemma for DYNQF is applied along similar lines as the corresponding lemma for DYNPROP. In the next subsection we will see several examples of how to use the lemma to prove lower bounds.

4.2.2   Applying the Generalized Substructure Lemma

For applying the Substructure Lemma for DYNQF, it is essential to find structures with suitable similar substructures. In Sect. 4.1.2 several techniques for finding suitable isomorphic substructures have been exhibited. Here we extend those techniques for finding similar substructures.

Using Counting

The counting technique for obtaining isomorphic substructures relies on the finiteness of the set of isomorphism types of fixed arity. Hence, a natural approach towards finding suitable similar substructures, is to rely on the finiteness of the set of similarity types. Here we use a simplified form of this approach to extend the lower bound for invariant initialization from Proposition 4.1.8 to quantifier-free programs with auxiliary functions: we aim at finding structures where the similarity type and the isomorphism type of relevant substructures coincide. Then the counting technique can be applied in the same way as in Sect. 4.1.2.

Exhibiting substructures where isomorphism types and similarity types coincide relies on a weakness of invariant initialization, namely functions initialized by invariant initialization can only point to *distinguished* nodes as formalized by the following lemma.

Lemma 4.2.5. *Let* $\mathcal{P} = (P, \text{INIT}, Q)$ *be a* DYNQF-*program with invariant initialization mapping* INIT *and auxiliary schema* τ_{aux}. *Further let* $\mathcal{I}$ *be an input structure for* $\mathcal{P}$ *whose domain contains* b *and* b' *with* $b \neq b'$. *If* $id[b, b']$ *is an isomorphism of* $\mathcal{I}$, *then* $f^{\text{INIT}(\mathcal{I})}(\bar{a}) \neq b$ *for all* k-*ary function symbols* $f \in \tau_{aux}$ *and all* k-*tuples* $\bar{a}$.

Proof. The claim follows immediately from the invariance of the initialization mapping.   □

The following lemma will be useful for the proof of the next theorem. A subset A of S is *closed* if $\mathcal{N}_\mathcal{S}^1(A) = A$. Obviously $\mathcal{N}_\mathcal{S}^m(A) = A$ for closed sets A and for every m.

Lemma 4.2.6. *Let $\mathcal{P}$ be a* DYNQF *program and $\mathcal{S}$ and $\mathcal{T}$ be states of $\mathcal{P}$ with domains S and T. Further let $A \subseteq S$ and $B \subseteq T$ be closed. If $\mathcal{S} \upharpoonright A$ and $\mathcal{T} \upharpoonright B$ are isomorphic via π then $P_\alpha(\mathcal{S}) \upharpoonright A$ and $P_\beta(\mathcal{T}) \upharpoonright B$ are isomorphic via π for all π-respecting modification sequences α, β on A and B.*

Proof. Observe that when A and B are closed and $\mathcal{S} \upharpoonright A$ and $\mathcal{T} \upharpoonright B$ are isomorphic via π then A and B are k-similar via π for arbitrary k. Thus the claim follows from Lemma 4.2.4. □

The following proposition is slightly more precise than Theorem 4.2.1.

Proposition 4.2.7. *s-t-REACH cannot be maintained in* DYNQF *with invariant initialization mapping. This holds even for 1-layered s-t-graphs.*

Proof. We adapt the argumentation of the proof of Proposition 4.1.8.

Towards a contradiction, assume that $\mathcal{P}$ is a DYNQF-program with auxiliary schema τ_{aux} and invariant initialization mapping INIT which maintains the s-t-reachability query for 1-layered s-t-graphs. Let m be the maximum arity of relation or function symbols in $\tau_{\mathrm{aux}} \cup \{E\}$. Further let n be the number of isomorphism types of structures with at most $m + 2$ elements.

We consider the complete 1-layered s-t-graphs $G_i = (V_i, E_i)$, $2 \le i \le n + 2$, with $V_i = \{s, t\} \cup A_i$ and $A_i = \{a_1, \ldots, a_i\}$. Further let $\mathcal{S}_i = (V_i, E_i, \mathcal{A}_i)$ be the state obtained by applying INIT to G_i.

We observe that $id[a, a']$ is an automorphism of G_i for all pairs (a, a') of nodes in A_i with $a \ne a'$. Thus, by Lemma 4.2.5, s and t are the only values that the auxiliary functions in $\mathcal{S}_i$ can assume, and therefore $\mathcal{S}_i \upharpoonright A \cup \{s, t\}$ is closed for any subset A of A_i. Hence, by Lemma 4.2.6, it is sufficient to find $\mathcal{S}_k$ and $\mathcal{S}_\ell$ with $k < \ell$ such that $\mathcal{S}_k$ is isomorphic to $\mathcal{S}_\ell \upharpoonright V_k$. The contradiction can now be obtained as in the proof of Proposition 4.1.8. □

Lower bounds for k-clique and k-colorability (where k is fixed) can be established via reductions to the dynamic s-t-reachability query for shallow graphs.

Corollary 4.2.8. *k-CLIQUE, for $k \ge 2$, and k-COL, for $k \ge 1$, cannot be maintained in* DYNQF *with invariant initialization.*

Proof. We prove that 3-CLIQUE cannot be maintained in DYNQF with invariant initialization using a similar idea as in the proof of Proposition 4.1.16. Afterwards we sketch the proof for k-CLIQUE, for arbitrary $k \ge 3$. We remark that the result for 2-CLIQUE follows from a closer inspection of the proof of Proposition 4.2.7. The graphs used in the proof have a k-Clique if and only if they are not $(k - 1)$-colorable. Therefore it follows that k-COL cannot be maintained in DYNQF with invariant initialization mapping for $k \ge 1$.

More precisely, we show that from DYNQF dynamic program $\mathcal{P}'$ with invariant initialization that maintains 3-CLIQUE one can construct a dynamic program $\mathcal{P}'$ that maintains the s-t-reachability query for 1-layered s-t-graphs. As the latter does not exist thanks to Proposition 4.2.7, we can conclude that the former does not exist either.

Let us thus assume that $\mathcal{P}' = (P', \text{INIT}', Q')$ is a dynamic program for 3-CLIQUE with invariant initialization mapping INIT' and auxiliary schema τ'_{aux}.

We use the following simple reduction. For a 1-layered graph $G = (\{s, t\} \cup A, E)$, let G' be the graph obtained from G by adding an edge (s, t). Clearly, G has a path from s to t if and only if G' has a 3-clique.

The dynamic program $\mathcal{P}$ uses the same auxiliary schema as $\mathcal{P}'$ and the same initialization mapping. The update formulas of $\mathcal{P}$ are obtained from those in $\mathcal{P}'$ by replacing every atomic formula $E'(x, y)$ by $(E(x, y) \vee (x = s \wedge y = t))$. Obviously, $\mathcal{P}$ is a dynamic program for s-t-reachability for 2-layered s-t-graphs if $\mathcal{P}'$ is a dynamic program for 3-CLIQUE, as desired.

For arbitrary k, the construction is similar. The idea is that $\mathcal{P}$ simulates on a graph G the behavior of $\mathcal{P}'$ on $G \otimes (K_{k-3}, K_{k-3})$, that is, the graph that results from G by adding two $(k - 3)$-cliques and completely connecting them with every node of G. The update formulas of $\mathcal{P}$ are exactly as in the previous reduction to 3-CLIQUE. However, INIT is not the same as $\text{INIT}'(G)$ but rather the projection of $\text{INIT}'(G \otimes (K_{k-3}, K_{k-3}))$ to the nodes of G. By Lemma 4.2.5, auxiliary functions in $\text{INIT}(G)$ do not take values from (K_{k-3}, K_{k-3}). Thus $\mathcal{P}$ is a dynamic program for s-t-reachability for 2-layered s-t-graphs if $\mathcal{P}'$ is a dynamic program for k-CLIQUE.   □

Using Ramsey's Theorem

The method of finding suitable substructures using Ramsey's Theorem presented in Sect. 4.1.2 can be extended for finding suitable similar substructures. After formalizing a Ramsey-like statement for structures with functions, we will see how to obtain lower bounds for k-clique and reachability in quantifier-free fragments with unary functions.

The following notion will be useful in what follows. The *m-similarity type* of a k-ary tuple $\bar{a}$ is the atomic τ-type of the m-neighborhood tuple $\bar{\mathcal{N}}_S^m(\bar{a})$ of $\bar{a}$. Recall that also constants and their functional values are contained in $\bar{\mathcal{N}}_S^m(\bar{a})$. For fixed m, k and τ there are only finitely many similarity types. Observe that two tuples $\bar{a}$ and $\bar{b}$ with the same m-similarity type are m-similar. This is certified by the bijection that maps $\bar{\mathcal{N}}_S^m(\bar{a})$ to $\bar{\mathcal{N}}_S^m(\bar{b})$ component-wise.

The following analogon of Corollary 4.1.23 for structures with unary functions can be used to exhibit similar substructures. Recall that $\log^{(k)}(n)$ denotes $\log(\log(\dots (\log n) \dots))$ with k many log's.

Lemma 4.2.9. *Let τ be a k-ary schema whose function symbols are of arity at most 1; and let $m \in \mathbb{N}$ be an arbitrary number. Then there is a function $g \in \Omega(\log^{(k-1)}(n))$ such that for every τ-structure S with domain S and every linear order $\prec$ on S, there is a subset $S' \subseteq S$ of size $g(|S|)$ such that all $\prec$-ordered k-tuples over S' are m-similar.*

Proof. The idea is to construct, from the structure S, a purely relational structure T such that the type of a tuple $\bar{a}$ in T encodes the type of the whole m-neighborhood of $\bar{a}$ in S. Then Corollary 4.1.23 is applied to the structure T in order to obtain S'.

For the construction of T we assume, without loss of generality, that the schema of S contains the equality symbol $=$. Denote by Γ the set of all k-ary m-similarity types. The structure T is over the same domain as S and uses the schema τ_Γ which contains a k-ary relation R_γ for every k-ary similarity type $\gamma \in \Gamma$. A relation R_γ^T contains all tuples $\bar{a}$ whose similarity type in S is γ.

Then, by Corollary 4.1.23, T contains an $\prec$-ordered τ-clique S' of size Ω $(\log^{(k-1)}(|S|))$. We show that all $\prec$-ordered k-tuples over S' are m-similar in the structure S. Therefore let $\bar{a}$ and $\bar{b}$ be two such tuples. By definition of S' they have the same type in T and therefore, by definition of T, their neighborhood tuples $\bar{\mathcal{N}}_S^m(\bar{a})$ and $\bar{\mathcal{N}}_S^m(\bar{b})$ have the same type in S. Hence, by the observation from above, the tuples $\bar{a}$ and $\bar{b}$ are m-similar. $\square$

Now, we prove that unary DYNQF cannot maintain s-t-reachability. Unfortunately, reusing the method from Proposition 4.1.14 where a lower bound for s-t-reachability for unary DYNPROP on 1-layered s-t-graphs was obtained is not possible, since lists can be represented by unary functions in a straightforward way.

Proposition 4.2.10. *s-t-REACH on 1-layered s-t-graphs can be maintained in unary* DYNPROP *with unary built-in functions. In particular, s-t-REACH on 1-layered s-t-graphs can be maintained in unary* DYNQF.

Proof sketch. We construct a DYNQF*-program $\mathcal{P}$ over relational auxiliary schema $\{Q, \mathrm{ConS}, \mathrm{ConT}, C\}$ and functional built-in schema $\{\mathrm{PRED}, \mathrm{SUCC}\}$, where Q is the query bit (i.e. a 0-ary relation symbol), ConS, ConT and C are unary relation symbols and PRED and SUCC are unary function symbols.

The basic idea is to interpret elements of D as numbers according to their position in the graph of SUCC. For simplicity, but without loss of generality, we therefore assume that the domain is of the form $D = \{0, \ldots, n-1\}$ with $s = 0$ and $t = n - 1$. For every state S, the built-in function SUCC^S is then the standard successor function on D (with $\mathrm{SUCC}^S(n-1) = n - 1$) and PRED^S is its corresponding predecessor function (with $\mathrm{PRED}^S(0) = 0$).

The second idea is to store the current number i of vertices connected to both s and t by letting $C^S = \{i\}$. If an edge-insertion connects an element to s and t then i is replaced by $i + 1$ in C^S with the help of PRED^S and SUCC^S. Analogously i is replaced by $i - 1$ for edge-removals that disconnect an element from s or t. The relations ConS^S and ConT^S store the elements currently connected to s and t, respectively.

For a given instance of the s-t-reachability query on 1-layered s-t-graphs the initialization mapping initializes the auxiliary relations accordingly.

Insertion of (a, b) **into** E. If $a = s$ then node b is inserted into ConS; if $b = t$ then node a is inserted into ConT. Further, if a or b is now in both S and T then the counter is incremented by 1:

$$\phi_{\mathrm{INS}_E}^{\mathrm{ConS}}(a, b; x) \stackrel{\mathrm{def}}{=} (a = s \wedge x = b) \vee \mathrm{ConS}(x)$$

$$\phi_{\mathrm{INS}_E}^{\mathrm{ConT}}(a, b; x) \stackrel{\mathrm{def}}{=} (b = t \wedge x = a) \vee \mathrm{ConT}(x)$$

$$\phi_{\mathrm{INS}_E}^{C}(a, b; x) \stackrel{\mathrm{def}}{=} (a = s \wedge \mathrm{ConT}(b) \wedge C(\mathrm{PRED}(x)))$$
$$\vee (b = t \wedge \mathrm{ConS}(a) \wedge C(\mathrm{PRED}(x)))$$
$$\vee (a = s \wedge \neg\mathrm{ConT}(b) \wedge C(x))$$
$$\vee (b = t \wedge \neg\mathrm{ConS}(a) \wedge C(x))$$

$$\phi_{\mathrm{INS}_E}^{Q}(a, b) \stackrel{\mathrm{def}}{=} \neg\phi_{\mathrm{INS}_E}^{C}(a, b; s)$$

Deletions can be maintained in a similar way.   □

Intuitively, unary functions cannot store the transitive closure relation of a directed path in such a way that the information can be extracted by a quantifier-free formula. The proof is simplified by the following observation.

Lemma 4.2.11. *If an ℓ-ary query Q can be maintained by a k-ary DYNQF-program, then Q can be maintained by a k-ary DYNQF-program with only one ℓ-ary auxiliary relation (used for storing the query result) on databases with at least two elements.*

The restriction to structures with at least two elements is harmless, as we only use this lemma in a context where structures indeed have at least two elements.

Proof sketch. In order to encode relations by functions, two constants (i.e., 0-ary functions) $c_\perp$ and $c_\top$ are used. Those constants are initialized by two distinct elements of the domain. Then a k-ary relation R can be easily encoded by a k-ary function f_R via $(a_1, \ldots, a_k) \in R$ if and only if $f_R(a_1, \ldots, a_k) = c_\top$.   □

Now we will prove Theorem 4.2.2, which we restate for the convenience of the reader.

Theorem 4.2.2 **(R).** *s-t-REACH cannot be maintained in unary DYNQF.*

Proof. Towards a contradiction, we assume that $\mathcal{P} = (P, \mathrm{INIT}, Q)$ is a unary DYNQF-program that maintains s-t-reachability over schema $\tau = \tau_{\mathrm{inp}} \cup \tau_{\mathrm{aux}}$ with unary τ_{aux}. By Lemma 4.2.11 we can assume that τ_{aux} contains only 0-ary and unary function symbols and one 0-ary relation symbol Q for storing the query result. The graphs used in this proof do not have self-loops and every node has at most one outgoing edge. Therefore we can assume, in order to simplify the presentation, that τ contains a unary function symbol e, such that in every state $\mathcal{S}$ the function $e^{\mathcal{S}}$ encodes the edge relation E as follows. If the single outgoing edge from u is (u, v) then $e(u) = v$ and if u has no outgoing edge then $e(u) = u$.

Let n be chosen sufficiently large with respect to τ and $\mathcal{P}$. Let $G = (V, E)$ be a graph where $V = \{s, t\} \cup A$ with $A = \{a_1, \ldots, a_n\}$ and $E = \{(a_i, a_{i+1}) \mid i \in \{1, \ldots, n - 1\}\}$, i.e., $G \upharpoonright A$ is a path of length $n - 1$ from a_1 to a_n. Further, let $\mathcal{S} = (V, E, \mathcal{A})$ be the state obtained by applying INIT to G.

Our goal is to find i and j with $i < j$ such that $(a, b) \approx_m (b, a)$ holds for the two nodes $a \stackrel{\text{def}}{=} a_i$ and $b \stackrel{\text{def}}{=} a_j$, where m is the number from the Substructure Lemma for DYNQF, for modification sequences of length 2.

Then the Substructure Lemma for DYNQF implies that the program $\mathcal{P}$ computes the same query result for the following two modification sequences:

(β_1) Insert edges (s, a) and (b, t).
(β_2) Insert edges (s, b) and (a, t).

However, applying the modification sequence β_1 yields a graph in which t is reachable from s, whereas β_2 yields a graph in which t is not reachable from s (see Fig. 4.8 for an illustration). This is the desired contradiction.

Thus it remains to show the existence of such i and j. To this end, applying Lemma 4.2.9 yields numbers $i_1 < i_2 < i_3$ such that (a_{i_1}, a_{i_2}), (a_{i_1}, a_{i_3}) and (a_{i_2}, a_{i_3}) are $(m+1)$-similar. Our goal is to show that also (a_{i_1}, a_{i_2}) and (a_{i_2}, a_{i_1}) are m-similar.

Note that $\bar{\mathcal{N}}_{\mathcal{S}}^{m+1}(a_{i_1}, a_{i_2})$, $\bar{\mathcal{N}}_{\mathcal{S}}^{m+1}(a_{i_1}, a_{i_3})$ and $\bar{\mathcal{N}}_{\mathcal{S}}^{m+1}(a_{i_2}, a_{i_3})$ have the same atomic type because (a_{i_1}, a_{i_2}), (a_{i_1}, a_{i_3}) and (a_{i_2}, a_{i_3}) are $(m + 1)$-similar; and that it is sufficient to show that the atomic types of $\bar{\mathcal{N}}_{\mathcal{S}}^{m}(a_{i_1}, a_{i_2})$ and $\bar{\mathcal{N}}_{\mathcal{S}}^{m}(a_{i_2}, a_{i_1})$ are equal.

Let $\mathcal{S}'$ be the structure obtained by removing the relation E from $\mathcal{S}$. Recall that all information about E is encoded in the unary function e. As an intermediate step we show that the atomic types $\bar{\mathcal{N}}_{\mathcal{S}'}^{m+1}(a_{i_1}, a_{i_2})$ and $\bar{\mathcal{N}}_{\mathcal{S}'}^{m+1}(a_{i_2}, a_{i_1})$ are equal. The atomic types certainly agree on the only relation $Q^{\mathcal{S}'}$ of $\mathcal{S}'$. Thus it remains to verify that $\bar{\mathcal{N}}_{\mathcal{S}}^{m+1}(a_{i_1}, a_{i_2})$ and $\bar{\mathcal{N}}_{\mathcal{S}'}^{m+1}(a_{i_2}, a_{i_1})$ have the same equality type.

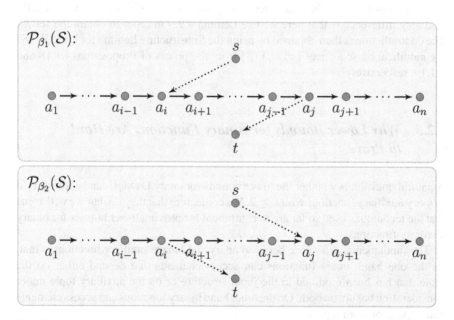

Fig. 4.8 The structures $\mathcal{P}_{\beta_1}(\mathcal{S})$ and $\mathcal{P}_{\beta_2}(\mathcal{S})$ from the proof of Theorem 4.2.2. Edges inserted by modification sequence β_1 and modification sequence β_2, respectively, are dotted.

To this end we show the following claim: if $t_1(a_{i_1}) = t_2(a_{i_2})$ holds for two terms t_1 and t_2 of depth at most $m + 1$, then also $t_1(a_{i_2}) = t_2(a_{i_1})$. We observe that if $t_1(a_{i_1}) = t_2(a_{i_2})$ then also $t_1(a_{i_1}) = t_2(a_{i_3})$ and $t_1(a_{i_2}) = t_2(a_{i_3})$ (since $\bar{\mathcal{N}}_{\mathcal{S}'}^{m+1}(a_{i_1}, a_{i_2})$, $\bar{\mathcal{N}}_{\mathcal{S}'}^{m+1}(a_{i_1}, a_{i_3})$, and $\bar{\mathcal{N}}_{\mathcal{S}'}^{m+1}(a_{i_2}, a_{i_3})$ have the same equality type). Hence, $t_1(a_{i_2}) = t_2(a_{i_2})$ and therefore $t_1(a_{i_2}) = t_2(a_{i_2}) = t_1(a_{i_1}) = t_2(a_{i_1})$. The latter equality follows as the equality types of $\bar{\mathcal{N}}_{\mathcal{S}'}^{m+1}(a_{i_1})$, and $\bar{\mathcal{N}}_{\mathcal{S}'}^{m+1}(a_{i_2})$ are equal. This concludes the proof of the claim.

To prove $\bar{\mathcal{N}}_{\mathcal{S}}^m(a_{i_1}, a_{i_2})$ and $\bar{\mathcal{N}}_{\mathcal{S}}^m(a_{i_2}, a_{i_1})$ it only remains to show that $(u, v) \in E$ if and only if $(u', v') \in E$, for two components u and v from $\bar{\mathcal{N}}_{\mathcal{S}}^m(a_{i_1}, a_{i_2})$ and their corresponding components u' and v' from $\bar{\mathcal{N}}_{\mathcal{S}}^m(a_{i_2}, a_{i_1})$. However, $(u, v) \in E$ if and only if $e(u) = v$, and analogously $(u', v') \in E$ if and only if $e(u') = v'$. Thus this claim follows already from the fact that $\bar{\mathcal{N}}_{\mathcal{S}}^{m+1}(a_{i_1}, a_{i_2}, s, t)$ and $\bar{\mathcal{N}}_{\mathcal{S}}^{m+1}(a_{i_2}, a_{i_1}, s, t)$ have the same equality type.   □

The lower bounds for k-clique and a $\exists^*\forall^*$FO-definable query, obtained in Propositions 4.1.18 and 4.1.19, respectively, can be generalized to DYNPROP with unary functions as well. For the convenience of the reader we restate the theorems.

Theorem 4.2.3 (R). *Under insertions, k-CLIQUE ($k \geq 3$) cannot be maintained in $(k - 2)$-ary DYNPROPwith unary auxiliary functions.*

Theorem 4.2.12. *There is a $\exists^*\forall^*$FO-definable query which cannot be maintained in DYNPROP with unary auxiliary functions.*

The proofs are along the same lines as the proofs of Propositions 4.1.18 and 4.1.19. The only difference is that here we use Lemma 4.2.9 in order to obtain the set A'. The contradiction is then obtained by using the Substructure Lemma for DYNQF and the modification sequences (α) and (β) from the proofs of Propositions 4.1.18 and 4.1.19, respectively.

4.2.3 Why Lower Bounds for Binary Functions Are Hard to Prove

A natural question is whether the lower bounds for unary DYNQF can be transferred to k-ary auxiliary functions with $k \geq 2$. We conjecture that they do, but we will argue that the techniques used so far are not sufficient for proving lower bounds for binary auxiliary functions.

The fundamental difference between unary and binary auxiliary functions is that, on the one hand, unary functions can access elements that depend either on the tuple that has been modified in the input structure or on the auxiliary tuple under consideration but not on both. On the other hand binary functions can access elements that depend on both tuples.

A consequence is that binary DYNQF can maintain every boolean graph property when the domain is large with respect to the actually used domain. We make this more precise. In the following we assume that all domains D are a disjoint union of a modifiable domain D^+ and a non-modifiable domain D^-, and that modifications may only involve tuples over D^+. Auxiliary data, however, may use the full domain. A dynamic complexity class C *profits from padding* if every boolean graph property can be maintained whenever the non-modifiable domain is sufficiently large in comparison to the modifiable domain[2].

Above we have seen that DYNPROP with unary auxiliary functions does not profit from padding.

Theorem 4.2.13. *Binary* DYNQF *profits from padding.*

Proof. First we show that ternary DYNQF profits from padding. Let Q be an arbitrary boolean graph property. In the following we construct a ternary DYNQF program $\mathcal{P}$ which maintains Q if $2^{|D^+|^2} = |D^-|$. The idea is to identify D^- with the set of all graphs over D^+, that is D^- contains an element c_G for every graph G over D^+. A unary relation R_Q stores those elements of D^- that correspond to graphs with the property Q. Finally the program maintains a pointer p to the element in D^- corresponding to the current graph over D^+. The pointer is updated upon edge modification by using ternary functions f_{INS} and f_{DEL} initialized by the initialization mapping in a suitable way.

The program $\mathcal{P}$ is over schema $\tau = \{Q, p, f_{\text{INS}}, f_{\text{DEL}}, R_Q\}$ where p is a constant, f_{INS} and f_{DEL} are ternary function symbols, R_Q is a unary relation symbol and Q is the designated query symbol.

We present the initialization mapping of $\mathcal{P}$ first. The initial state S for a graph H is defined as follows. The functions f_{INS} and f_{DEL} are independent of H and defined via

$$f^S_{\text{INS}}(a, b, c_G) = c_{G+(a,b)}$$
$$f^S_{\text{DEL}}(a, b, c_G) = c_{G-(a,b)}$$

for $a, b \in D^+$ and $c_G \in D^-$. For all other arguments the value of the functions is arbitrary. Here $G + (a, b)$ and $G - (a, b)$ denote the graphs obtained by adding the edge (a, b) to G and removing the edge (a, b) from G, respectively. The relation R^S_Q contains all c_G with $G \in Q$. Finally the constant p^S points to c_H.

It remains to exhibit the update formulas. After a modification, the pointer p is moved to the node corresponding to the modified graph, and the query bit is updated accordingly:

$$t^p_{\text{INS}}(u, v) = f_{\text{INS}}(u, v, p) \qquad t^Q_{\text{INS}}(u, v) = R_Q(f_{\text{INS}}(u, v, p))$$
$$t^p_{\text{DEL}}(u, v) = f_{\text{DEL}}(u, v, p) \qquad t^Q_{\text{DEL}}(u, v) = R_Q(f_{\text{DEL}}(u, v, p))$$

---

[2]Note that this type of padding differs from the padding technique used by Patnaik and Immerman for maintaining a PTIME-complete problem in DYNFO [PI97].

Now we sketch how to modify this construction for binary DYNQF. The binary DYNQF program maintains $\mathcal{Q}$ on an extended non-modifiable domain that contains

- an element c_G for every graph G over D^+, and
- elements $c_{G,a,\text{INS}}$ and $c_{G,a,\text{DEL}}$ for every graph G over D^+ and every $a \in D^+$.

The intuition is that when an edge (a, b) is inserted into the graph G then the pointer p is moved from c_G to the element $c_{G+(a,b)}$ using the intermediate element $c_{G,a,\text{INS}}$.

For insertion modifications the binary DYNQF program maintaining $\mathcal{Q}$ uses two binary functions f_{INS} and s_{INS} that are initialized as

$$f_{\text{INS}}^{\mathcal{S}}(a, c_G) = c_{G,a,\text{INS}}$$
$$s_{\text{INS}}^{\mathcal{S}}(b, c_{G,a,\text{INS}}) = c_{G+(a,b)}$$

for $a, b \in D^+$ and $c_G, c_{G,a,\text{INS}} \in D^-$. For all other arguments the value of the functions is arbitrary.

When an insertion occurs, the pointer and the query bit are updated via

$$t_{\text{INS}}^{p}(u, v) = s_{\text{INS}}(v, f_{\text{INS}}(u, p))$$
$$t_{\text{INS}}^{\mathcal{Q}}(u, v) = R_{\mathcal{Q}}(s_{\text{INS}}(v, f_{\text{INS}}(u, p)))$$

The update formulas and terms for deletions are analogous.   □

Hence the ability to profit from padding distinguishes binary DYNQF and DYNPROP extended by unary functions. Although the proof of the preceding theorem requires the non-modifiable domain to be of exponential size with respect to the modifiable domain, the construction also explains why the lower bound technique for k-clique cannot be immediately applied to binary DYNQF. In that lower bound construction only tuples over the set A are modified, while tuples containing elements from $C = [a]^k$ are not modified. Thus, by treating C as a non-modifiable domain, it can be used to store information as in the proof above. As the modification sequences used in the lower bounds are of length k^2, finding similar substructures in structures with binary auxiliary functions becomes much harder.

4.3 First-Order Update Programs

As argued in the introduction of this chapter, lower bounds for DYNFO are notoriously hard to prove. So far we have seen lower bounds for the syntactic restriction DYNPROP and for its extension by auxiliary functions. In this section we discuss several approaches for proving lower bounds for DYNFO.

The first approach to be discussed is the application of static lower bounds in order to obtain dynamic lower bounds. It is used in a straightforward way: assume that there is a DYNFO-program for some query and deduce a contradiction to a well-known static lower bound from this upper bound. In previous work, this approach has been applied successfully to prove, for example, that the transitive closure cannot be maintained using unary auxiliary relations as well as one binary auxiliary relation that stores the transitive closure [DS98, DLW03]; and that there is an arity hierarchy for dynamic programs with first-order updates [DS98]. Although both results employ quite different static lower bounds, the underlying technique is the same. We will make this technique explicit by introducing the notion of a query being *expressible with help relations*. Then, looking from this perspective, we will reprove the above results and the following small new result.

Theorem 4.3.1. *There is a context-free language that cannot be maintained in unary* DYNFO.

This theorem is joint work with Nils Vortmeier and already appeared in his master's thesis [Vor13], though with a different proof.

Two new approaches towards lower bounds for DYNFO will be discussed in detail. The first employs simulation in order to separate dynamic complexity classes from static complexity classes. We outline how it can be used to obtain lower bounds for DYNFO with restricted initialization settings. The second approach uses a weakness in the original initialization setting of Patnaik and Immerman to prove lower bounds in this setting for several queries. Unfortunately the lower bounds proved with these two approaches are not very strong. Yet we hope that the approaches can be used to obtain better lower bounds in the future.

While working on lower bounds for DYNFO we also tried to employ Ehrenfeucht-Fraïssé-like games. Ehrenfeucht-Fraïssé games played a major role for standardizing inexpressibility proofs for (static) logics. In particular, they can be used for proving that a property cannot be expressed on finite structures (see [Lib04] for a very accessible introduction to those games). Therefore it is natural, to try to develop an Ehrenfeucht-Fraïssé-like game for dynamic complexity. One such attempt has been made by Stephan Kreutzer, Thomas Schwentick, Sebastian Siebertz and the author. Unfortunately, so far the game has not been used for obtaining new lower bounds. Most lower bounds from the literature can be proved using the game, though only in the weak setting of history-independent dynamic programs. For details on this method we refer to Nils Vortmeier's master's thesis [Vor13] which also contains several example applications.

The rest of this section is structured as follows. In the next subsection, we present a unified perspective on dynamic lower bounds relying on static lower bounds. Afterwards, in Subsect. 4.3.2, we explain the two approaches for proving lower bounds for restricted initialization settings.

4.3.1 Applying Static Lower Bound Methods

As already mentioned in the introduction of this chapter, several techniques for proving lower bounds in the static setting are available. Most dynamic lower bounds for DYNFO have been proved drawing on those techniques. In this subsection we present a unified view on how to prove dynamic lower bounds by falling back to static lower bound results.

Most of the lower bounds for DYNFO found in the literature are captured by this unified perspective. A notable exception is the technique used by Grädel and Siebertz in [GS12] for proving lower bounds for DYNFO with logical initialization. However, also those results are shown by falling back to methods for proving inexpressibility results for first-order logic.

The basic idea for establishing many dynamic lower bounds for DYNFO is to infer a contradiction to a known static lower bound from a hypothetic dynamic upper bound. More precisely, the fact that a query $\mathcal{Q}_{\text{static}}$ is not expressible (with help relations) in some fragment of first-order logic is used to obtain a dynamic lower bound by showing that if there was a dynamic program for a particular query $\mathcal{Q}_{\text{dynamic}}$, then $\mathcal{Q}_{\text{static}}$ would be expressible. The unified view presented here makes this idea explicit.

The following notion captures the essence of the technique. A query $\mathcal{Q}$ over schema τ is *expressible with help relations*[3] by a formula φ over schema $\tau \cup \tau_{\text{help}}$ if for every τ-structure $\mathcal{S}$ there is a τ_{help}-structure $\mathcal{S}_{\text{help}}$ over the same domain such that $\text{ANS}(\mathcal{Q}, \mathcal{S}) = \text{ANS}(\varphi, (\mathcal{S}, \mathcal{S}_{\text{help}}))$. The schema τ_{help} is called *helping schema*.

Observe that every k-ary query can be expressed by using a single k-ary help relation. We will use inexpressibility results where a k-ary query cannot be expressed using k'-ary help relations for $k' < k$.

In the following we present three example applications that obtain dynamic lower bounds by relying on static lower bounds for the expressibility with help relations. In each of those applications we will first sketch a proof of the static lower bound, and then show how it can be used to prove a dynamic lower bound.

The first example is that the transitive closure of a binary relation R cannot be maintained in unary DYNFO. We follow the argument of Dong, Libkin and Wong [DLW03]; yet we make the use of a query which is not expressible with help relations explicit.

A graph (V, E) is a simple path if $V = \{v_1, \ldots v_n\}$ and $E = \{(v_{i_1}, v_{i_2}), (v_{i_2}, v_{i_3}), \ldots (v_{i_{n-1}}, v_{i_n})\}$ where all i_j are pairwise distinct.

Lemma 4.3.2. *The transitive closure of simple paths cannot be expressed by a first-order formula with unary help relations.*

Proof sketch. This follows from a standard locality argument, similar to the argument that reachability is not expressible in monadic, existential second-order logic, see, e.g., [Lib04, Proposition 7.14]. We only give a very rough proof sketch.

Assume that there is a first-order formula φ that expresses the transitive closure of simple paths using unary help relations. The unary help relations can be seen as a coloring of the nodes of a graph. Now, in a very long colored path one can

---

[3]We note that this notion differs from the notion of describability introduced in Sect. 3.1. Help relations can depend on the whole structure whereas for describability the additional relations may only depend on the domain.

find two nodes whose neighborhoods have the same color-pattern. Those two nodes cannot be distinguished by φ if the neighborhoods are large enough; and therefore the transitive closure cannot be expressed for such paths, even in the presence of unary help relations.   □

Theorem 4.3.3. *Transitive closure cannot be maintained in unary* DYNFO *with a binary designated query relation.*

Proof. Assume that there is a unary DYNFO-program $\mathcal{P}$ that maintains the transitive closure of a graph in the designated query relation T. We claim that from $\mathcal{P}$ one can construct a first-order formula φ that expresses the transitive closure of simple paths using unary help relations. This contradicts the preceding lemma.

Let $G = (V, E)$ be a simple path with first node u and last node v. Consider the graph $G' \stackrel{\text{def}}{=} G + (v, u)$ and let $\mathcal{S}_{G'}$ be a state with input database G' which is reachable by $\mathcal{P}$. Then $T^{\mathcal{S}_{G'}}$ is exactly V^2. Observe that u, v and V^2 are first-order definable for simple paths, and let $\varphi_{\text{first}}(x)$, $\varphi_{\text{last}}(x)$ and $\varphi_{V^2}(x, y)$ be first-order formulas that define the relations $\{u\}$, $\{v\}$ and V^2 for simple paths.

When removing the edge (v, u) from G' the update formula $\phi^T_{\text{DEL}_E}$ defines the transitive closure of G, because $\mathcal{P}$ maintains the transitive closure of E. Thus the formula φ can be constructed from $\phi^T_{\text{DEL}_E}$, by simulating the removal of edge (v, u) from $G + (v, u)$.

More precisely, the formula φ uses helping schema $\tau_{\text{help}} \stackrel{\text{def}}{=} \tau_{\text{aux}}$ and is defined by

$$\varphi(x, y) \stackrel{\text{def}}{=} \exists u \exists v \left(\varphi_{\text{first}}(u) \wedge \varphi_{\text{last}}(v) \wedge \psi^T_{\text{DEL}_E}(v, u; x, y) \right)$$

where $\psi^T_{\text{DEL}_E}$ is obtained from $\phi^T_{\text{DEL}_E}$ by substituting literals $T(w_1, w_2)$ by $\varphi_{V^2}(w_1, w_2)$ and literals $E(w_1, w_2)$ by $E(w_1, w_2) \vee (w_1 = v \wedge w_2 = u)$. The help relations for a graph G are the corresponding auxiliary relations in $\mathcal{S}_{G'}$.   □

In a similar way one can show that there is a context-free language that cannot be maintained in unary DYNFO. This example has previously appeared in the master's thesis of Vortmeier [Vor13, Satz 5.2] though with a different proof. It should be contrasted with Hesse's result that all regular languages can be maintained in unary DYNFO [Hes03b], and with the result by Gelade, Marquardt and Schwentick that all context-free languages can be maintained in 4-ary DYNFO [GMS12] (see also Sect. 2.6).

Lemma 4.3.4. *The following binary query* $\mathcal{Q}_{\text{dist}}$ *over linearly ordered structures* $(D, <)$ *cannot be expressed by a first-order formula with unary help relations. The query* $\mathcal{Q}_{\text{dist}}$ *selects, for all k, the tuple (a, b) such that a is the kth and b is the k-last element with respect to $<$.*

Proof sketch. The argument is again a standard locality argument and very similar to the argument from Lemma 4.3.2. Assume that there is a first-order formula φ that expresses $\mathcal{Q}_{\text{dist}}$ using unary help relations. Again we interpret the unary help relations as a coloring of the elements of the domain. If the domain is large enough, then there are two elements a_1 and a_2 such that a_1 and a_2 are in the first third of D with respect to $<$ and large neighborhoods of a_1 and a_2 have the same color-pattern.

Suppose that a_1 is the kth element of D. Let b be the k-last element of D. Since D is large and a_1 and a_2 are in the first third of D, all three elements a_1, a_2 and b are far apart with respect to $<$. Hence the pairs (a_1, b) and (a_2, b) cannot be distinguished by φ, but (a_1, b) is in $\mathrm{ANS}(\mathcal{Q}_{\mathrm{dist}}, (D, <))$ while (a_2, b) is not. □

Theorem 4.3.1 (R). *There is a context-free language that cannot be maintained in unary* DYNFO.

Proof sketch. We show that the language of palindromes

$$L_{\mathrm{pali}} \stackrel{\mathrm{def}}{=} \{ww^R \mid w \in \{a, b\}^*\}$$

cannot be maintained in unary DYNFO. Recall that strings are encoded by structures with a linear order $<$ (representing the order on the positions) and two unary relations A and B (representing the letters a and b).

Assume that $\mathcal{P}$ is a unary DYNFO-program that maintains L_{pali} using auxiliary schema τ_{aux}. From $\mathcal{P}$ a formula φ can be constructed that expresses $\mathcal{Q}_{\mathrm{dist}}$ using unary help relations:

$$\varphi(x, y) \stackrel{\mathrm{def}}{=} \psi^{\mathcal{Q}}_{\mathrm{INS}_B \mathrm{INS}_B}(x, y)$$

Here the formula $\psi^{\mathcal{Q}}_{\mathrm{INS}_B \mathrm{INS}_B}(x, y)$ simulates the computation of the new query bit of $\mathcal{P}$ after inserting the letter b at position x and position y. Furthermore every occurrence of a literal $A(x)$ is replaced by $\top$.

The unary help relations for φ for a structure $(D, <)$ are the unary auxiliary relations of $\mathcal{P}$ for the initial state for the word $a^{|D|}$. The formula φ expresses $\mathcal{Q}_{\mathrm{dist}}$ with unary help relations. This contradicts the preceding lemma. □

A slightly different example for the help-relation technique relies on a circuit lower bound due to Cai [Cai90]. Using this circuit bound, one can show that, for every k, a certain k-ary query over a $6k$-ary schema cannot be expressed with help relations of arity $k - 1$. This static lower bound for expressivity is used for obtaining an arity hierarchy for DYNFO in a similar way as in the preceding theorems. An analogous result for FOIES has already been proved by Dong and Su in [DS98] where it was attributed to Peter Bro Miltersen. We follow their argument, but explicitly use a query which is not expressible with help relations.

The following theorem states the circuit lower bound to be used; its formulation is from [DS98].

Theorem 4.3.5 [Cai90]. *Let $m \in \mathbb{N}$ and let $X = \{x_{ij} \mid 1 \le i \le m, 1 \le j \le m^5\}$ be a set of Boolean variables. Further let C be a circuit of depth d with unbounded fan-in that computes the m parity functions $x_{i1} \oplus \ldots \oplus x_{im^5}$ for every $1 \le i \le m$. Assume further that C also takes as input $m - 1$ arbitrary precomputed values, called help bits, which can depend on the values of the variables in X in any desired way. Then the circuit C must have size $\ge 2^{m^c}$ where c is a constant depending on d.*

The help bits in the statement of the theorem play a similar role as help relations. Therefore it is not surprising that Cai's theorem has a formulation in terms of expressibility with help relations.

For $k \in \mathbb{N}$ let $\mathcal{Q}_k$ be the k-ary query defined over a $6k$-ary relation symbol S as follows. For every $\{S\}$-structure $\mathcal{S}$, the result $\text{ANS}(\mathcal{Q}_k, \mathcal{S})$ of $\mathcal{Q}_k$ contains all k-ary tuples $\bar{a}$ such that the number of $5k$-ary tuples $\bar{b}$ with $(\bar{a}, \bar{b}) \in R^{\mathcal{S}}$ is divisible by 2.

Corollary 4.3.6. *Let $k \in \mathbb{N}$. There is no first-order formula φ that expresses $\mathcal{Q}_k$ with $(k - 1)$-ary help relations.*

Proof sketch. Assume, towards a contradiction, that there is such a first-order formula φ over schema $\{S\} \cup \tau_{\text{help}}$ where τ_{help} is $(k - 1)$-ary. One can easily construct a polynomial-size constant-depth circuit family $(C_i)_{i \in \mathbb{N}}$ that evaluates φ.

For evaluating φ over domains of size n, the circuit C_N with $N \stackrel{\text{def}}{=} n^{6k} + |\tau_{\text{help}}| \cdot n^{k-1}$ input bits is used, where n^{6k} bits $X = \{x_{ij} \mid 1 \leq i \leq m, 1 \leq j \leq m^5\}$ are used to encode the relation S and $|\tau_{\text{help}}| \cdot n^{k-1}$ bits are used to encode the relations from τ_{help}. Here we assume, without loss of generality, that all $S \in \tau_{\text{help}}$ are of arity $k - 1$.

Let $S^{\mathcal{S}}$ be the relation corresponding to a valuation v of X. Then using the encoding of the help relations for $S^{\mathcal{S}}$ as help bits, the circuit C_N computes the m parity functions $x_{i1} \oplus \ldots \oplus x_{im^5}$ for the valuation v. Let c be the constant from Cai's theorem depending on the depth of the family $(C_i)_{i \in \mathbb{N}}$.

One can find an n large enough such that for $m \stackrel{\text{def}}{=} n^k$ the number $|\tau_{\text{help}}| \cdot n^{k-1}$ of help bits needed by C_N is smaller than m, and the size of the circuit C_N is less than 2^{m^c}. This contradicts Cai's theorem. $\square$

The following theorem is basically from [DS98]. We state a slightly generalized variant for boolean queries.

Theorem 4.3.7 [DS98]. *Let $k \geq 2$. There is a boolean query over a $(6k + 1)$-ary schema that can be maintained in k-ary DYNFO, but not in $(k - 1)$-ary DYNFO. In particular, DYNFO has a strict arity hierarchy.*

Proof. We first exhibit a k-ary query $\mathcal{Q}'_k$ such that $\mathcal{Q}'_k$ is in k-ary DYNFO but not in $(k - 1)$-ary DYNFO with a k-ary designated query relation. The latter will be shown by assuming the existence of such a DYNFO-program, and constructing from this a first-order formula φ that expresses $\mathcal{Q}_k$ using $(k - 1)$-ary help relations. This contradicts the preceding corollary. Afterwards we present a boolean query $\mathcal{Q}''_k$ that satisfies the theorem statement.

The k-ary query $\mathcal{Q}'_k$ is very similar to the query $\mathcal{Q}_k$. It is defined over a $(6k + 1)$-ary relation symbol T and $\text{ANS}(\mathcal{Q}'_k, \mathcal{T})$ contains, for every $\{T\}$-structure $\mathcal{T}$, all k-ary tuples $\bar{a}$ such that the number of $(5k + 1)$-ary tuples $\bar{b}$ with $(\bar{a}, \bar{b}) \in T^{\mathcal{T}}$ is divisible by 4.

Towards a contradiction, assume that $\mathcal{Q}'_k$ can be maintained by a $(k - 1)$-ary DYNFO-program $\mathcal{P}$ with designated query relation Q. Let $\mathcal{S}$ be a $\{S\}$-structure over a domain D that contains at least four distinguished elements $\{c_1, c_2, c_3, c_4\}$ (for simplicity we assume that $\mathcal{P}$ stores them in constants of the same name). Consider a state $\mathcal{T}$ of $\mathcal{P}$ over domain D reachable by $\mathcal{P}$ where T is interpreted as follows:

$$T^{\mathcal{T}} = D^k \times \{c_1\}^{5k+1} \cup \{(\bar{d}, c_2), (\bar{d}, c_3) \mid \bar{d} \in S^{\mathcal{S}}\}$$

Then for each k-ary tuple $\bar{a}$, the number of $(5k+1)$-ary tuples $\bar{b}$ such that $(\bar{a}, \bar{b}) \in T^{\mathcal{T}}$ is either 1 or 3 modulo 4. It is 1 modulo 4 if the number of $5k$-ary tuples $\bar{b}'$ with $(\bar{a}, \bar{b}') \in S^{\mathcal{S}}$ is even, and it is 3 modulo 4 otherwise.

The following observation is crucial. The answer of $\mathcal{Q}'_k$ for the tuple $\bar{a}$ after inserting the tuple $(\bar{a}, c_4, \ldots, c_4)$ into $T^{\mathcal{T}}$ is exactly the negation of the answer given by $\mathcal{Q}_k$ for $\bar{a}$ evaluated on the structure $\mathcal{S}$. This can be used to define a formula φ that expresses $\mathcal{Q}_k$ with $(k-1)$-ary help relations from the update formula $\phi^Q_{\mathrm{INS}_T}$.

To this end we note that the construction of $T^{\mathcal{T}}$ from $S^{\mathcal{S}}$ as described above is first-order definable. Let $\varphi_T(\bar{x})$ be a $(6k+1)$-ary formula over schema $\{S, c_1, c_2, c_3, c_4\}$ that defines T from S.

Then $\mathcal{Q}_k$ can be expressed by the $\{S\}$-formula

$$\varphi(\bar{x}) \stackrel{\mathrm{def}}{=} \neg \psi^Q_{\mathrm{INS}_T}(\bar{x}, c_4, \ldots, c_4; \bar{x})$$

where $\psi^Q_{\mathrm{INS}_T}$ is obtained from $\phi^Q_{\mathrm{INS}_T}$ by substituting literals $T(\bar{x})$ by $\varphi_T(\bar{x})$. The help relations for φ are obtained from the corresponding auxiliary relations in $T^{\mathcal{T}}$. The constants $c_1, \ldots, c_4$ can be removed from φ by using additional unary help relations.

As the formula φ contradicts the preceding corollary, the query $\mathcal{Q}'_k$ is not maintainable by a $(k-1)$-ary DYNFO-program with a k-ary designated query relation.

Now we exhibit a boolean query $\mathcal{Q}''_k$ over a $(6k+1)$-ary schema which is not maintainable by a $(k-1)$-ary DYNFO-program. The query $\mathcal{Q}''_k$ is over schema $\{T, U_1, \ldots, U_k\}$ where T is a $(6k+1)$-ary relation symbol and all U_i are unary relation symbols. If, in a structure $\mathcal{S}$, each of the relations $U_i^{\mathcal{S}}$ contains exactly one element u_i, then $\mathcal{Q}''_k$ evaluates to true if and only if the tuple $(u_1, \ldots, u_k)$ is contained in the result of $\mathcal{Q}'_k$ on $T^{\mathcal{S}}$. If one of the relations $U_i^{\mathcal{S}}$ does not contain exactly one element, then the result of $\mathcal{Q}''_k$ is false.

The query $\mathcal{Q}''_k$ can be easily maintained by a k-ary DYNFO program by maintaining the query result for $\mathcal{Q}'_k$ by counting modulo 4 for every k-ary tuple; and extracting the result for $(u_1, \ldots, u_m)$ (if all those u_i exist and are unique).

On the other hand, it is easy to see that from a $(k-1)$-ary DYNFO-program $\mathcal{P}''$ for $\mathcal{Q}''_k$, a $(k-1)$-ary program $\mathcal{P}'$ for $\mathcal{Q}'_k$ with k-ary designated query symbol can be constructed. The program $\mathcal{P}'$ maintains all auxiliary relations of $\mathcal{P}''$ using their respective update formulas from $\mathcal{P}''$, under the assumption that the relations $U_1, \ldots, U_k$ are empty (those relations are not present in $\mathcal{P}'$). Additionally it maintains the k-ary designated query relation Q' as follows. If a tuple is inserted into or deleted from T, then in order to determine whether a tuple $\bar{x} = (x_1, \ldots, x_k)$ is in Q', the update formula for Q' simulates inserting $x_1, \ldots, x_k$ into $U_1, \ldots, U_k$, respectively, using the update formulas of $\mathcal{P}''$. The tuple $\bar{x}$ is contained in Q' if and only if the value of the query relation Q'' of $\mathcal{P}''$ after this insertion sequence is true. The detailed construction is straightforward though tedious. This is a contradiction to the lower bound for $\mathcal{Q}'_k$ proved above. Hence $\mathcal{Q}''_k$ cannot be maintained by a $(k-1)$-ary DYNFO-program.   □

4.3.2 Two Approaches for Restricted Initializations

Two approaches aimed at proving lower bounds for DYNFO will be discussed in this subsection. One of them is based on simulating dynamic programs by algorithms, the other is based on finding a property which is satisfied by all queries maintained by some fragment of DYNFO but which is not satisfied by certain queries. The simulation-based approach is inspired by a remark by William Hesse. He proposed to use diagonalization to separate static from dynamic complexity classes.

Most lower bounds in the dynamic world so far have been proved for fragments of DYNFO obtained by either restricting the arity of the auxiliary relations or by restricting first-order update formulas syntactically. Both approaches to be presented here are exemplary used to prove lower bounds for DYNFO with restricted initialization settings instead.

Some prior work on restricted initializations has been done. Grädel and Siebertz showed that the equal cardinality query for two unary relations is not in DYNFO when the initial input database can be arbitrary and the initialization for the auxiliary database is defined by some logical formalism [GS12]. This lower bound strongly depends on the restriction of the initialization. In Sects. 4.1 and 4.2 we have seen further lower bounds for restricted initializations though for quantifier-free dynamic programs only.

The two approaches presented here will be applied to the original initialization setting of Patnaik and Immerman, where queries are maintained from scratch using first-order update formulas. Recall that a program maintains a query from scratch if it starts from an initially empty input database and from auxiliary relations initialized by first-order formulas.

Simulating Dynamic Programs

Every query Q maintained by some DYNFO-program P from scratch, can also be evaluated by a polynomial time algorithm. Given some domain and database over that domain, such an algorithm can simply simulate P for the modification sequence that inserts all tuples from the database into an initially empty database. It starts by initializing the auxiliary relations by evaluating the initialization formulas, and then updates the auxiliary relations by evaluating the update formulas for every modification. This can be achieved in time $O(n^\ell)$ for some $\ell \in \mathbb{N}$ where we assume that the input size n is the sum of the size of the domain and the amount of space necessary to store the database. The constant ℓ depends, among others, on the arity of P. Hence DYNFO with initialization from scratch is contained in PTIME.

A natural follow-up question is whether this containment is strict. If all such programs could be simulated in time $O(n^\ell)$ for some uniform $\ell \in \mathbb{N}$ then this would indeed be the case: the time hierarchy theorem guarantees the existence of a query that can be computed in time $O(n^{\ell+1})$ but not in time $O(n^\ell)$. Unfortunately a simulation with uniform time bound $O(n^\ell)$ is not possible in a naïve way since the arity of DYNFO-programs is not bounded.

The approach, however, works for space-restricted complexity classes. In the following we will see that every query that can be maintained by a DYNFO-program from scratch can be evaluated by an $O(n^\ell)$-space algorithm for some $\ell \in \mathbb{N}$ where ℓ depends not on the DYNFO-program at hand. The space hierarchy theorem then implies that DYNFO with this kind of initialization is strictly contained in PSPACE. After proving the following theorem, we shortly discuss the limits of this approach.

Theorem 4.3.8. *There is an $\ell \in \mathbb{N}$ such that every query that can be maintained by a DYNFO-program from scratch can be evaluated by an $O(n^\ell)$-space algorithm.*

Proof. We exhibit an algorithm for the following slightly more general evaluation problem for a DYNFO-program $\mathcal{P}$: Given a domain D, a modification sequence α on D, a relation symbol R from $\mathcal{P}$ and a tuple $\bar{d}$ over D of the same arity as R. Is $\bar{d} \in R^\mathcal{S}$ where $\mathcal{S} \overset{\text{def}}{=} \mathcal{P}_\alpha(\mathcal{S}_0)$ and $\mathcal{S}_0$ is the initial state for domain D?

Recall that the combined complexity of the evaluation problem for first-order logic is in PSPACE. The standard recursive evaluation algorithm for first-order logic does, however, not immediately yield a uniform polynomial space-bound for evaluating DYNFO-programs. Naïve evaluation of a DYNFO-program $\mathcal{P}$ for a given modification sequence uses $|D|^k$ space for storing the auxiliary relations, where k is the largest arity of an auxiliary relation occurring in $\mathcal{P}$. Since the arity of dynamic programs is not bounded, this yields no uniform space-bound.

Yet a well-known trick for space-bounded algorithms can be applied. Instead of storing the auxiliary relations explicitly, the algorithm can recompute an auxiliary bit when necessary. The idea is as follows. For evaluating whether a tuple $\bar{d}$ is in a relation R after application of a modification sequence $\alpha = \alpha_1 \ldots \alpha_m$ with $\alpha_i = \delta_i(\bar{a}_i)$, the algorithm starts to evaluate $\phi^R_{\delta_m}(\bar{a}_m; \bar{d})$. The evaluation is with respect to the state $\mathcal{S}_{m-1}$ reached by $\mathcal{P}$ after application of $\alpha_1 \ldots \alpha_{m-1}$. Whenever the evaluation requires to know whether a tuple $\bar{d}'$ is contained in some relation R' in state $\mathcal{S}_{m-1}$, the formula $\phi^{R'}_{\delta_{m-1}}$ is evaluated recursively for $(\bar{a}_{m-1}, \bar{d}')$.

This idea is made precise in Algorithm 2. The procedure EVAL$_\mathcal{P}$ implements the actual evaluation algorithm for a DYNFO-program $\mathcal{P}$. For empty modification sequences the procedure returns the value of the initialization mapping, which can be obtained by application of the standard evaluation algorithm EVAL$_{\text{FO}}$. For all other sequences the evaluation is delegated to the procedure EVAL$'_{\text{FO}}$, that evaluates the update formula corresponding to the last modification in the modification sequence. The evaluation of the update formula is done as in the usual evaluation of first-order formulas, except that required information about the structure is computed by recursive calls to EVAL$_\mathcal{P}$.

The correctness of the algorithm can be shown by a straightforward induction over the length of modification sequences.

We show that for every DYNFO-program $\mathcal{P}$ the algorithm uses $O(m|D|)$ space. To this end, we first argue that the call tree of EVAL$_\mathcal{P}$ for evaluating a modification sequence α of length m is of depth at most cm for some constant c that depends on $\mathcal{P}$ only. The procedure EVAL$_\mathcal{P}$ is called at most m times in every branch of the call tree. Furthermore, the procedure EVAL$'_{FO}$ is called at most once from each invocation of EVAL$_\mathcal{P}$. The number of successive recursive calls of EVAL$'_{FO}$ (without a call of EVAL$_\mathcal{P}$ in between) can be at most c' for some constant c' that depends on the update

---

Algorithm 2. A PSPACE-algorithm for evaluating a DYNFO-program $\mathcal{P}$. Here $\alpha = \alpha_1 \ldots \alpha_m$ with $\alpha_i = \delta_i(\bar{a}_i)$ is a modification sequence on a domain D; R is a relation symbol from $\mathcal{P}$; and $\bar{d}$ is a tuple over D of the same arity as R.

```
1: procedure EVALₚ(α, R, d̄)
2:      ▷ Evaluates whether d̄ is in relation R after applying α.
3:      if |α| = 0 then
4:          Return INIT(R, d̄).
5:      else
6:          Return EVAL'FO(φᴿ_δₘ, (āₘ, d̄), δ₁(ā₁)...δₘ₋₁(āₘ₋₁))
7:      end if
8: end procedure
9: procedure EVAL'FO(φ, ā, α)
10:     ▷ Evaluates whether ā satisfies φ after applying α.
11:     if φ(x₁, ..., xₗ) = R'(xᵢ₁, ..., xᵢₗ') then
12:         Assume ā = (a₁, ..., aₗ)
13:         Let d̄' ≝ (aᵢ₁, ..., aᵢₗ')
14:         Return EVALₚ(α, R', d̄')
15:     else if φ = ¬ψ then
16:         Return NOT EVAL'FO(ψ, d̄, α)
17:     else if ... then
18:         ... (All other cases are as in the standard FO-evaluation
19:             algorithm.)
20:     end if
21: end procedure
```

---

formulas of $\mathcal{P}$. Each branch of the call tree ends with at most c'' additional calls for the evaluation of an initialization formula of $\mathcal{P}$ where c'' is some constant that, again, only depends on $\mathcal{P}$. Hence all in all the depth of the call tree of EVALₚ is at most $c'' + c'm$ and therefore of the form cm for some c.

We now argue that only one branch has to be stored and that each node of a branch can be stored in a linear amount of space. Observe that all branches are independent, that is, after computing the result of a branch starting from a node v of the call tree, it is sufficient to store the result in node v and proceed with the next branch starting from v. Therefore at every point of time, the algorithm stores at most one branch of the call tree and each node of this branch stores at most one tuple $\bar{a}$ of domain elements. The arity of $\bar{a}$ is bounded by a constant d that only depends on $\mathcal{P}$. Thus the algorithm uses space $O(m|D|)$ for every program $\mathcal{P}$.

For evaluating a query $\mathcal{Q}$ maintained from scratch by a DYNFO-program $\mathcal{P}$, the procedure EVALₚ is called for the modification sequence that inserts all tuples of a given database. Thus this sequence is of length at most n where n is the sum of the size of the domain and the amount of space necessary to store the database. Therefore $\mathcal{Q}$ can be evaluated in space $O(n^2)$.   □

The theorem also holds for other initialization settings as long as the initialization can be computed in the given space bound. Thus, for example, if the initialization mapping may use $O(|D|^\ell)$ space to compute one bit of the auxiliary data, then the same proof goes through.

The simulation-based approach, however, has two drawbacks. First, presumably, for DYNFO only separation from PSPACE can be proved. A uniform $O(n^\ell)$-time bound for simulating DYNFO-programs would yield a $O(n^\ell)$-time algorithm for the evaluation problem for first-order formulas with combined complexity. Yet this problem is PSPACE-complete, and therefore such a time bound is very unlikely. Second, as we will see in the next part of this subsection, the separation of DYNFO from PSPACE can also be obtained much easier for the initialization setting of Patnaik and Immerman. Also for initializations computable in space $O(|D|^\ell)$ a separation can be obtained easier. The idea here is as follows. The space hierarchy already holds for unary languages [Sze94, Theorem 11.1.1]. Let L be a unary language over $\Sigma \stackrel{\text{def}}{=} \{a\}$ that can be decided in space $O(n^{\ell+1})$ but not in space $O(n^\ell)$. Let Q_L be the boolean query that is true if and only if $a^{|D|} \in L$ where D is the domain of the database. Then DYNFO with $O(|D|^\ell)$-space initialization mapping cannot maintain this query (as already the initialization has to be incorrect).

Despite those drawbacks, the approach to prove lower bounds via simulation might be useful because it is quite robust. For example, fast simulation algorithms for fragments of DYNFO, e.g. DYNPROP and DYNQF, might yield new lower bounds for those fragments.

Using Domain Independence

Next we aim at an application of the following very simple idea. Assume that all queries maintainable in some dynamic complexity class DYNC satisfy a certain property. Now, if one can show that a given query does not have this property, then the query is not maintainable in DYNC.

Here we apply this idea to DYNFO with initialization from scratch. Very simple queries cannot be maintained in this setting. Consider, for example, the boolean query which is true for domains of even size and false otherwise. It cannot be maintained in DYNFO from scratch because a first-order formula cannot tell domains of even and odd size apart for large, empty structures. More generally, queries that depend on domain elements that are not used in the input database cannot be maintained in DYNFO from scratch.

Next we generalize this argument. Recall that the active domain of a state consists of all elements of the domain that are contained in a tuple of an input relation. The *non-active domain* contains all elements of the domain that are not in the active domain. Let $f : \mathbb{N} \to \mathbb{N}$ be a function. A boolean query Q is f-*domain independent* if the answer of Q is the same for all structures S and S' over domains D, D' with $D \subseteq D'$ that have the same active domain, agree on their active domain and whose non-active domain is of size at least $f(|D_{\text{ACT}}|)$ where D_{ACT} denotes the active domain. Thus, intuitively, the result of an f-domain independent query Q does not depend on the non-active domain as long as the size of the non-active domain is larger than $f(|D_{\text{ACT}}|)$.

The following lemma can be used to prove lower bounds for DYNFO with initialization from scratch for queries that are not c-domain independent for any $c \in \mathbb{N}$. We postpone its technical proof to the end of this subsection.

Lemma 4.3.9. *If a boolean query Q can be maintained in DYNFO from scratch, then Q is c-domain independent for some constant $c \in \mathbb{N}$.*

Corollary 4.3.10. *The following queries cannot be maintained in* DYNFO *from scratch:*

(a) The domain is of even size.

(b) The number of elements not contained in a unary relation U is of size $f(|U|)$ where f is an arbitrary monotonically increasing function.

Thus proving lower bounds in the original setting of Patnaik and Immerman is not too hard for queries that strongly depend on the non-active domain.

We observe that part (b) of the preceding theorem implies that the boolean query on a unary relation U which is true if and only if $|U| = |D \setminus U|$ cannot be maintained in DYNFO from scratch. We shortly discuss the relation of this observation to Theorem 4.2 in [GS12]. In this theorem, it is shown that the equal cardinality query for two unary relations cannot be maintained in DYNFO with arbitrary initial input databases and logical initialization of the auxiliary data. Although DYNFO with computation from scratch also has logical initialization, the observation is not a special case of the setting used by Grädel and Siebertz. The reason is, that when arbitrary initial input databases are allowed, it is sufficient to show that the logical initialization is not very powerful for certain specific initial input databases. This is used in the proof of Theorem 4.2 in [GS12]. Actually, the equal cardinality query can be easily maintained from scratch in $DynFO$: build a linear order on the active domain and maintain counters for the two unary relations.

It remains to prove Lemma 4.3.9. It is immediately implied by the following more general lemma. For a DYNFO-program $\mathcal{P}$, let $c_{\mathcal{P}}$ be the sum of the maximal arity of all input relations, the maximal arity of all auxiliary relations and the maximal number of quantifiers occurring in an update or initialization formula of $\mathcal{P}$. Recall that an element a is touched by a modification $\alpha(\bar{b})$ if a is contained in $\bar{b}$.

Lemma 4.3.11. *Let D and D' be two domains with $D \subseteq D'$, and let $U \subseteq D$ and $c \in \mathbb{N}$ be such that $|U| + c \leq |D|$. If $\mathcal{P}$ is a* DYNFO-*program that starts from scratch such that $c_{\mathcal{P}} \leq c$ and α is a modification sequence that only touches elements from U then $\mathcal{P}_\alpha(\mathcal{S}_0)$ and $\mathcal{P}_\alpha(\mathcal{S}_0')$ agree on the 0-ary relations where $\mathcal{S}_0$ and $\mathcal{S}_0'$ are the initial states of $\mathcal{P}$ for the domains D and D', respectively.*

Proof. A function μ is U-invariant, if $\mu(a_i) = a_i$ whenever $a_i \in U$. We aim at proving that $\mathcal{P}_\alpha(\mathcal{S}_0) \simeq_\mu \mathcal{P}_\alpha(\mathcal{S}_0') \upharpoonright X_\mu$ for all modification sequences α and all U-invariant injective functions $\mu : D \to D'$ with $X_\mu \overset{\text{def}}{=} \mu(D)$. This, in particular, implies that the two structures $\mathcal{P}_\alpha(\mathcal{S}_0)$ and $\mathcal{P}_\alpha(\mathcal{S}_0')$ agree on the 0-ary relations.

We first prove the following claim. Let $\mathcal{S}$ and $\mathcal{S}'$ be states over D and D', respectively. If $\mathcal{S} \simeq_\mu \mathcal{S}' \upharpoonright X_\mu$ for all U-invariant injective functions $\mu : D \to D'$ then

$$(\mathcal{S}, \bar{b}) \models \varphi \text{ if and only if } (\mathcal{S}', \pi(\bar{b})) \models \varphi$$

for all m-tuples $\bar{b}$, all U-invariant injective functions π and all first-order formulas φ of quantifier-depth q with $m + q \leq c$.

Towards proving the claim let $\bar{b}$, π and φ be as described above. Let A be the elements of $D \setminus U$ that are not contained in $\bar{b}$ and, analogously, let A' be the elements of $D' \setminus U$ that are not contained in $\pi(\bar{b})$. We prove the claim by sketching a winning strategy for Duplicator in a q-round Ehrenfeucht-Fraïssé game. Duplicator replies a move c on $(\mathcal{S}, \bar{b})$ by Spoiler with a move d on $(\mathcal{S}', \pi(\bar{b}))$ where (1) $d \stackrel{\text{def}}{=} c$ if $c \in U$, (2) $d \stackrel{\text{def}}{=} \pi(c)$ if d is in $\bar{b}$, and (3) d is an element from A' if c is an element from A (if c has been used before, then Duplicator uses the previous response to c). Duplicator responds similarly when Spoiler's move is on the structure $(\mathcal{S}', \pi(\bar{b}))$. Observe that since $m + q \leq c$ there are sufficiently many fresh elements in A and A'. We claim that the partial bijection π' induced by the corresponding choices of Spoiler and Duplicator is actually a U-invariant partial isomorphism of the structures $(\mathcal{S}, \bar{b})$ and $(\mathcal{S}', \pi(\bar{b}))$, and therefore Duplicator wins the game. The function π' is U-invariant due to (1). It can be extended to a U-invariant injective function π'' from D to D'. By the assumption $\mathcal{S} \simeq_{\pi''} \mathcal{S}' \restriction X_{\pi''}$ and therefore π' is a partial isomorphism.

Now we prove the statement of the lemma. Inductively over the length of α we prove that $\mathcal{P}_\alpha(\mathcal{S}_0) \simeq_\mu \mathcal{P}_\alpha(\mathcal{S}'_0) \restriction X_\mu$ for an arbitrary U-invariant injective function $\mu : D \to D'$ with $X_\mu \stackrel{\text{def}}{=} \mu(D)$. The induction hypothesis is satisfied in the initial structures $\mathcal{S}_0$ and $\mathcal{S}'_0$, as the initial input database is empty and the auxiliary relations are initialized by first-order formulas of quantifier-depth $\leq c_\mathcal{P}$. Now, if the states $\mathcal{S}_i$ and $\mathcal{S}'_i$ — obtained by applying the first i modifications in α — satisfy the hypothesis, then so do $\mathcal{S}_{i+1}$ and $\mathcal{S}'_{i+1}$. To see this let $\delta(\bar{b})$ be the $(i+1)$st modification in α, let R be an arbitrary ℓ-ary auxiliary relation symbol and $\bar{c}$ an ℓ-ary tuple over D. Then $(\mathcal{S}_i, \bar{b}, \bar{c}) \models \phi_\delta^R(\bar{u}; \bar{x})$ if and only if $(\mathcal{S}_i, \bar{b}, \mu(\bar{c})) \models \phi_{\delta_i}^R(\bar{u}; \bar{x})$, due to the induction hypothesis, the claim proved above and because $|\bar{u}| + |\bar{x}| + q \leq c_\mathcal{P}$. Therefore $\mathcal{P}_\alpha(\mathcal{S}_{i+1}) \simeq_\mu \mathcal{P}_\alpha(\mathcal{S}'_{i+1}) \restriction X_\mu$.   □

4.4 Outlook and Bibliographic Remarks

In this chapter methods for proving lower bounds in the dynamic complexity framework have been presented. For DYNPROP and DYNQF, the Substructure Lemma and combinatorial tools have been used to obtain new lower bounds for the reachability query and the k-clique query. For DYNFO, a unified perspective on static lower bounds has been introduced, and two new approaches for proving dynamic lower bounds for restricted initialization settings have been discussed.

While proving lower bounds for full DYNFO — a major long-term goal in dynamic descriptive complexity — might be really hard to achieve, we believe that the following goals are suitable for both developing new lower bound methods and for improving the current methods.

We start with possible goals for quantifier-free complexity classes. A general quantifier-free lower bound for the reachability query and the k-clique query remains open. We have seen that both queries cannot be maintained in binary DYNPROP. We conjecture that neither the 3-clique query nor the reachability query can be maintained in DYNPROP under insertions and deletions. Such lower bounds would be interesting as still very few general lower bounds for DYNPROP are known, and therefore lower bounds for those two queries could contribute to finding a general framework for proving lower bounds for this fragment.

For DYNQF, the current methods for proving lower bounds have been applied only to fragments with unary auxiliary functions. In Subsect. 4.2.3 we argued why those methods cannot be easily generalized to obtain lower bounds for binary DYNQF. Proving lower bounds for this fragment seems feasible due to the severe restrictions posed by DYNQF. A first step towards such lower bounds could be to study binary DYNQF-programs that start from scratch.

For quantifier-free dynamic complexity classes, we have seen that combinatorial tools such as the theorems of Ramsey and Higman played an important role for lower bound proofs. Therefore it appears to be promising to study the applicability of other combinatorial tools in this context.

For (full) first-order updates a major challenge is the development of lower bound tools. Most of the current techniques are in some sense not fully dynamic: either results from static descriptive complexity are applied to constant-length modification sequences (see Subsect. 4.3.1); or non-constant but very regular modification sequences are used. In the latter case, the modifications do not depend on previous changes to the auxiliary data (as, e.g., in [GS12] and in Sect. 4.1). Finding techniques that adapt to changes could be a good starting point. Here, the Ehrenfeucht-Fraïssé game discussed in the introduction of Sect. 4.3 could be a good starting point.

We think that the power of the two techniques presented in Subsect. 4.3.2 have not been completely exhausted here, and finding further applications of them is possible.

Another promising direction is to substantiate that proving lower bounds for DYNFO is hard, for example, by showing that a certain lower bound for DYNFO implies the separation of two well-known static complexity classes.

Bibliographic Remarks

The Substructure Lemma has already been introduced in [GMS09]; here we use a new formulation of this result. Most lower bound results from Sects. 4.1 and 4.2 have been published in [ZS13, Zeu14a]. The former work includes all lower bounds for arbitrary modifications and is joint work with Thomas Schwentick. The latter work contains lower bounds for insertions only and is solely by the author. Proposition 4.1.19 will appear in [Zeu14b], the full version of [Zeu14a]. It resulted from discussions with Samir Datta. The separations of fragments of DYNPROP have been announced in [ZS14], the proofs will be published in the full version of [ZS15].

The results for DYNFO are attributed as follows. The results using static lower bounds in Sect. 4.3.1 have all been presented elsewhere before. We contributed a new unified presentation of their proofs. Theorem 4.3.3 is from [DLW03] originally; Theorem 4.3.7 has been published in [DS98]. Theorem 4.3.1 is joint work with Nils Vortmeier and has been proved, though in a different way, in his master's thesis. The two approaches in Sect. 4.3.2 are part of (so far) unpublished joint work with Thomas Schwentick and Nils Vortmeier on algorithmic properties of dynamic programs. The idea to use simulations is inspired by William Hesse.

Chapter 5
Conclusion

In the decade after its introduction in the early 1990s, dynamic descriptive complexity has seen many results; including results for the maintainability of specific queries as well as lower bounds for restricted dynamic programs. Yet, after Hesse's proof that reachability can be maintained in DYNTC^0 [Hes03b], work in the area stopped almost completely. Probably the focus of the community shifted to other fields because further progress on maintaining reachability was not foreseeable and proving lower bounds for other dynamic complexity classes seemed unattainable.

In the last few years, however, new progress on both topics — lower bounds and reachability — has been achieved. We shortly recapitulate those results and their relation to this thesis.

Two new lower bounds, one for the quantifier-free fragment [GMS09] and one for logical initialization mappings [GS12], indicated that approaches orthogonal to the study of bounded-arity DYNFO might foster better understanding of dynamic complexity; and, in the long term, maybe even lead to stronger lower bounds.

Those two results motivated us to study small dynamic complexity classes in more detail. We have seen how several small dynamic complexity classes relate to each other and how they relate to static complexity classes (see Chap. 3). Further some new attempts to prove lower bounds for such small classes have (see Chap. 4). In particular new lower bounds for the quantifier-free fragment have been obtained by using the basic technique from [GMS12] in conjunction with suitable combinatorial tools, and a unified view on lower bounds for DYNFO has been presented.

While we were studying lower bounds for small fragments, progress on maintaining reachability was made by Samir Datta, William Hesse and Raghav Kulkarni. In a breakthrough result for dynamic descriptive complexity, they showed that reachability can be maintained by non-uniform AC^0 with parity gates [DHK14]. Only recently, by a different approach, reachability was shown to be maintainable using first-order update formulas by Samir Datta, Raghav Kulkarni, Anish Mukherjee, Thomas Schwentick and the author [DKM+15]. We have seen a short overview of

© Springer-Verlag GmbH Germany 2017
T. Zeume, *Small Dynamic Complexity Classes*, LNCS 10110
DOI: 10.1007/978-3-662-54314-6_5

the proof in Sect. 2.6, and the detailed construction for one of the three key steps has been presented in Sect. 3.4.

Although this thesis is not focused on upper bounds, we have seen how the latter result can be applied in order to maintain regular path queries (see Chap. 1). Also more expressive path queries have been studied here, though for restricted graph classes.

Thus, in the last couple of years, significant progress has been achieved for both lower bounds and reachability. We hope that those results help to spark a wider interest in dynamic descriptive complexity.

At the end of each chapter we already discussed open questions and further directions for the topic of the chapter. In the following we indicate other possible directions for future research.

New Applications

The recent result on the maintainability of Reachability raises hopes that dynamic complexity can be applied to many other fields of interest in computer science. This is, on the one hand, because reachability as well as the closely related problem of computing the transitive closure of a relation is the basis for many computational problems. On the other hand, the technique used for maintaining Reachability in [DKM+15] seems to yield more insights. In the following we shortly discuss those two aspects.

As an example of applying the result itself we have seen how regular path queries can be evaluated dynamically. Other problems that rely on maintaining the transitive closure can now be studied as well. Examples for such problems are dynamic LTL model checking and query evaluation under ontologies.

The former problem has already been studied in [KW03], where dynamic LTL model checking was shown to be in DynTC^0. The reduction to reachability used in the proof does not immediately transfer to DynFO. However, if reachability is maintainable when nodes can be (de)activated, then LTL model checking can be maintained in DynFO as well.

Query evaluation under ontologies has been studied a lot in the description logic community in the last decade (see, e.g., [CDL+13, LW12]). In this setting, the input is a database, an ontology and a query, and one is interested in answering the query on the database extended by ontological knowledge. The data complexity for different description logics used as ontology language varies a lot, among others examples for AC^0, NLOGSPACE and PTIME are known [CDL+13]. Extending a database by ontological knowledge is very related to the computation of a transitive closure. Therefore query evaluation under ontologies that have static data complexity in NLOGSPACE could be a good first candidate for studying the dynamic complexity of query answering.

We now turn to possible applications of the technique used for maintaining Reachability in [DKM+15]. Maintainability of Reachability was reduced to maintaining the rank of a matrix, which in turn was maintained using first-order updates. Thus linear algebraic problems seem to be interesting candidates for further studies. Problems from algebra and linear algebra have not been studied in dynamic complexity so far, with the exception of the observation that multiplication of two n bit numbers encoded by unary relations can be maintained in DYNFO [PI94]. We plan to pursue this path more systematically. Candidate problems to start with are division and iterated multiplication, as they are in TC^0 but not in AC^0.

Generalized Modifications

The choice of allowing only single deletions and insertions is rather restricted. Changes to a database are often induced by an SQL-query that specifies which tuples shall be modified, deleted or inserted. Looking at the dynamic complexity of problems when more elaborated modifications are possible is therefore another interesting direction for future research. This was already noted by different authors, among them Patnaik and Immerman [PI97] and Etessami [Ete98].

Preliminary work on some simple generalized modifications has already been done. Dong and Pang studied maintainability of Reachability under edge-set and node-set deletions [DP97]; edge contractions have been studied by Siebertz [Sie11]. A framework for general modifications was introduced by Weber and Schwentick [WS07].

Generalized modifications might also offer new insights into the traditional dynamic complexity setting. Above we have already mentioned that maintainability of reachability in DYNFO under node (de)activations (which roughly corresponds to node insertions and deletions) implies that LTL model checking can be maintained in DYNFO. Another problem that might be tackled by having a closer look at generalized modifications is the following. The dynamic maintenance of many queries is difficult because one change in the input database influences the query result at several places. Examples for such queries are the dynamic model checking problem for CTL* and the evaluation problem for the graph query language nSPARQL [PAG10]. A CTL* formula can, for example, ask if there is a path p starting from some initial node such that at every node v along p a path p_v with a certain property starts. Then a single change in the Kripke structure possibly influences many of the paths p_v. The query language nSPARQL can express similar properties and therefore dynamic evaluation leads to related challenges. A thorough understanding of generalized modifications might lead to new approaches for maintaining such queries.

Finally a systematic study of first-order defined modifications might yield new approaches for proving lower bounds.

Transfer of Techniques

We believe that dynamic complexity can profit a lot from other fields of theoretical computer science, and vice versa.

So far several techniques used in dynamic complexity have been imported from other areas. For example, an Euler tour construction due to Henzinger and King [HK99] was used by Hesse to maintain undirected reachability in DYNFO with unary functions [Hes03b]. The derandomized Isolation Lemma due to Reinhardt and Allender [RA00] was used by Datta et al. to maintain the size of maximum matchings in DYNFO (with arbitrary initialization) [DKM+15].

On the other hand, techniques for maintaining reachability for restricted graph classes in the dynamic descriptive complexity framework have been used in a logical framework for shape analysis [RSL10]. The techniques were used for keeping information in an abstraction as precise as possible during a sequence of modifications.

Those transfers indicate that dynamic complexity can both profit from and contribute to other fields. We advocate for an active study of further transfers of techniques.

References

[ACP12]   Arenas, M., Conca, S., Pérez, J.: Counting beyond a yottabyte, or how SPARQL 1.1 property paths will prevent adoption of the standard. In: Proceedings of the 21st World Wide Web Conference 2012, WWW 2012, Lyon, France, 16–20 April 2012, pp. 629–638 (2012)

[AHV95]   Abiteboul, S., Hull, R., Vianu, V.: Foundations of Databases, vol. 8. Addison-Wesley, Reading (1995)

[Ajt83]   Ajtai, M.: Σ_1^1-formulae on finite structures. Ann. Pure Appl. Logic **24**(1), 1–48 (1983)

[AV99]   Abiteboul, S., Vianu, V.: Regular path queries with constraints. J. Comput. Syst. Sci. **58**(3), 428–452 (1999)

[Bae13]   Barceló Baeza, P.: Querying graph databases. In: Hull, R., Fan, W. (eds.) Proceedings of the 32nd ACM SIGMOD-SIGACT-SIGART Symposium on Principles of Database Systems, PODS 2013, New York, NY, USA, 22–27 June 2013, pp. 175–188. ACM (2013)

[BIS90]   Mix Barrington, D.A., Immerman, N., Straubing, H.: On uniformity within NC^1. J. Comput. Syst. Sci. **41**(3), 274–306 (1990)

[BLLW12]   Barceló, P., Libkin, L., Widjaja Lin, A., Wood, P.T.: Expressive languages for path queries over graph-structured data. ACM Trans. Database Syst. **37**(4), 31 (2012)

[Cai90]   Cai, J.: Lower bounds for constant-depth circuits in the presence of help bits. Inf. Process. Lett. **36**(2), 79–83 (1990)

[CDL+13]   Calvanese, D., De Giacomo, G., Lembo, D., Lenzerini, M., Rosati, R.: Data complexity of query answering in description logics. Artif. Intell. **195**, 335–360 (2013)

[CM77]   Chandra, A.K., Merlin, P.M.: Optimal implementation of conjunctive queries in relational data bases. In: Proceedings of the Ninth Annual ACM Symposium on Theory of Computing, pp. 77–90. ACM (1977)

[Cod70]   Codd, E.F.: A relational model of data for large shared data banks. Commun. ACM **13**(6), 377–387 (1970)

[DHK14]   Datta, S., Hesse, W., Kulkarni, R.: Dynamic complexity of directed reachability and other problems. In: Esparza, J., Fraigniaud, P., Husfeldt, T., Koutsoupias, E. (eds.) ICALP 2014. LNCS, vol. 8572, pp. 356–367. Springer, Heidelberg (2014). doi:10. 1007/978-3-662-43948-7_30

[DI08]   Demetrescu, C., Italiano, G.F.: Mantaining dynamic matrices for fully dynamic transitive closure. Algorithmica **51**(4), 387–427 (2008)

T. Zeume, *Small Dynamic Complexity Classes*, LNCS 10110
DOI: 10.1007/978-3-662-54314-6

[DKM+15] Datta, S., Kulkarni, R., Mukherjee, A., Schwentick, T., Zeume, T.: Reachability is
          in DynFO. In: Halldórsson, M.M., Iwama, K., Kobayashi, N., Speckmann, B. (eds.)
          ICALP 2015. LNCS, vol. 9135, pp. 159–170. Springer, Heidelberg (2015). doi:10.
          1007/978-3-662-47666-6_13
 [DLR95] Duffus, D., Lefmann, H., Rödl, V.: Shift graphs and lower bounds on Ramsey numbers
          $r_k(l;r)$. Discrete Math. **137**(1–3), 177–187 (1995)
[DLSW99] Dong, G., Libkin, L., Su, J., Wong, L.: Maintaining the transitive closure of graphs
          in SQL. Int. J. Inf. Technol. **5** (1999)
 [DLW03] Dong, G., Libkin, L., Wong, L.: Incremental recomputation in local languages. Inf.
          Comput. **181**(2), 88–98 (2003)
  [DP97] Dong, G., Pang, C.: Maintaining transitive closure in first order after node-set and
          edge-set deletions. Inf. Process. Lett. **62**(4), 193–199 (1997)
  [DR97] Dong, G., Ramamohanarao, K.: Maintaining constrained transitive closure by con-
          junctive queries. In: Bry, F., Ramakrishnan, R., Ramamohanarao, K. (eds.) DOOD
          1997. LNCS, vol. 1341, pp. 35–51. Springer, Heidelberg (1997). doi:10.1007/3-540-
          63792-3_7
  [DS93] Dong, G., Su, J.: First-order incremental evaluation of datalog queries. In: Beeri,
          C., Ohori, A., Shasha, D. (eds.) Database Programming Languages (DBPL-4), pp.
          295–308. Springer, Heidelberg (1993)
  [DS95] Dong, G., Jianwen, S.: Incremental and decremental evaluation of transitive closure
          by first-order queries. Inf. Comput. **120**(1), 101–106 (1995)
  [DS97] Dong, G., Jianwen, S.: Deterministic FOIES are strictly weaker. Ann. Math. Artif.
          Intell. **19**(1–2), 127–146 (1997)
  [DS98] Dong, G., Jianwen, S.: Arity bounds in first-order incremental evaluation and def-
          inition of polynomial time database queries. J. Comput. Syst. Sci. **57**(3), 289–308
          (1998)
  [DT92] Dong, G., Topor, R.W.: Incremental evaluation of datalog queries. In: Biskup, J.,
          Hull, R. (eds.) Database Theory - ICDT 1992. Lecture Notes in Computer Science,
          vol. 646, pp. 282–296. Springer, Heidelberg (1992)
  [EF05] Ebbinghaus, H.-D., Flum, J.: Finite Model Theory. Perspectives in Mathematical
          Logic. Springer, Heidelberg (2005)
 [EHR65] Erdös, P., Hajnal, A., Rado, R.: Partition relations for cardinal numbers. Acta Math-
          ematica Hungarica **16**(1), 93–196 (1965)
  [ER52] Erdös, P., Rado, R.: Combinatorial theorems on classifications of subsets of a given
          set. Proc. Lond. Math. Soc. **3**(2), 417–439 (1952)
 [Ete98] Etessami, K.: Dynamic tree isomorphism via first-order updates. In: Mendelzon,
          A.O., Paredaens, J. (eds.) Proceedings of the Seventeenth ACM SIGACT-SIGMOD-
          SIGART Symposium on Principles of Database Systems, Seattle, Washington, USA,
          1–3 June 1998, pp. 235–243. ACM Press (1998)
 [FSS84] Furst, M., Saxe, J.B., Sipser, M.: Parity, circuits, and the polynomial-time hierarchy.
          Math. Syst. Theor. **17**(1), 13–27 (1984)
 [GMS93] Gupta, A., Mumick, I.S., Subrahmanian, V.S.: Maintaining views incrementally. In:
          Buneman, P., Jajodia, S. (eds.) Proceedings of the 1993 ACM SIGMOD International
          Conference on Management of Data, Washington, DC, 26–28 May 1993, pp. 157–
          166. ACM Press (1993)
 [GMS09] Gelade, W., Marquardt, M., Schwentick, T.: The dynamic complexity of formal lan-
          guages. In: Albers, S., Marion, J.-Y. (eds.) Proceedings of 26th International Sym-
          posium on Theoretical Aspects of Computer Science, STACS 2009, Freiburg, Ger-
          many, 26–28 February 2009. LIPIcs, vol. 3, pp. 481–492. Schloss Dagstuhl - Leibniz-
          Zentrum fuer Informatik, Germany (2009)
 [GMS12] Gelade, W., Marquardt, M., Schwentick, T.: The dynamic complexity of formal lan-
          guages. ACM Trans. Comput. Log. **13**(3), 19 (2012)
  [GS12] Grädel, E., Siebertz, S.: Dynamic definability. In: Deutsch, A. (ed.) 15th International
          Conference on Database Theory, ICDT 2012, Berlin, Germany, 26–29 March 2012,
          pp. 236–248. ACM (2012)

[Hes03a] Hesse, W.: The dynamic complexity of transitive closure is in DynTC^0. Theor. Comput. Sci. **296**(3), 473–485 (2003)

[Hes03b] Hesse, W.: Dynamic computational complexity. Ph.D. thesis, University of Massachusetts Amherst (2003)

[HI02] Hesse, W., Immerman, N.: Complete problems for dynamic complexity classes. In: Proceedings of 17th IEEE Symposium on Logic in Computer Science (LICS 2002), Copenhagen, Denmark, 22–25 July 2002, p. 313. IEEE Computer Society (2002)

[HK99] Monika Rauch Henzinger and Valerie King: Randomized fully dynamic graph algorithms with polylogarithmic time per operation. J. ACM **46**(4), 502–516 (1999)

[KAK+14] Koch, C., Ahmad, Y., Kennedy, O., Nikolic, M., Nötzli, A., Lupei, D., Shaikhha, A.: DBToaster: higher-order delta processing for dynamic, frequently fresh views. VLDB J. **23**(2), 253–278 (2014)

[Koc10] Koch, C.: Incremental query evaluation in a ring of databases. In: Paredaens, J., Van Gucht, D. (eds.) Proceedings of the Twenty-Ninth ACM SIGMOD-SIGACT-SIGART Symposium on Principles of Database Systems, PODS, Indianapolis, Indiana, USA, 6–11 June 2010, pp. 87–98. ACM (2010)

[KW03] Kähler, D., Wilke, T.: Program complexity of dynamic LTL model checking. In: Baaz, M., Makowsky, J.A. (eds.) CSL 2003. LNCS, vol. 2803, pp. 271–284. Springer, Heidelberg (2003). doi:10.1007/978-3-540-45220-1_23

[Lib04] Libkin, L.: Elements of Finite Model Theory. Texts in Theoretical Computer Science. An Eatcs Series. Springer, Heidelberg (2004)

[LM13] Losemann, K., Martens, W.: The complexity of regular expressions and property paths in SPARQL. ACM Trans. Database Syst. **38**(4), 24 (2013)

[LW97a] Libkin, L., Wong, L.: Incremental recomputation of recursive queries with nested sets and aggregate functions. In: Cluet, S., Hull, R. (eds.) DBPL 1997. LNCS, vol. 1369, pp. 222–238. Springer, Heidelberg (1998). doi:10.1007/3-540-64823-2_13

[LW97b] Libkin, L., Wong, L.: Query languages for bags and aggregate functions. J. Comput. Syst. Sci. **55**(2), 241–272 (1997)

[LW99] Libkin, L., Wong, L.: On the power of incremental evaluation in SQL-like languages. In: Connor, R., Mendelzon, A. (eds.) DBPL 1999. LNCS, vol. 1949, pp. 17–30. Springer, Heidelberg (2000). doi:10.1007/3-540-44543-9_2

[LW12] Lutz, C., Wolter, F.: Non-uniform data complexity of query answering in description logics. In: Brewka, G., Eiter, T., McIlraith, S.A. (eds.) Principles of Knowledge Representation and Reasoning: Proceedings of the Thirteenth International Conference, KR 2012, Rome, Italy, 10–14 June 2012. AAAI Press (2012)

[Mil99] Miltersen, P.B.: Cell probe complexity-a survey. In: 19th Conference on the Foundations of Software Technology and Theoretical Computer Science (FSTTCS) (1999)

[MSVT94] Miltersen, P.B., Subramanian, S., Vitter, J.S., Scott, J., Tamassia, R.: Complexity models for incremental computation. Theor. Comput. Sci. **130**(1), 203–236 (1994)

[MW95] Mendelzon, A.O., Wood, P.T.: Finding regular simple paths in graph databases. SIAM J. Comput. **24**(6), 1235–1258 (1995)

[PAG10] Pérez, J., Arenas, M., Gutierrez, C.: nsparql: a navigational language for RDF. J. Web Sem. **8**(4), 255–270 (2010)

[PI94] Patnaik, S., Immerman, N.: Dyn-FO: a parallel, dynamic complexity class. In: PODS, pp. 210–221. ACM Press (1994)

[PI97] Patnaik, S., Immerman, N.: Dyn-FO: a parallel, dynamic complexity class. J. Comput. Syst. Sci. **55**(2), 199–209 (1997)

[Pot03] Potter, B.: The Tale of Squirrel Nutkin. Original Peter Rabbit Books. F. Warne & Company, Incorporated, New York (1903)

[RA00] Reinhardt, K., Allender, E.: Making nondeterminism unambiguous. SIAM J. Comput. **29**(4), 1118–1131 (2000)

[RSL10] Reps, T.W., Sagiv, M., Loginov, A.: Finite differencing of logical formulas for static analysis. ACM Trans. Program. Lang. Syst. **32**(6), 24:1–24:55 (2010). doi:10.1145/1749608.1749613

[RZ08]   Roditty, L., Zwick, U.: Improved dynamic reachability algorithms for directed graphs. SIAM J. Comput. **37**(5), 1455–1471 (2008)

[SI84]   Shmueli, O., Itai, A.: Maintenance of views. In: Yormark, B. (ed.) SIGMOD 1984, Proceedings of Annual Meeting, Boston, Massachusetts, 18–21 June 1984, pp. 240–255. ACM Press (1984)

[Sie11]   Siebertz, S.: Dynamic definability. Master's thesis, RWTH Aachen (2011)

[SS11]   Schmitz, S., Schnoebelen, P.: Multiply-recursive upper bounds with Higman's lemma. In: Aceto, L., Henzinger, L., Sgall, J. (eds.) Proceedings of Automata, Languages and Programming. Lecture Notes in Computer Science, vol. 6756, pp. 441–452. Springer, Heidelberg (2011)

[Sze94]   Szepietowski, A. (ed.): Turing Machines with Sublogarithmic Space. Lecture Notes in Computer Science, vol. 843. Springer, Heidelberg (1994)

[Vol99]   Vollmer, H.: Introduction to Circuit Complexity: A Uniform Approach. Springer, Heidelberg (1999)

[Vor13]   Vortmeier, N.L Komplexitätstheorie verlaufsunabhängiger dynamischer Programme. Master's thesis, TU Dortmund University (2013)

[Woo12]   Wood, P.T.: Query languages for graph databases. ACM SIGMOD Rec. **41**(1), 50–60 (2012)

[WS07]   Weber, V., Schwentick, T.: Dynamic complexity theory revisited. Theor. Comput. Syst. **40**(4), 355–377 (2007)

[Zeu14a] Zeume, T.: The dynamic descriptive complexity of k-Clique. In: Csuhaj-Varjú, E., Dietzfelbinger, M., Ésik, Z. (eds.) MFCS 2014. LNCS, vol. 8634, pp. 547–558. Springer, Heidelberg (2014). doi:10.1007/978-3-662-44522-8_46

[Zeu14b] Zeume, T.: The dynamic descriptive complexity of k-clique. In: Acctepted to Information and Computation Special Issue MFCS 2014 (2014)

[ZS13]   Zeume, T., Schwentick, T.: On the quantifier-free dynamic complexity of reachability. In: Chatterjee, K., Sgall, J. (eds.) MFCS 2013. LNCS, vol. 8087, pp. 837–848. Springer, Heidelberg (2013). doi:10.1007/978-3-642-40313-2_73

[ZS14]   Zeume, T., Schwentick, T.: Dynamic conjunctive queries. In: Schweikardt, N., Christophides, V., Leroy, V. (eds.) Proceedings 17th International Conference on Database Theory (ICDT), Athens, Greece, 24–28 March 2014, pp. 38–49. OpenProceedings.org (2014)

[ZS15]   Zeume, T., Schwentick, T.: On the quantifier-free dynamic complexity of reachability. Inf. Comput. **240**, 108–129 (2015)

Subject Index

Symbols

$\phi_\delta^R(\bar{u}; \bar{x})$, 14

Δ-semantics, 37, 60

Δ-update program, 60

$\exists^1 \text{FO}$, 68

$\prec$-ordered τ-clique, 93

$\prec$-ordered tuple, 12

$\prec$-homogeneous, *see* homogeneous

τ_{aux}, 14

τ_{inp}, 14

A

A-$\prec$-homogeneous, *see* homogeneous

Absolute semantics, 14, 37, 60

AC^0, 5, 76

Active domain, 21, 77

Algorithmic approach, 1

Arity, 12

Atomic formula, 12

Atomic type, 13

Auxiliary data, 1

Auxiliary database, 14

Auxiliary schema, 14

C

Closed under isomorphisms, 13

Composed formula, 12

Conjunctive query, 36, 40

  union of, 36, 40

Constant, 12

CRPQ, *see* regular path query

D

Database, 12

Declarative approach, 1

Definable, 13

Dependency graph, 15, 71, 110

Describable query, 53

Domain, 12

Domain independence, 77

  f-domain independent, 134

Dynamic descriptive complexity
  framework, 3

Dynamic instance, 14

Dynamic program, 3, 14

Dynamic schema, 14

DynC, 16

DynFO, 3, 15

DynProp, 17

DynQF, 19

E

Equivalence of dynamic programs, 15

Existential prefix form, 69

Expressible, 13

  with help relations, 126

F

First-order formula, 12

First-order incremental evaluation
  system, 21

First-order logic, 12

FOIES, *see* first-order incremental
  evaluation systems

From scratch, *see* initialization
  from scratch

© Springer-Verlag GmbH Germany 2017

T. Zeume, *Small Dynamic Complexity Classes*, LNCS 10110

DOI: 10.1007/978-3-662-54314-6

G
Graph, 13
   k-layered, 13
   as structure, 13
Graph database, 24

H
Higman's Lemma, 93
Homogeneous
   with respect to $\prec$, 93
   with respect to $\prec$ and A, 96
Honest modification, 110

I
Initialization, 22
   arbitrary, 22
   from scratch, 23
   invariant, 22, 91
   with built-in arithmetic, 76
Input schema, 14
Isomorphism, 12

K
k-clique query, 13, 87
k-colorability query, 13

L
Lower bound
   for k-clique, 92, 99, 101
   for k-colorability, 92, 99
   for an $\exists^*\forall^*$FO-query, 102
   for reachability, 91, 93, 94

M
Maintenance of a query, 14
Modification, 14

N
Neighborhood, 114
Nesting depth, 114
Non-recursive dynamic program, 68

P
$P_\alpha(\mathcal{S})$, 14
Parity query, 15
PRAM, 5
Preprocessing technique, 42, 47
Preservation, 12
Program state, 14

Q
Query, 13
Query symbol, 14

R
Ramsey number
   bounds for hypergraphs, 104
   for hypergraphs, 103
   for structures, 93
Ramsey's Theorem
   for hypergraphs, 104
   for structures, 93
Reachability query, 13, 87
Regular path query, 24
   conjunction of, 24
Relational database, 4, 12
Replacement technique, 42, 45–47, 62
RPQ, *see* regular path query

S
Schema
   functional, 18
   helping, 126
   relational, 12
Similar, 114
SQL, 4
Squirrel technique, 43, 44, 65, 69
State, *see* program state
Structure, 12
Subsequence, 93
Substructure, 12
Substructure Lemma
   for DYNPROP, 86, 89
   for DYNQF, 113, 115

T
$t_\delta^f(\bar{x}; \bar{y})$, 19
Topological sorting, 71
Touched element, 77
Tower function, 103

U

Union of conjunctive queries,
    see conjunctive query
Update formula, 14
Update program, 14
Update term, 19

Upper bound
    reachability under insertions, 3

W

Weak maintainability, 53

Printed in the United States
By Bookmasters